No Questions Asked

No Questions Asked

News Coverage since 9/11

Lisa Finnegan

Foreword by Norman Solomon

Democracy and the News

Jeffrey Scheuer, Series Editor

Westport, Connecticut
London

Library of Congress Cataloging-in-Publication Data

Finnegan, Lisa.
    No questions asked : news coverage since 9/11 / Lisa Finnegan; foreword by Norman Solomon.
        p. cm. — (Democracy and the news, ISSN 1932–6947)
    Includes bibliographical references and index.
    ISBN 0–275–99335–3 (alk. paper)
    1. Government and the press—United States—History—21st century.
    2. Journalism—United States—History—21st century. I. Title.
    PN4738.F56 2007
    071'.3090051—dc22   2006028548

British Library Cataloguing in Publication Data is available.

Library of Congress Catalog Card Number: 2006028548
ISBN: 0–275–99335–3
ISSN: 1932–6947

First published in 2007

Praeger Publishers, 88 Post Road West, Westport, CT 06881
An imprint of Greenwood Publishing Group, Inc.
www.praeger.com

Printed in the United States of America

The paper used in this book complies with the
Permanent Paper Standard issued by the National
Information Standards Organization (Z39.48-1984).

10 9 8 7 6 5 4 3 2 1

For my husband, Farhad Abdolian, who is the best person I know.

Contents

Series Foreword

On September 11, 2001, an enormous sea change occurred in our national political culture. The onset of that change can be traced further back, at least in part, to the disputed 2000 presidential election and the sporadic but portentous terrorist attacks on American lives and property during the 1990s. In recent months, new threats against the lives of air passengers have been discovered.

The 1990s now seem like a distant prelapsarian Eden, before the fall of the twin towers and the attendant collapse of our sense of security. Yet we remain at the very beginning of an era that will likely last for decades. We have not begun to measure the extent of the changes we see—in our personal lives and psyches, our communities, our nation, and the world; it will take years to fully comprehend where we are. As G. W. F. Hegel noted in the *Philosophy of Right*, wisdom comes in hindsight: "The owl of Minerva spreads its wings only with the falling of the dusk."

It is one of the burdens of journalism—including timely nonfiction books—to minimize this disparity between our situation and our understanding: to provide rolling accounts of events as they flow. It is no easy thing. But it is a burden for which journalists must be held accountable because such timely and time-constrained explanations are part of journalism's debt to democracy. Without them we cannot begin to figure out where we have come from and where we are going.

Even from the limited perspective of the present, we can look back over the past five years and see that a new climate of fear and insecurity has infected our politics; in some cases, it has been the politics of exploiting, or even propagating, fear and insecurity. Here, too, the national media are responsible as gatekeepers, along with public figures and the public in general. All share responsibility—but journalists are responsible most of all—for the quality and climate of information.

It is a premise of this series—and an axiom of modern life—that all politics is mediated. So to explore any change in our political culture is also to look at how it might have been mediated differently. To understand what is going on around us with any confidence, we must all be media critics not just capable of partisan sniping or finding bias under every journalistic rock but also capable of discerning good and bad journalism through a wider lens than our own political beliefs.

Thus, to understand the political sea change, we are still undergoing inevitably means exploring all aspects of the media's coverage of those still-unfolding events. To be sure, we await the verdicts of historians decades and centuries hence; but we don't have the luxury of merely sitting back and waiting for them. We must understand what is going on right now, with all the advantages and disadvantages of our immediacy to events. Our very democracy depends on it. For some things, such as the supposed weapons of mass destruction in Saddam Hussein's arsenal, knowledge has arrived too late.

As the only known alternative to force and fear, democracy is an endless process of criticism and countercriticism, and examination and cross-examination. It demands that we simultaneously use, observe, and critique our mediating institutions because, in gathering information and holding public institutions accountable, they represent us; we must talk and argue about their performance, just as we talk and argue about the performance of our political representatives. Both, for better or worse, are essential to the democratic process.

In any debate, it is important to be candid and critical about the facts. Being candid means finding the relevant facts and stating them clearly; being critical means keeping facts and values apart as much as possible. To the extent we can do that, we can have democratic debates—which by definition involve talking to, and not past, people with whom we disagree.

However, facts alone don't generally win or constitute arguments, at least not interesting ones. Facts are crucial nodes of agreement across partisan lines; they may embarrass particular policies or strategies but they seldom embarrass value systems. Only when the facts are abundantly clear, and point overwhelmingly in one direction, do they truly speak for themselves and acquire critical moral mass. And that is the case here; that is what makes the book you are about to read extraordinary and important.

Lisa Finnegan has performed an estimable service in laying out important facts (including the crucial subclass of revealing quotations by important players) regarding the performance of the American media since 9/11. She does so in a remarkably methodical, accessible, and non-polemical fashion. Those who would defend that performance, in regard to crucial issues of foreign policy, national security, and civil liberties, will confront a significant challenge here: a veritable wall of factual evidence of media failure. And much of the argument is made by journalists.

Indeed, the singular strength of *No Questions Asked* is that the facts that Ms. Finnegan marshal speak so eloquently for themselves, without partisan embellishment. And they tell a story of gross failure on the part of much of the American press corps. That is not to say countervailing facts might not be brought to light, or their importance debated. We must have that national conversation.

But while the significance of facts may be disputed, their existence cannot be denied, else all conversation stops.

That debate will further unfold in the coming years, as the Bush presidency becomes history and its astonishing effects on American life play out well into the twenty-first century. I believe *No Questions Asked* will be a key resource and point of entry for discussion, documenting the failed lenses of the national media for understanding our times. Students and scholars, journalists, and citizens will benefit both from this book and from the broader, clearer discussion it makes possible about the direction of our nation in this fateful time.

Jeffrey Scheuer, Series Editor
September 2006

Foreword

This book focuses on the scarcity of tough questions that has plagued the news media of the United States for many years. Real journalism thrives only when it scrutinizes the claims and actions of the powerful. But especially after the events of September 11, 2001, what we have gotten from major news outlets is more akin to stenography for the movers and shakers in Washington.

Of course, reporters should keep the public informed about what official sources have to say. But to stop there—to mainly convey the statements and information provided by officialdom—is to fail the true test of journalism. That test is independence.

When they function independently, journalists rely on a multiplicity of sources. By probing, searching, exploring, and excavating, journalists expose to the light of day what might otherwise remain hidden.

But in its prevalent forms, what we call journalism has a strong tendency to blend into the normalized scenery. In the short run, that's apt to seem like the "professional" thing to do. Most gainfully employed reporters want to be a bit ahead of the curve—without going too far out on a limb. In such an atmosphere, it takes a conscious act of will to look at the big picture and challenge the supposed truisms that might not be true.

Lisa Finnegan describes that professional atmosphere well. Journalists, she points out, "read and listen to each other's reports and compare and contrast the information in them. They note the presentation and the play of their peers' stories and compare them with their own. They often socialize together and sometimes with the politicians they cover. White House and Pentagon reporters often share their perspective through 'pool' reports, in which one reporter is given access to information and is expected to summarize it for others on the beat. As such, they are susceptible to groupthink..."

Anyone who is out of step—straying from conventional media wisdom—may lose access to official sources and coveted exclusive interviews. When journalists anger people in high places, the media career risks can be appreciable. But when journalists are careful to avoid angering people in high places, something is seriously amiss.

Too often we're encouraged to view high-quality journalism as nonconfrontational, in keeping with expectations that media professionals should do their jobs with rigorous neutrality. But passive acceptance of being spun—going along to get along with sources at places like the White House and the Pentagon—is a form of de facto advocacy. It has the effect of advocating by serving the interests of those sources.

Asking key questions is essential to the scrutiny process, which is the crux of journalism. Only by questioning what's on the surface can reporters and pundits shed meaningful light on profound choices to be made by individuals and institutions. Journalism can't answer the most important questions. But journalism should ask them.

Major U.S. media outlets have overwhelmingly failed to ask key questions in recent years. In this book, Finnegan documents how devastating that failure has been—for the quality of day-to-day news coverage and for the possibilities of wide-ranging democratic discourse in the United States.

To vigorously question is to enliven the body politic. To question only sluggishly, or not at all, is to facilitate the blockages that prevent the vital circulation of facts and ideas. Those blockages can be lethal for democracy.

Such patterns of media constriction have been long-standing. And the first years of the 21st century have made matters worse. As the author observes, "the American press corps enabled the Bush administration to cocoon the public to such an extent that it had only a vague notion about alternative viewpoints and policy options, or the consequences of American policy decisions worldwide." She quotes CBS anchor Dan Rather's succinct comment—a full decade before 9/11—that "suck-up coverage is in."

The launch of the ongoing "war on terror" enabled U.S. foreign policy—and American media coverage—to center on what Finnegan aptly describes as the "vague concept" behind it. A war against a defined enemy can end; a war against an undefined threat may not.

After 9/11, the label of terrorism quickly became so elastic that it could be stretched to suit the administration's preferences at any time. Big U.S. news outlets, far too eager to stay in sync with those preferences, have shown little interest in focusing on insights along the lines of those expressed by retired U.S. Army General William Odom, who told viewers of C-SPAN's *Washington Journal* on November 24, 2002: "Terrorism is not an enemy. It cannot be defeated. It's a tactic. It's about as sensible to say we declare war on night attacks and expect we're going to win that war." Continuing his heretical comment, Odom said: "We're not going to win the war on terrorism. And it does whip up fear. Acts of terror have never brought down liberal democracies. Acts of parliament have closed a few."

While some journalists grew to express skepticism about the nonstop "anti-terror" rhetoric from the White House and its supporters, the overall stance of news media has involved routinely embracing the assumption that the U.S. government is at war with terrorism. Along the way, that means ignoring how civilians in Afghanistan and Iraq have experienced terror as a result of American firepower.

We can now point to quite a few journalists who have gotten tough on the president's refusal to address substantive criticism without reverting to anti-terror rhetoric to tar his critics. But on the whole—and most egregiously in routine news coverage on front pages and news shows—the reporting has accepted and propagated the basic world view from Washington.

Only as journalists stop cowering and start reporting on the basic flaws of the "war on terror" will the body politic benefit from the free circulation of ideas and information—the lifeblood of democracy. And only then will there be appreciable media space to really explore why so many people have become violently angry with America.

No Questions Asked: News Coverage since 9/11 provides a valuable map of the media terrain that we will need to understand and explore to invigorate the role of journalism in our society.

Norman Solomon

Preface

Those who can make you believe absurdities can make you commit atrocities.
—Voltaire

Journalism is not an easy profession, but it is an important one. Without a vigilant press, government secrecy thrives and democracy suffers. The fourth estate is an important part of the checks and balances system in the United States.

Unfortunately, in the midst of the chaotic 9/11 hijackings and in the years that followed the first major foreign terrorist attack on U.S. soil, members of the press forgot that their role is to observe what happens, to ask difficult questions, and to report what they see and hear. Instead, journalists minimized alternative viewpoints, amplified the administration's perspective, and presented half-truths that misled the American public.

A survey from January through September 2003, released in October 2003, found that most Americans were extremely confused about the facts:

- Sixty-nine percent said they believed Iraq played an important role in the 9/11 attacks, with 13 percent claiming they had seen clear evidence of such a link.
- Fifty-two percent said they believed a link had been found between Saddam Hussein and al Qaeda.
- Twenty-two percent said the United States had found (WMD) weapons of mass destruction in Iraq, with 20 percent saying they believed biological and chemical weapons have been used against U.S. troops.

Most alarming of all, despite protests in cities across the globe, the majority of those polled believed the United States had worldwide support for the invasion of Iraq.[1] All of these assumptions were incorrect.

Where did Americans get the false information? They got it from the media. The same study revealed that the more an individual watched commercial television news in the United States, the more likely he or she was to be wrong about the facts surrounding the Iraq war and its aftermath. The study also found that the more misperceptions a person held, the more likely he or she was to support the war—and to rely on television news for information about the war. Overall, 60 percent of the people surveyed held at least one of the misperceptions mentioned above.

I want to be clear that the central point of this book is that the media did not do its job and report the news fairly, completely, and accurately—not that the press was insufficiently critical of the Bush administration. My goal was to write a facts-based book that critically examines the media's coverage of events since the 9/11 attacks.

American journalists claim they are not responsible for public policy or public support or rejection of a policy. The fact is they help determine how a policy is perceived by the public and are—whether they like it or not—part of the political process.

Ultimately, the question comes down to this: What is a journalist's job? Is it to provide a voice—and amplify the voice unchallenged—for an administration and its policy? To question everything an administration says and does? To read reports, analyze information, question administration officials, and educate the public? To act as the public's watchdog? To provide commentary that enhances dialogue? To simply report what everybody says and leave it at that?

The answer is complicated. I believe a journalist should certainly give a voice to the president and tell the public what he (and perhaps someday she) believes politically and personally. But responsibility should not stop there—that is, where the line is drawn between what state-controlled publications do and "free," democratic ones.

In democracies reporters have the responsibility to listen, analyze, question officials, question outside sources, consider all the information, call officials back for clarification if necessary, and write balanced stories that present all sides as fairly and accurately as possible.

Most importantly, a journalist must find a way to tell the public that an official is lying or that the facts are being skewed. This is tricky and most American journalists would claim that calling a politician a liar is exhibiting bias. It is difficult to ask high-level officials (or anyone) uncomfortable questions, but it is a journalist's job. Skeptical examination of information presented by officials is not biased reporting, but balanced reporting. At the very least information should be checked for accuracy before landing on the front page or leading the evening news.

If a president says the sky is falling, it should certainly lead the story. But the reporter should also look up, point out the sky seems fine and ask why the president thinks the sky is falling. A second and third opinion about the feasibility of the sky falling would also be a good idea.

There is another question to be pondered: What happened to the free press in the United States? Again, this is not an easy question to answer. Corporate ownership has played a role, as has a shrinking market share and a fierce fight for an audience.

But since September 11, 2001, other factors have emerged: fear, personal attacks on those who present alternative viewpoints, editors who allow themselves to be bullied by administration officials, and a general disregard for hard-charging journalism that includes the pursuit of difficult truths.

According to Christiane Amanpour, international correspondent for CNN, the press was "intimidated" by the Bush administration and Fox News. "I think the press was muzzled," she said, "and I think the press self-muzzled. I'm sorry to say, but certainly television—and perhaps, to a certain extent, my station—was intimidated by the administration and its foot soldiers at Fox News. And it did, in fact, put a climate of fear and self-censorship, in my view, in terms of the kind of broadcast work we did."[2]

Rather than bristling at the accusation, Fox News' Irena Briganti countered: "Given the choice, it's better to be viewed as a foot soldier for Bush than a spokeswoman for al-Qaeda."[3] Although it is difficult to understand how an entire press corps could be so easily bullied, Briganti's retort provides a hint. It suggests that an effective psychological campaign was launched against the American public and the media after the September 11 attacks. The media, like the rest of the world, was, as Bush so simply put it, "either with us or...with the terrorists." Given the choice, and his sudden popularity after the attacks, the press decided it was with the president.

The line was drawn in the sand early, and members of the media chose to fall in step. An emotional veteran newsman Dan Rather wept with talk show host David Letterman a few days after the 9/11 attacks and pledged: "George Bush is the president.... Wherever he wants me to line up, just tell me where."[4]

Many people, including members of the media itself, say the press has failed to do its job. Very few news reports filled in the basic blanks—the who, what, where, when, and whys—about U.S. foreign policy, the USA Patriot Act, the administration's insistence on the need for secrecy and for more power, the truth about WMD in Iraq, and the need for our soldiers to topple another country's dictator and send a tenuous region into dangerous imbalance. Very few reports are filling in those blanks now.

In this book I present examples of how the American media failed and some explanations why. I highlight the errors of those in the profession who should have known better. It is easy for journalists to blame corporate conglomerates, a lack of public interest, and groupthink for their decisions to skew the news after the 9/11 attacks. But make no mistake about it, members of the media made choices and the American public has suffered because of those choices. They deserve to be held accountable. If they are not forced to take responsibility, then they will continue to do a haphazard job reporting the news.

Finally, this book focuses on the media, but that does not mean I believe journalists are the sole guardians of truth and democracy. Reporters are one of several players in the checks and balances system in the United States. A democracy is "by the people, for the people," and the public has a responsibility to keep an eye on its government. The drafters of the Constitution made it clear that without public involvement, the system would fail.

Members of Congress should also be held accountable for legislation they pass without vigorous debate and for any breeches to the checks and balances. It is their job to ensure government remains open and honest. They (or their staffers) also need to pay closer attention to legislation they pass. Somebody, besides lobbyists, needs to read the legislation that is passing through the halls of Congress.

Acknowledgments

I was fortunate to have had an excellent first editor. Margie Freaney taught me the basics of news reporting and provided me with a sturdy journalistic foundation. I still remember her tough lessons and used much of what she taught me when analyzing news reports for this book. She is an excellent editor and teacher, and her careful reading of the book helped me tremendously.

Barbara Bromberg, Kerry O'Rourke and Chris and MaryJo McArthy all were patient readers whose suggestions helped shape the book, and I owe them all a big thanks.

Professor Harold Takooshian helped me to understand the theories of social psychology I mention in the book. He has been an excellent teacher, and I am extremely grateful for his guidance.

My goddaughter Kellyrose Andrews is always an inspiration. Her strength and courage amazes me. My godson Collin Sullivan's wit and determination reminded me of the importance of staying focused.

Hilary Claggett at Praeger and Jeffrey Scheuer, series editor, saw the book's potential, and I appreciate their feedback and support.

Finally, I want to thank my husband Farhad Abdolian, who remained patient and kind throughout the ups and downs of the publishing process. I couldn't have done it without him.

Introduction: A Patriotic Press

Every government is run by liars, and nothing they say should be believed.
                    —I. F. Stone, legendary investigative journalist

The day after George W. Bush was elected to a second term in office, the British *Daily Mirror* covered its front page with the headline: "How Could 59,054,057 People Be So Dumb?"

The headline stands in stark contrast to the empathy and support expressed by the world after the September 11, 2001, attacks. The day after the attacks, the *Mirror*'s headline was "War On The World." The French daily newspaper *Le Monde* ran an editorial with the headline: "We Are All Americans." The prime ministers of Germany and Sweden made similar statements.

Four years later, these sentiments have become reversed. Opinion in the United States and Europe, as the *Daily Mirror*'s post-election headline illustrates, is very different.

A January 2005 report by the Pew Research Center for the People and the Press stated that,

> Anti-Americanism is deeper and broader now than at any time in modern history. It is most acute in the Muslim world, but it spans the globe—from Europe to Asia, from South America to Africa. And while much of the animus is aimed directly at

President Bush and his policies, especially the war in Iraq, this new global hardening
of attitudes amounts to something larger than a thumbs down on the current occu-
pant of the White House.[1]

What happened to the feelings of unity expressed after the attacks? Why is the
thinking inside the United States and the support of George W. Bush so different
from beliefs outside the country such a short time later?

There are a number of answers, but the most relevant is that the information
people use to make their decisions, and how it is presented, was—and remains
—different in the United States and abroad.

After the terrorist attacks, journalists in the United States asked few questions, instead passively accepting and promoting the administration's point of
view. Alarmist statements by Bush and his staff led stories and opinions that cast
doubt on the administration's explanations were minimized or omitted. There
was little critical examination of the way officials framed events, threats, and
policy options, and the American media did little to provide the public with a
balanced perspective.[2]

Though the public does not base its decisions solely on information from the
media, the repetition of information by media outlets undeniably influences public opinion and election outcomes. Americans incorporated the media's one-
sided reports into their own biases and opinions, and re-elected George W. Bush.
People outside the United States took this to mean Americans supported his policy decisions after the 9/11 attacks, including the war in Iraq.

Journalists from other countries were more persistent with questions to their
own government officials and members of the Bush administration. They followed more leads, provided more viewpoints, and presented data that cast doubt
on the information provided by the Bush administration. This led many people
living abroad to believe the White House had misled the American public and
the world about a number of issues, including the purported links between Saddam Hussein and Osama bin Laden and the need to go to war in Iraq. People
who read these stories wondered how the American public could re-elect Bush.

Did the president mislead the public? The answer is the topic for another
book.

What is clear, however, is that the American press corps enabled the Bush
administration to cocoon the public to such an extent that it had only a vague
notion about alternative viewpoints and policy options, or the consequences of
American policy decisions worldwide.

Journalists have some basic responsibilities when covering a story: to record
the facts, to get as many details as possible, to gather as much background information as possible, and to use as much of this information as necessary to explain
what happened, what it means, and why it occurred. Good journalists also sort
fact from fiction and alert their audience when speculation or rumor is presented
as fact.

When the story reported is life altering, such as the 9/11 attacks, recording even the smallest details is important because the information may be useful in analyzing the situation later. If nothing else, it is important to have an accurate account of such an historic day.

Reporters with the president on the morning of the attacks failed to gather not only the small details that enhance a story but also some basic facts that would have enhanced understanding as the story progressed. National reporters who travel with the president and some local journalists covered Bush's elementary school visit that morning. The carelessness exhibited by the press that day foreshadowed the media's poor performance in the years to come.

Most reporters with Bush knew the planes had hit the World Trade Center towers soon after it happened. Because they were covering the president, they were among the first people their news organizations contacted. They understood, very early on, that it was a significant day in the history of the country. The first plane hit the tower before Bush arrived at the school, yet few reporters took note of the president's actions upon arrival. With whom did he speak? Was he ushered into another room where he was briefed about the situation? Did he look concerned? When and how did he learn about the hijackings?

When the second plane hit the World Trade Center, reporters' pagers and cell phones rang almost immediately with the news. Yet these reporters did not chronicle what happened in the classroom soon afterward, such as when the president's chief of staff, Andrew Card, whispered in Bush's ear that the second plane had hit, and how long after that the president left the room. Most reports say Card approached the president between 9:05 and 9:07, and that Bush left the classroom 6–15 minutes later. The *New York Times* account has Card breaking the news at 9:05 and the president leaving "abruptly" at 9:12.[3] However, there is no consensus about the facts among the journalists in the room that day.

The information was not difficult to obtain. The Emma E. Booker Elementary School has a videotape of the president sitting in the classroom with the children. According to the videotape, he was in the room for 15 minutes.

Looking back with the added knowledge that the president had received warnings about potential terrorist attacks—including an August 2001 daily briefing memo headed "Bin Laden Determined to Strike in U.S."—the value of a detailed account of Bush's actions that morning becomes clear. Years later, when the National Commission on Terrorist Attacks upon the United States (commonly known as the 9/11 Commission) investigated the calamitous day, its members said the administration was not cooperating and that they were having trouble collecting some information that journalists should have recorded that morning.

Additionally, reporters never asked for clarification of contradictory explanations by officials in the days after the event. For example, Bush told reporters he saw the first plane hit while watching television before entering the classroom that morning and thought the pilot had made a mistake. He later said Card had told him about the attack. Journalists were also told that Condoleezza Rice broke the news to him, that senior adviser Karl Rove told him, and that a teacher approached him with information about the crash when he arrived at the school. We still do not know how he learned about the first foreign terrorist attack on U.S. soil.

Knowing how Bush learned of the attacks is not irrelevant. The media's passivity in pursuing the details of that day illustrates three things: Journalists were shaken and decided not to ask questions that could be considered trivial; they did not want to cast doubt on officials' authority in a time of crisis; and they were focused on the fact that the United States was vulnerable, and deemed everything else unimportant.

While this may explain why journalists made the decisions they did, it does not mean the decisions were correct. When anyone contradicts an earlier statement or gives conflicting accounts of an event, journalists should pursue the issue further. The chances are good that the contradictions will lead to a story; at the least, reporters will learn which information is correct. This is important for several reasons; including that without knowing what happened, errors in the system cannot be corrected. The terrorists' success clearly shows there were flaws that needed to be fixed.

Additionally, if the media cannot obtain the answers to simple questions, how will it manage the more difficult ones?

By being so passive about collecting information and questioning the president's actions, the media allowed the administration to change the image of Bush over time from someone who did not appear to take control of the situation to that of a decisive, strong leader who took immediate action. The administration literally rewrote history. It was not until after Hurricane Katrina destroyed New Orleans in 2005 that the press discussed Bush's lack of leadership in times of crisis.

Members of the administration made several attempts to revise the public's understanding of the president's actions the morning of 9/11. In each telling, the president becomes more authoritative. Listen to Card tell reporter Brian Williams how the president reacted after Card whispered that a second plane had hit the WTC and "America is under attack": "I pulled away from the president, and *not that many seconds later, the president excused himself* from the classroom, and we gathered in the holding room and talked about the situation"[4] (emphasis added).

Bush spent much more than "not that many seconds" with the children after being told about the second strike.

A year later, Card wrote a column about his experience that morning. After whispering in the president's ear, he said, "*It was only a matter of seconds, but it seemed like minutes,*" before Bush looked up, "excused himself very politely to the teacher and to the students, and he left"[5] (emphasis added). It *seemed like minutes* because it was. The elementary school videotape shows it was 15 minutes.

PERCEPTION AND REALITY

Cognitive psychologists understand that perceptions are influenced by what is heard most often and that societal opinions are often based on misperceptions. These misperceptions are very often the result of media coverage. For example, the 1999 Columbine school shooting in Colorado led to an abundance of media stories questioning the safety of schools around the country. The media reports naturally left parents concerned about their children's safety, and there were calls for improved security at schools. What was not mentioned in the reports was that American schools were actually pretty safe. Information at the time of the tragedy, according to Glenn Muschert, a professor at Ohio's Miami University, revealed that

> one child in 2 million would be fatally shot at school per year—the same odds as being struck by lightning....A year later, the statistic was revised downward to one child in 3 million....There is a higher probability that a child will be victimized at home, involved in drug abuse, or die from drunk driving. Our schools are relatively safe, but Columbine created fear and terror in Americans for their children at school.[6]

Muschert contends that the way the media framed the event contributed greatly to the nation's panic and led to the false perception that schools were dangerous. Much of the media's focus was on the cause of the shootings and how the community had reacted, which made the crime seem less important than the reasons for the crime. "The search for this meaning then became a priority for people throughout the country so they could apply that information to their schools and communities."[7] What followed was intense scrutiny of school bullying and general teenage angst.

After the September 11 attacks, opinions that strayed from the administration's message were effectively minimized, resulting in a perception of unity. Members of Congress later said they felt bullied and were called dangerous and unpatriotic if they questioned even the smallest decision or statement by the president.

"No one would ever overtly question your patriotism," one reporter said in March 2002. "But there is a little sense of, 'this is wartime, how dare you ask those questions?'"[8]

The administration repeatedly said that "evil" enemies who were jealous of America's freedom had perpetrated the attacks. The explanation—as incomplete as it is—was echoed by the media and in time was perceived as reality. Very few other possibilities were discussed, and very few alternatives to the president's plans to hunt down terrorists around the world were debated. These unexplored explanations, and the fear and paranoia that accompanied them enabled the administration to convince the public of many things, including the fact that Hussein was its enemy (because of his complicity in the 9/11 attacks) and that unless he was removed from power, the United States was in grave danger. A means to convey this message was the U.S. media, and it was a very effective means.

IMAGES OF WAR

During World War II, *Life* magazine became famous for its pictures showing war in all its glory and all its brutality as well. The public embraced the pictures partly because it believed the country was fighting a just war.

Pictures of the current wars are much more anesthetized; they show little, if any, blood or pain. Civilian death and destruction caused by American troops in Afghanistan and Iraq are largely absent from American coverage. So are images of American soldiers and allied troops taking gunfire in the war zones.

The deaths of and injuries to American soldiers are mentioned, but few details are provided, and pictures rarely show their suffering. Ted Koppel, who was the anchor of ABC's *Nightline*, was severely criticized for dedicating an April 30, 2004, program to reading the names of the dead American soldiers as their pictures flashed across the screen. Sinclair Broadcast Group ordered its eight ABC affiliates to pull the program off the air.

Koppel said the program was inspired in part by the June 27, 1969, edition of *Life* magazine, which published pictures of 217 of the 242 Americans killed in action in a week in Vietnam.

The decision to read the names brought accusations of bias, and Koppel was accused of politicizing the war. He concluded the broadcast by saying: "Our goal tonight was to elevate the fallen above the politics and the daily journalism. The reading tonight of those 721 names was neither intended to provoke opposition to the war nor was it meant as an endorsement."[9]

When somber pictures of a military plane full of flag-draped coffins ran in the *Seattle Times*, they became among the most controversial images of the war even though no blood or chaos was shown; in fact, the pictures were eerily calm and serene. Like Koppel's broadcast, however, the images were met with discomfort.

Defense Secretary Donald Rumsfeld summed up the reaction well when he said, "Death has a tendency to encourage a depressing view of war."

Many newspaper editors would argue that they do not run pictures of bloody corpses or of those injured in the war because the images are not appropriate for "family" publications. However, the same media outlets chose to run grisly pictures of Hussein's dead sons, Uday and Qusay. The bloody and bruised faces of the dead men covered the full front page of some publications. The justification came straight from the Pentagon, which convinced journalists that the pictures should run because they helped prove the identity of the men. Unsaid was the fact that they also helped validate claims that the United States was on the road to victory.

The results of this type of easy acceptance of official explanation could influence journalism for years to come, as illustrated by the classroom experiences of Auburn University Professor Dale Harrison. Harrison showed his Media Law and Ethics class the pictures of Uday and Qusay that ran in newspapers and asked whether editors had made the correct decision in publishing them. Students almost unanimously said editors were right in running the pictures and echoed the Pentagon's reasoning that they helped identify the men and confirm their death.

However, when shown images of American contractors whose charred bodies were dragged from their burning vehicles and hung from a bridge in Iraq, students said editors had made a mistake in running the photos because the victims' families may not have been notified and the images were too disturbing.

Rather than basing their decisions on whether the images were newsworthy or too graphic to run, they personalized the content of the pictures as Americans and made their decisions accordingly.

"The age-old question is whether a journalist is a citizen or journalist first," Harrison said. "Their reaction has been as Americans and not as students of journalism."[10]

Harrison said he had expected more diversity in the students' reactions and closer attention to bias and objectivity in the decision-making process. Since the 9/11 attacks, he has often had to argue the opposing view in classroom discussions. "Normally, the students do that for you, but to a large extent, it has been a chorus of 'America the Beautiful,'....It's almost impossible to get students to see there is an opposite point of view. [For them], there is no other point of view."[11]

MEDIA MANIPULATION GAINING GROUND

The Project for Excellence in Journalism's report on the State of the News Media 2004 found that those who are trying to manipulate the media are gaining ground. The project's study notes that reporters are facing an increased workload as organizations cut costs and the "simple supply and demand" pressure of a 24-hour news cycle makes it a "seller's market for information." The growth of blogs, Internet news sites, cable news shows, and talk radio has led the mainstream media to pick up questionable stories it would have ignored years ago.

A good example is the Swift Boat Veterans for Truth's disparaging allegations about Democratic candidate John Kerry's Vietnam war record. The allegations dominated the 2004 presidential election campaign for months.

The *New York Times* stenographically wrote about the allegations for more than five months before debunking them in stories that chronicled the relationship members of the group had to the Republican party or the Bush family. Alison Mitchell, deputy national editor of the *New York Times*, said the paper would have ignored the story a few years ago but was forced to cover the allegations so it did not lose readers or appear to be biased. "I'm not sure that in an era of no cable television, we would even have looked into it," she said.[12]

In the aftermath of the 9/11 attacks, many journalists came to believe their job was to report what government officials said or believed, and increasingly confused skepticism and questions with bias. This philosophy can be seen in everything from news stories about the terrorist attacks to allegations about WMD in Iraq. In short, journalists stopped being critical news gatherers and became more like official messengers.

After the September 11 attacks, journalists were perfectly willing to keep their questions in check for what they were told by officials was the safety of the nation and were submissive enough to present information as fact, even if there were doubts about its accuracy. Dozens of questions remain unanswered about September 11, 2001.

For instance, were the planes hijacked with plastic knives and box cutters, as claimed by the administration and the FAA (Federal Aviation Administration), or with knives, guns, and bombs, as reported by those on board the aircraft that day? Information about what happened on those planes is still unclear. My point in introducing this information is not to state as fact that the hijackers had guns and bombs, but to highlight that the media never persistently pursued the truth, got the facts, and reported them accurately.

Information casting doubt on the plastic knife version of events was available in newspaper archives and in bits of information reported in fringe publications. Occasionally, the material was reported in mainstream outlets, but for the most part, it was ignored.

UPI (United Press International) reported that a leaked FAA memo written the night of September 11 said a passenger on Flight 11 had been shot. The FAA deleted any reference to gunfire on board in its final version of the memo and said the original was only a draft. The draft memo said that passenger Daniel Lewin was shot. Lewin was later "identified as a former member of the Israel Defense Force Sayeret Matkal, a top-secret counter-terrorist unit, whose Unit 269 specializes in counter-terrorism activities outside of Israel." The shooting incident was not mentioned in later UPI stories and was largely ignored by the mainstream press.[13] The 9/11 Commission report said Lewin was stabbed.

The AP (Associated Press) reported that Boston's Logan Airport (where two of the hijacked planes originated) had been plagued with security problems for years.

> In 1999 the major airlines at Logan and the Port Authority were fined a total of $178,000 for at least 136 security violations over the previous two years. In the majority of incidents, screeners hired by the airlines for checkpoints in terminals routinely failed to detect test items, such as pipe bombs and guns. Also in 1999, a teen-ager...allegedly sliced through a fence and settled into an empty seat on a British Airways jet and flew to London.[14]

It is possible that the AP story received minimal play because the country was still raw with pain and shock, and much of the focus at that time was on the search for possible survivors. While this may help explain the media's decisions, it does not excuse them. A journalist's job is to remain clearheaded during times of trouble and to ferret out important truths. Without understanding the severity of airport security problems, it is difficult to know how to correct them and protect against future terrorist attacks.

Five months after the attacks, a special agent with the FAA, Bogdan Dzakovic, became a controversial whistle-blower when he came forward with information claiming he had tried to correct security problems at airports for 14 years. *USA Today* reported in February 2002:

As a member of the Federal Aviation Administration's undercover security team, Dzakovic documented failure after failure to detect simulated bombs or other weapons at airports worldwide. In a complaint filed with the federal government he alleges, "The more severe the security problem we identified, the more the FAA tried to bury the information."[15]

He told Congress:

In 1998, the Red Team completed extensive testing of screening checkpoints at a large number of domestic airports. We were successful in getting major weapons [guns and bombs] through screening checkpoints with relative ease at least 85 percent of the time in most cases. At one airport, we had a 97 percent success rate in breaching the screening checkpoint. No action was taken to remedy this security problem, and we have never been back to any airport to test security in this manner. In 1999, our testing results of the approximately million dollar per unit CTX bomb detection machine was so poor that my boss ordered the Red Team to start notifying local FAA management several days before we were to conduct tests at a given airport....Our government is now poised to spend $2 billion on these machines.[16]

Rather than attack the issues raised by Dzakovic with hard-hitting questions to high-level officials, the following month, the *Washington Post* and the *New York Times* both reported that airport officials had done all they could to stop the terrorists on September 11. Airport security was so efficient, the papers said, that several of the hijackers had been stopped on the morning of the attacks for additional baggage checks.

The *Times* reported,

Nine of the 19 terrorists who hijacked four jetliners on September 11 had been singled out for special scrutiny that morning under aviation-security guidelines, government officials said today, as they looked back sadly at what might have been. But because their baggage contained no explosives, the hijackers were allowed to board....Although details were sketchy, they seemed to tell a story not of ineptitude but of security procedures overtaken by new terrorist tactics.[17]

The timing of the information's release should have caused editors to pause for reflection. Why not ask about Dzakovic's allegations and include an official's response in the story?

Additionally, despite assurances from the airline industry, it does not appear that security has significantly improved.

In August 2003, a woman was arrested in Philadelphia when she tried to board a second plane with a loaded .357 magnum handgun in her carry-on. She had just gotten off a plane from Atlanta with the gun in her bag. In January 2004, a woman flew from New York's LaGuardia Airport to Denver with a knife and stun gun in her carry-on bag. She realized her mistake during a layover and alerted authorities. Airports have also admitted that cargo luggage is loaded into the holds of passenger airplanes without being examined.

Did the hijackers have guns and bombs? Is airport security safer? Is the United States relying on the CTX bomb detection machines that Dzakovic and his team found ineffective?

In September 2003, 75 percent of Americans said they were satisfied that the government was doing a good job of protecting them from terrorists. The question is, however: Can they really know if they are safer if they don't have the necessary facts?[18]

WHERE WERE THE FOLLOW-UP QUESTIONS?

The press has a history of suspending its skepticism and supporting the government during times of war. With the onset of war, readership skyrockets and television news ratings rise. Reporters become excited about the possibility of following troops to the war zones. It is perceived as an adventure that casts a spotlight on them and their work.

After a conflict has ended, however, reporters are often their own most outspoken critics. But this does not stop them from repeating their errors.

Here is CBS anchor Dan Rather's description of the media's pro-government coverage of Grenada, Panama, and the Persian Gulf wars:

> Some of what happened was because of a lack of will, a lack of guts to speak up, to speak out, speak our minds. . . .Obviously politicians have learned ways to intimidate individual reporters, news organizations, and the press in general.[19]

He added that, during times of national crisis, reporters

> begin to think less in terms of responsibility and integrity, which get you in trouble . . .and more in terms of power and money. . . .Increasingly, anybody who subscribes to this idea that the job is not to curry favor with people you cover. . .finds himself as a kind of lone wolf [who] probably ought to wear one of those shirts that says "last of the independents," and will be in the minority. . . .Suck-up coverage is in.[20]

While there were some reporters who remained independent and skeptical after the 9/11 attacks—most notably the *New Yorker*'s Seymour M. Hersh, the *Washington Post*'s Dana Milbank and Knight Ridder Washington bureau reporters Warren Strobel and Jonathan Landay—most did not. What is telling is that many in the media continued to bow to administration officials even after publicly acknowledging their failures.

During a conference a year after the 9/11 attacks, Rather disparaged reporters for their passivity.

"The height of patriotism," he said, "is asking the tough questions....We haven't been patriotic enough....It is our responsibility to knock on doors every day and ask what's going on in there even if it makes us unpopular."[21]

During a BBC interview Rather acknowledged that nationalism can become overwhelming in the heat of battle: "One finds oneself saying: 'I know the right question, but...this is not exactly the right time to ask it.'"[22]

A government official may refuse to answer a question, but a reporter is paid to ask regardless. Rather's comments were so startling to Europeans that he made the front page of several British newspapers. His comments barely made a ripple in the United States, and most Americans never heard his remarks.

He was not the only journalist who voiced such criticism. CNN's Aaron Brown recalled the internment camps that held Japanese-Americans during World War II and worried that the lack of oversight by a passive press might lead to another national embarrassment.

"We need to raise questions about the [Afghan] detainees, how they are being treated and about due process, and we need to follow these stories....This is the nature of our role in a free society," he said.[23]

Christiane Amanpour, CNN's chief international correspondent, famously declared that news agencies were "intimidated" by the Bush administration and Fox News.[24]

However, even as journalists claimed to recognize their errors, they remained silent when the administration began building its case for war in Iraq. The White House began linking Hussein and bin Laden and making claims about Iraq's WMD shortly after Rather, Brown, and others vowed to ask more questions and exhibit more skepticism about government policy.

The information to cast doubt on many of the administration's statements about WMD was available from reliable sources, including current and former U.N. weapons inspectors, and was reported in European publications. Even Colin Powell had stated publicly that Iraq's weapons program had been crippled by years of sanctions. But this information was largely absent from coverage of the debate in the United States

This propensity to bow to the administration was not diminished even as the war in Iraq moved from a "cakewalk" to an expensive, prolonged commitment of troops.

ACCESS DENIED

As a result of the media's passivity and "patriotism," some long-standing rules regarding access to public information—the basic tool of its trade—were weakened and will hamper journalists for years to come.

At least two major tools used to obtain information about government policy and decisions were gutted by the administration with barely a ripple of notice in the press: the FOIA (Freedom of Information Act) and the 1978 Presidential Records Act. Congress passed both laws after the Watergate scandal when it realized that unchecked presidential power could lead to abuse. Both have since been used by journalists, academics, and the public to monitor the government's actions.

Among other things, FOIA requests were responsible for Ford's pulling its Pinto car off the market in 1978 after information about its defective gas tank became public, the acknowledgement that Agent Orange was used in Vietnam, and the resignation of Vice President Spiro Agnew after George Washington University students forced the release of 2,500 pages of state and federal documents.[25] It is an invaluable tool for journalists and the American public alike.

Yet the media did not put up a fight when Attorney General John Ashcroft sent out a memo on October 12, 2001, announcing a new policy directive restricting access to information available under FOIA.

Ashcroft reversed a decades-old policy of open access to government documents when he advised all executive agencies to refuse requests for information whenever possible. All court challenges would be vigorously defended by the Justice Department, he said in a memo.

"Previously," a lawyers group complained, "the Department of Justice would defend an agency's refusal to release information under FOIA only when it could be argued that releasing the information would result in 'foreseeable harm.' Under the new directive, however, Ashcroft urged agency employees to consider all potential reasons for non-disclosure."[26]

Rather than report the policy change with stories describing the history of the act and its use to protect the public and prevent government abuses, a handful of papers ran short stories on inside pages. The broadcast media barely uttered a word about FOIA.

On October 17, 2001, the *Washington Post* ran an AP story about the policy reversal on page A15 with the headline "Ashcroft Urges Caution With FOIA Requests." The *New York Times* did not broach the subject on either its editorial or its news pages until January 2003.[27]

Editorial writer and columnist Ruth Rosen summed up the situation three months after the policy change in a January 7, 2002, column in the *San Francisco Chronicle*:

> The President didn't ask the networks for television time. The attorney general didn't hold a press conference. The media didn't report any dramatic change in governmental policy. As a result, most Americans had no idea that one of their most precious freedoms disappeared on Oct. 12. Yet it happened. In a memo that slipped beneath the political radar, U.S. Attorney General John Ashcroft vigorously urged federal agencies to resist most Freedom of Information Act requests made by American citizens.[28]

In November 2002, most information collected under the Homeland Security Act was exempted from FOIA regulations. "Critical infrastructure information" voluntarily provided to the Department of Homeland Security is not subject to disclosure under FOIA. Critical infrastructure includes telecommunications, energy production, banking and finance, transportation, water systems, and emergency services. All 22 federal agencies within the Department of Homeland Security and its more than 170,000 employees do not have to comply with FOIA.

Another major action that went largely unreported was President Bush's reversal of the 1978 Presidential Records Act. The 1978 Presidential Records Act was created amid concern that Richard Nixon would never allow public access to his records. Without such access, Congress feared, presidents could rule in secret.

Under the Act presidential papers were to be made available to the public 12 years after the president left office. The executive order that Bush signed on November 1, 2001, reinterprets the Act, giving the White House and former presidents the right to veto the release of any White House documents.

What does that mean? Bush and Cheney's papers prior to the September 11 attack through the war in Iraq are now protected. Bush's new executive order was never announced, yet it prompted members of Congress from both parties to urge the president to reconsider. He refused. The order covers Presidents Ronald Reagan, George H.W. Bush, Bill Clinton, and George W. Bush, their vice presidents, and all future presidents and vice presidents.

Most of the changes made by Bush's executive order have no expiration date and thus would continue in effect long after he is gone.

More than *two years* after the federal squeeze on information, the media decided that perhaps it had made a mistake in not covering the administration's actions more vigorously. Washington journalists held a luncheon and vowed to fight for their fading right to access government data.

"Press efforts to thwart government secrecy are moving forward on two fronts as Washington bureau chiefs unite to more aggressively cover federal government attempts to hide information and the head of Associated Press offers plans for a new open government lobbying center in Washington, D.C.," *Editor & Publisher*, a magazine for the publishing industry wrote in June 2004.[29] Bureau chiefs said they would urge reporters to get more information on the record, reporters would be trained to look for secrecy abuses in government and bring any denial of access to their bosses for review, and AP would open a media advocacy center to lobby for access.[30]

Vickie Walton-James, the *Chicago Tribune*'s Washington bureau chief said, "The real issue is telling our readers what it is they are not getting. We need to pay attention to this, and not just when a big case pops up."[31]

It is good that members of the press decided to fight for their rights, but it took too long. Once again, the members of the media looked back at their passivity during a time of national crisis with regret. Walton-James demonstrates that journalists recognize their failures quite clearly, but they do little to correct the problems that led to these failures, and so the cycle continues.

Part of the problem is that many political reporters have become confused about what constitutes a story. This is especially true for those covering the nation's capital. Throughout the years, focus has turned from the very practical —how does this law, regulation, or policy affect my readers or viewers—to the more trivial scandal-driven, he said/she said bickering of partisan politicians.

Many journalists covering Washington are simply too close to their sources. As the lines blur and reporters are drawn into the bubble-world of insider tidbits and politicians' quarrels and infidelities, they lose sight of the real stories and their responsibilities as journalists.

The *Washington Post*'s Bob Woodward is a good example of what can happen when reporters become too close to their sources. During the buildup to the Iraq war, Woodward was writing a book about the administration and had information that there were concerns about the validity of the intelligence being used. He knew that some officials did not believe that Iraq had WMD and were concerned about where the president was getting his information. Instead of sharing this with his editors, however, he wrote pro-Bush stories that ran on the front page of the paper. The few stories written by *Post* reporters who questioned the intelligence information were delegated to back pages. Woodward later said he should have shared his information.

Woodward did not learn from his mistake. Years later, when special prosecutor Patrick Fitzgerald was investigating who revealed the identity of secret CIA (Central Intelligence Agency) agent Valerie Plame, he did not tell his editors or Fitzgerald that he was most likely the first journalist to receive the leaked information from administration officials. Woodward told his editor months later, right before Lewis "Scooter" Libby was indicted for perjury and obstructing justice. He apologized to his editor, but not to his readers. "I explained in detail that I was trying to protect my sources. That's job number one in a case like this."

Woodward did more than protect his sources, he denigrated Fitzgerald's probe during television and radio interviews and denounced him as a "junkyard dog" who "turns over rocks, and rocks under rocks." Actually, it's also a reporter's job to "turn over rocks and rocks under rocks." Woodward had obviously confused his role as independent news gatherer with that of an author and political insider.

While it is useful for a reporter to know the background of politicians, the knowledge is more useful if it helps shed light on an issue of relevance. In other words, the partisan bickering or personal infidelity should not always be the story—the results and implications of the political maneuvering should be— and that is rarely the case anymore.

The situation is compounded by the struggle for an audience in a shrinking market and fierce competition from talk radio and pundits. Journalism is not an easy job, however, without the press pausing for an objective—and sometimes critical—look at a situation and asking the tough questions, it is difficult for the public to get the information it needs to make informed decisions. Without an informed constituency, governments rule unchecked.

THE WAR ON TERROR

A good example of journalists' enhancing public ignorance rather than providing clarity is the lack of questions that followed President Bush's declaration of a war on terrorism (later shortened to a war on terror) and the belief that a war against a concept could be won or lost on a battlefield.

American philosopher William James said, "War is the only force that can discipline a whole community." This applies not only to the public but to journalists as well.

The day after the 9/11 attacks, Bush said: "The deliberate and deadly attacks which were carried out yesterday against our country were more than acts of terror; they were acts of war. This will require our country to unite in steadfast determination and resolve....This will be a monumental struggle of good versus evil, but good will prevail."[32] The president ordered the country to be disciplined or risk falling prey to "evil" forces like the terrorists responsible for the attacks, which he framed as "an act of war" and a conflict between "good and evil."

North Carolina State University Professor Robert Entman writes:

> Framing is the central process by which government officials and journalists exercise political influence over each other and over the public. Successful political communication requires the framing of events, issues, and actors in ways that promote perceptions and interpretations that benefit one side while hindering the other.... Framing entails selecting and highlighting some facets of events or issues, and making connections among them so as to promote a particular interpretation, evaluation, and/or solution.[33]

Certainly, the media has a responsibility to report what the president and his top officials say, but the statements should also be analyzed, clarified, and debated.

When the president declared a "war on terror," the American media allowed him and his administration to frame the issue without asking for a definition of a war on terror or terrorism. The parameters of a war on terror were never explained.

The definition of terrorism may seem clear: Flying a commercial plane full of passengers into a building full of civilians is an act of terrorism. But what else falls under the category of "terrorism"?

In July 2002, a U.S. military plane dropped bombs on a village in Afghanistan. More than 100 people attending a wedding party lost their lives. The *New York Times* article about the incident was headlined, "Hunt for Taliban Leaves

Village With Horror." Should the Afghan civilians attacked that day consider what happened an act of terrorism?

Is the IRA (Irish Republican Army) a terrorist group? The British government believes the IRA is responsible for a December 2004 bank robbery in Belfast that netted $39 million. If the IRA is a terrorist group, then the money it obtained from the robbery should be a source of concern. What should the U.S. response be?

Should immigrants from Middle Eastern countries who remain in the United States after their visas expire be considered terrorists, as Ashcroft believes?

Where do you draw the line if you do not have a clear definition?

Few journalists have pointed out that America's enemy in this "war on terror" is not a person, a country, or even an ideology—it is a methodology. Terrorism is a tool that has been used by the desperate for decades. One very valid question largely ignored by mainstream journalists is, how do you fight a concept? Ronald Spiers, a retired diplomat who served as U.S. ambassador to Turkey and Pakistan and as Assistant Secretary of State for Intelligence, put it this way:

> A "war on terrorism" is a war without an end in sight, without an exit strategy, with enemies specified not by their aims but by their tactics. Relying principally on military means is like trying to eliminate a cloud of mosquitoes with a machine gun. "Terrorism" by its nature can't and won't be eradicated or abolished as long as there are grievances that the aggrieved believe cannot be resolved nonviolently.[34]

The *Times Union* of Albany, New York, was one of the few newspapers in the nation to print an editorial looking at the waging of a war with no concrete enemy.

> In only his second address before Congress since taking office last January, President Bush faced the difficult task of defining a war that defies conventional definition, and preparing the American people to pay its price in resources and young lives. Other presidents have summoned the nation to war before, but under vastly different circumstances. The enemies, and the battlefields, were identifiable. So were the military tactics necessary for victory....The administration is defining a war that cannot be won, that will never end....To eliminate the possibility of terror you would have to eliminate the human race, hardly an acceptable solution.[35]

The first moves in the war on terror were straightforward and were reported as such by the press. Bush announced that bin Laden and al Qaeda were responsible for the attacks, and were primarily based in Afghanistan. Other countries cooperated with the United States in attempts to financially stifle the offending groups. The United States launched an attack on Afghanistan.

But things soon became more complicated. The terminology used to frame an event or issue depends on the context in which it is introduced. Because a "war on terror" is such a vague concept, the administration was able to categorize a country or regime as part of the war or not part of it at will. There were no specifications to qualify the decisions and therefore no way to determine whether the terrorist label was correct.[36]

In this way, the Iraq war became part of the war on terror, as did the search for WMD and the hunt for Islamic extremists there. North Korea, which acknowledged possessing a nuclear weapon, was called a "terrorist regime" but was excluded from the war on terror. Iran and Syria "harbored" terrorists and were a part of the war on terror.

On the home front, immigrants who overstayed their visas became threats to national security and hence a part of the war on terror, as were Muslims who behaved "suspiciously" and drug dealers and racketeers caught by using the Justice Department's new tool, the USA Patriot Act.

It became difficult for journalists to understand who a terrorist was because the context kept changing.

Journalists should have recognized the problem of placing a generalized label on a complex topic because they were clearly warned early on. But rather than question the officials about it, reporters covered the issue as a political jousting match.

In March 2002, after the administration had requested a military budget of $4.7 trillion over a 10-year period, then-Senate Minority Leader Tom Daschle said he was concerned that Congress was not getting enough information about the war on terror.

> What I'm simply saying is that I think the time has come for us to be asking a lot more questions. We have a constitutional obligation to ask those questions. The right questions are, "How do you define success? How do you ensure that what it is we're doing is ultimately going to lead to success? What will Phase Two require, and how many troops are there going to be there? Will our allies be involved? How do we define success in the out years? How much is it going to cost? How long will they stay?"[37]

Daschle essentially did half of the media's job by pointing out the relevant questions that needed to be answered. Yet, rather than ask, reporters focused on the subsequent war of words that took place among members of Congress. The slew of stories that followed his remarks reported the Republicans' "disgust" with his lack of patriotism and chronicled what members of Congress said about his comments.

Senator Trent Lott got a lot of press when he said, "How dare Senator Daschle criticize President Bush while we are fighting our war on terrorism, especially when we have troops in the field?" Articles mentioned the fact that Daschle was a potential presidential candidate and had waffled on issues in the past. This information may be relevant, but so are the questions he asked. No reporter was persistent enough to get answers to Daschle's questions from administration officials.

Journalists are not the sole guardians of truth or the sole investigators in the political process. Daschle and other Democrats were correct in highlighting questions they had, and journalists were correct in reporting them. But journalists have the added responsibility to question the president and his representatives during open forums and to get officials on the record with answers to important questions (or even the acknowledgement that they do not have the answers). How we win a war on terrorism is a very valid question that the president should have been forced to answer.

About a week after Daschle's comments, Bush made what the *New York Times* called a "forceful" speech outlining the second phase of the war on terror.

I have set a clear policy in the second stage of the war on terror: America encourages and expects governments everywhere to help remove the terrorist parasites that threaten their own countries and the peace of the world. If governments need training or resources to meet this commitment, America will help.[38]

Daschle again provided journalists with the follow-up questions that were never asked. He told the *Times:* "'I think he defined the goals. [But] I think we still have a lot of work to do in making sure we understand how we reach those goals.'" Daschle's "questions were now specifically focused on Mr. Bush's pledge to provide any nation with military training and aid in the campaign against terrorism. 'How do we do that?' Mr. Daschle asked. 'What is the cost and the time frame, and who are we talking about?'"[39]

A few months later, Bush said that the United States "must uncover terror cells in 60 or more countries," or roughly one-third of the world. The *Washington Post* said,

The speech was the broadest definition to date of the way Bush sees America's new role in the world after the September 11 attacks. He said that not only will the United States impose pre-emptive, unilateral military force when and where it chooses, the nation will also punish those who engage in terror and aggression and work to impose a universal moral clarity between good and evil.[40]

The article did not include statements from any sources questioning the legality of U.S. use of pre-emptive force "when and where it chooses" or what some of the potential ramifications of such a policy might be. It did not address how the United States would pay for uncovering terror cells in 60 or more countries. Nor did the paper run any other article addressing these questions.

The United States is divided over issues of "moral clarity" such as gay marriage and stem cell research. A legitimate question is, who determines what is morally right and morally wrong on contentious issues such as these? How can anyone "impose a universal moral clarity" on a diverse world?

Helen Thomas, who spent 40 years as UPI's White House correspondent and is now a columnist with Hearst publications, said the media has ignored very basic questions about the war on terrorism. "9/11 instilled in everyone that we have to be patriotic. You get out of that by demanding answers: What is terrorism? What is terror? If you can't get to the root of a problem, how can you solve it? There aren't enough guns in the world to kill hatred."[41]

Thomas said reporters have yet to become forceful in their questions. She has been removed from her long-held front row seat at White House press conferences and briefings, and reassigned to the back row where her questions remain unasked.

> He won't call on me, and I'm in the back row now, so I'm ignored....They don't like my questions. That's okay, just so somebody asks them, but they just don't want me to ask questions....If I was a favored columnist, I'm sure I'd be in the front row again....I do think all of us [in the press] have laid down on the job early on [after 9/11]. Some of us are coming out of a coma. But nobody's being challenging enough. We are adversarial, we aren't there to worship at anybody's shrine. We're there for accountability.[42]

While there has been some debate about why she lost her seat (some believe it is because she became an opinion writer rather than a news reporter), Thomas is right. If she cannot ask the questions, someone else should. Unfortunately, few of her colleagues have her courage, least of all those at the agenda-setting papers like the *Washington Post* and the *New York Times*.

A HUMBLE PRESS

The problem seems to be that as the war on terror progressed and morphed, the press also lost its focus. The fear that journalist Rather mentioned appears to have played a role. Reporters have said they were afraid to appear unpatriotic, afraid to anger readers and viewers who they believed were in a nationalistic fervor, afraid to ask the wrong question, and afraid to anger Bush and lose their access to officials on his staff.

Nowhere was this fear and passivity more obvious than at the president's press conference on the eve of the war in Iraq on March 6, 2003. Reporters were escorted into the room in pairs and when the president entered the room, he ignored the raised hands and said he was only calling on those on his pre-approved list, in the pre-approved order. Unauthorized question were unacceptable. "This is a scripted press conference," he said at one point.

And what did reporters ask the president as he prepared to launch a war? Should Americans pray? Did he lay awake at night worrying about his responsibilities to the nation? How was his faith guiding him? Little information was dispensed at the press conference, and listeners were left with no greater understanding of the issues.

Former NPR *Morning Edition* host Bob Edwards later wrote: "You can't hold a press conference without the press, yet the president almost did. Where were they that night?"

Elisabeth Bumiller, the *New York Times* White House correspondent, said:

> I think we were very deferential because...it's live, it's very intense, it's frightening to stand up there. Think about it, you're standing up on prime-time live TV asking the president of the United States a question when the country's about to go to war. There was a very serious, somber tone that evening, and no one wanted to get into an argument with the president at this very serious time.[43]

It is undoubtedly intimidating to stand before the president on the eve of a war and ask an uncomfortable question that is broadcast live to the entire nation. Very few people like conflict, and the reporter would have been criticized for asking such a question. But journalists are paid to ask the uncomfortable questions, no matter how intimidating or difficult it may be.

A few relevant questions—such as how do we quantify success if we go to war in Iraq—would have been appropriate. Time has shown that killing individual terrorists, the course of action pursued by the administration after the 9/11 attacks, is not effective in stunting terrorism. In fact, the opposite holds true. The capture of Hussein resulted in an abundance of terrorist activity in Iraq. In fact, terrorist attacks have plagued the world. In Madrid, 200 died and 1,500 were injured in coordinated bomb attacks on a commuter train the morning of March 11, 2004. On July 7, 2005, 52 people were killed and 770 injured in a coordinated bomb attack in London.

Philosopher George Santayana's famous statement that, "Those who cannot remember the past are condemned to repeat it" should be the mantra of the American press.

In his memoirs, published in 1998, George H. W. Bush said the United States did not continue into Iraq after the Gulf war because it would have been a disaster.

> Trying to eliminate Saddam, extending the ground war into an occupation of Iraq ...would have incurred incalculable human and political costs....We would have been forced to occupy Iraq and, in effect, rule Iraq....There was no viable "exit strategy" we could see....Had we gone the invasion route, the United States could conceivably still be an occupying power in a bitterly hostile land. It would have been a dramatically different—and perhaps barren—outcome.[44]

Many of the same journalists who covered the Gulf war are now covering the Iraq war—some of them should have some archival knowledge. Even a small town paper has an editor who can recall the tiniest detail about a crooked planning project that occurred 20 years ago. Why couldn't Dan Rather, Peter Jennings, Tom Brokaw, or any *New York Times* or *Washington Post* reporter remember George H.W. Bush's words about invading Iraq and ask his son about his exit strategy?

CHAPTER 1

A Fearful Press

I'm the commander—see, I don't need to explain—I do not need to explain why I say things. That's the interesting thing about being president. Maybe somebody needs to explain to me why they say something, but I don't feel like I owe anybody an explanation.

—George W. Bush[1]

Immediately after the bombing of several commuter trains in Madrid, the Spanish government blamed the incident on the Basque separatist movement, ETA (Euskadi Ta Askatasuna). Journalists who investigated the March 11, 2004, attacks noted historic differences between the way in which ETA operated and the way the Madrid bombings had been carried out, and they questioned the government's view.

Reporters peppered officials with difficult questions and ran stories that undermined their explanation. The government refused to acknowledge that it was likely an al Qaeda attack and continued to claim ETA was a suspect. Heated debates between those who supported and those who opposed the government's view were broadcast daily on Spanish radio and television programs. Editorials criticized attempts to hide information about the perpetrators of the attack and alleged that the government's support of the war in Iraq was the reason why 200 civilians had been killed and 1,500 injured in the Madrid attack.

Eventually, reporters uncovered information revealing that the bombings were carried out by a group of al Qaeda operatives in the country, and government officials were forced to acknowledge that al Qaeda was responsible for the commuter train bombings. Despite U.S. officials' repeated claims that the terrorist group was attempting to win the war on terror by manipulating the Spanish people and frightening them into withdrawing troops from Iraq, the next election led to a change in leadership and the removal of Spanish soldiers from Iraq.

This type of hard-nosed journalism was something American reporters avoided in the aftermath of the 9/11 attacks. In part, that fact has to do with the history of the countries. Spain has had experience with terrorist bombs exploding on its soil, and its people have a more pragmatic approach to dealing with such events. Terrorist acts are considered crimes, and journalists approach their job in covering them from that perspective. They pursue information in much the same way a U.S. journalist would pursue information in a sensational murder trial.

As such, the public sees the violence and chaos that result from the terrorist acts reported in the media, followed by a proactive response from journalists who demand answers, and this coverage shapes the public's perceptions about the event and its consequences.

This did not occur in the United States after the 9/11 terrorist attacks.

Most Americans received information about the attacks and their aftermath from television news. A nationwide survey from September 14 through September 16, 2001, found that Americans watched an average of 8.1 hours of television news on the day of the attacks. Eighteen percent of those polled watched at least 13 hours of television that day.[2]

Media scholars argue that the television news format for a live, breaking story causes viewers to respond on an emotional level in both positive and negative ways. The format provides powerful imagery—often juxtaposed with images from past tragedies—accompanied by alarmist language that triggers reactions.

A study about the emotional tone of media reports on the 9/11 attacks and the audience response noted that "emotional response to a social issue may be the result of exposure to televised news coverage, which then motivates political action and civic participation. Based on the literature in political psychology, we can also expect that emotional responses can function as a heuristic device in forming opinions and attitudes."[3]

After the terrorist attacks in Madrid, Spaniards saw fierce opposition to their leader's decision to mislead them. They subsequently elected a different leader.

After the attacks in the United States, Americans saw the media line up behind their president and their country. Journalists wore flag pins on their lapels while reporting the news, and stories hailed President Bush as a strong leader of a great nation. Americans responded by supporting their leader and continued to do so years later, even after information pointing to official deception was presented.

There is a Danish proverb that says those who are afraid to ask questions are afraid to learn the truth. Journalists knew that the 9/11 attacks was one of the stories of the century. A *Denver Post* editor said that despite a tight budget and an abundance of wire stories, the paper decided to send staff reporters to an assortment of cities to cover the terrorist attack and U.S. responses to it because "no story is more local than the one that changes every one of our readers' lives. The events of 9/11 did just that."[4]

Despite this knowledge, American journalists did not focus on the problems that led to the tragedy. Certainly, the 9/11 attacks were of a greater magnitude than the Madrid bombings. But unlike the forceful push for accountability in Spain, journalists in the United States did not pursue questions that would clarify how the world's greatest military power had allowed so many men to board commercial airplanes and ram them into landmark buildings.

There are still no clear answers about what happened in the United States that day, why it happened, and what corrective action should be taken to prevent another such catastrophic attack.

One explanation is that fear played a role in the media's passive behavior. Fear was palpable on September 11, and several panicked journalists lost their composure on camera. The attack was bold and vicious and hit the nation on a crystal clear day—the damage could be seen from miles away. Like the rest of the world, journalists were bombarded with images of the twin towers collapsing, panicked people fleeing through the streets of Manhattan, a wall of smoke pouring out of the Pentagon, and a hole in the ground in Pennsylvania.

Journalists had the added trauma of taking the photographs, filming the towers crumbling, and interviewing survivors and victims' family members. Many of them wrote articles about "running for their lives" in downtown New York that day, believing they would not survive.

It is not unusual for reporters to find themselves in dangerous situations, and, on 9/11, as people ran away from the towers in Manhattan, reporters ran toward the scene. What is unusual is that even experienced war correspondents say the 9/11 terrorist attacks were personal and affected them deeply. For the first time, Americans faced the reality of a terrorist strike at home, changing the perception that the country was immune to foreign attack. The victims were not strangers in a foreign land but friends and family members, and journalists had difficulty disconnecting the events they were experiencing from their jobs as objective observers.

REPORTERS TRAUMATIZED

Susan Watts, a photographer for the *New York Daily News*, survived a kidnapping and murder attempt in Honduras but told an *Editor & Publisher* reporter that she found the 9/11 attacks more terrifying.

When those buildings were coming down and we were running for our lives, we weren't journalists anymore—we were victims. We became part of the story. Everything became surreal—and it still is. There's a hole in the sky, and your compass is gone. You lost your sense of place.[5]

According to the story, Watts had phoned her editor that morning and reported that she thought they "were all going to die."

"The most jarring thing was seeing myself and my colleagues just fall apart on the job," she said.

That never happened before. You never saw photographers being emotional. After 9/11, I'd be at funerals and memorials and my colleagues' eyes would be bloodshot, tears running down their faces. Hardened, seasoned photographers who'd seen war, been in Vietnam. It was utterly disturbing to me.[6]

Adam Lisberg, a reporter for the *Record* in Hackensack, New Jersey, said:

That morning, the adrenaline was flowing. I knew what I was doing. Then, all of a sudden, once the building came down, everything changed...It broke down that wall between yourself and what you're covering that you always put up...I'm not the same reporter I used to be.[7]

Media studies have shown that images of violence on television news can alter the viewer's perception of danger. Renowned media scholar George Gerbner spent years studying the influence of television on viewers and found that the more hours a person spent watching TV, the more insecure and vulnerable he or she felt. He labeled these feelings "mean world syndrome" and wrote,

if you are growing up in a home where there is more than say three hours of television per day, for all practical purposes you live in a meaner world—and act accordingly—than your next-door neighbor who lives in the same world but watches less television. The programming reinforces the worst fears and apprehensions and paranoia of people.[8]

This applies to those who watch television news as well. After a devastating earthquake in California's Santa Cruz Mountains, researchers found that "increased exposure to television news [about the quake] corresponded to higher levels of fear for respondents in the affected area. Increased viewing also reflected higher estimates of damage and destruction."[9]

A national survey conducted on the weekend after the 9/11 attacks found a strong correlation between stress and television viewing habits. Those who had watched more television news about the terrorist attacks reported more symptoms of stress.[10] Another study found that those who had watched news about the attacks more closely were angrier than those who had paid less attention.[11]

Exposure to these images is no different for the people reporting the news. In fact, seeing the World Trade Center towers fall may have enhanced the feelings of insecurity. People struggle to understand how a new danger fits into their perception of reality and cope in a variety of ways, including becoming fearful and angry. The terrorist attacks altered Americans' perceptions of safety. And the images that appeared on television screens showing the terror of those fleeing the scenes were difficult to escape.

The attacks were followed by the equally terrifying threat of a biological attack in the form of anthrax. A reporter for a tabloid newspaper in Florida was killed when he was exposed to the agent while opening his mail. A postal worker died after being exposed while sorting the mail. Officials warned about the potential for attacks on water and food supplies, spreading the fear to small communities far from New York and Washington, D.C.

The Justice Department repeatedly told Americans that al Qaeda operatives living in the United States were planning another attack. The public perception—fostered by media coverage of official warnings—was that another large attack was likely.

However, the reality is that more people in the United States die each year from preventable diseases stemming from obesity and smoking than have ever been killed by terrorists. In 2001, terrorists killed 2,978 people in the United States. That year, 2,911 people below the age of 20 were killed by guns in the country; heart disease killed 700,142, cancer 553,768, and accidents 101,537.[12] The likelihood of being killed by a terrorist in the United States is very small.

But fear is a difficult thing to control. The magnitude and implications of the 9/11 attacks were so overwhelming, and the images were so terrifying, that many reporters had trouble disengaging from their fear. The result was stories that highlighted the strength of the president and his staff—the very people responsible for protecting the country.

The change in journalists' portrayal of the president and the administration after 9/11 was immediate. As often occurs during times of crisis, the president was described as the strong leader of a great nation. Newspapers that ran critical articles and editorials about Bush in August for taking a month-long vacation after only six months on the job hailed his leadership ability in September. He was no longer a bumbling novice prone to mispronunciations—overnight, he had become a mighty commander leading his country in the darkest of times.[13]

"At the moment the first fireball seared the crystalline Manhattan sky last week, the entire impulse to distrust government that has become so central to U.S. politics seemed instantly anachronistic," said a *Los Angeles Times* column, "The Government, Once Scorned, Becomes Savior," published six days after the attacks.[14]

"Government to the Rescue," read the *Wall Street Journal* on September 27, 2001: "As America braces for a war on terrorism...it's time to declare a moratorium on government-bashing....September 11 has underscored the centrality of government in our lives."[15]

An editorial in the *Washington Post* said that Bush's "simple, almost Truman-esque tones" during his first speech after the attacks were just what the country needed. "The public does not suspect Bush of verbal guile."[16]

Anecdotal stories about Bush's competence were abundant. The *New York Times* detected a "new gravitas" in the president because he held a live press conference a month after the attacks. The paper said in an editorial that Bush "seemed more confident, determined and sure of his purpose and was in full command of the complex array of political and military challenges that he faces in the wake of the terrible terrorist attacks of September 11."[17]

He had grown into his role as commander-in-chief within weeks, the media assured the American public. *Fortune* magazine said, "almost everyone agrees that George W. Bush is a different President than he was two months ago," a contrast from "the easygoing, back-slapping fellow who never showed much interest in the rest of the world."[18]

As if words were not enough to convey the change in the Bush administration, *Vanity Fair* ran a series of Annie Leibovitz pictures of staffers that evoked images of Greek gods. "Trust these people" was the subliminal message.

The message was received. A *Washington Post* poll released on September 27, 2001, found 64 percent of Americans "trust the government in Washington to do what is right" "just about always" or "most of the time." The last time the *Post* conducted such a poll, in 1997, only 27 percent said they trusted the government.[19]

Another study, in November, found that 82 percent believed Pentagon officials were being honest and disclosing as much information as they could, including all the bad news. Eighty percent had confidence that the government was giving an accurate picture of the war in Afghanistan.[20] Almost 90 percent approved of the president and his actions. The numbers were astonishingly high and led to another round of positive media stories.

"Suddenly, Americans Trust Uncle Sam," a *New York Times* headline read. "Cynicism is out and trust in government is up to levels not seen since the height of the Vietnam War," reported the Scripps Howard News Service.[21]

There are several possible reasons the media and the public reacted the way they did. When a new threat enters a previously safe environment, the immediate decision is simply whether to approach it or avoid it: the instinctive fight-or-flight mechanism. In the case of the 9/11 attacks, it was impossible to escape the reality of the event. But it was very possible to avoid the reasons behind the attacks and to craft a more comfortable reality.

The media stories and editorials influenced public opinion and helped create the Bush administration's image as strong, trustworthy, and reliable. The press also helped the administration convince the American public that the country had been attacked because of its freedom and democracy—not because of its foreign policy, as bin Laden claimed. This explanation enabled Americans to avoid responsibility while simultaneously preparing to fight to protect their way of life.

Recent books and statements by former high-level Bush cabinet members have provided some insight into how this misconception flourished in the post-September 11 climate of fear. Those who worked closely with Bush say he demanded unquestioning acceptance of his decisions, many of them based on his "gut instincts." Some say he intimidated those who did not agree with him and that he considered dissent betrayal.

Ron Suskind described the president's style in a *New York Times Magazine* article:

> A cluster of particularly vivid qualities was shaping [Bush's] White House through the summer of 2001: a disdain for contemplation or deliberation, an embrace of decisiveness, a retreat from empiricism, a sometimes bullying impatience with doubters and even friendly questioners. Already Bush was saying, "have faith in me, and my decisions, and you'll be rewarded." All through the White House, people were channeling the boss. He didn't second-guess himself, why should they?[22]

This was not the first time the White House had been in this state. John Dean, counsel to President Richard Nixon, said staffers were united in their beliefs about covering up the Watergate break-in and protecting the president. Nixon and his aides did not waver from their position and did not consider alternative positions, which led to a unanimous but confused perspective, Dean said.

He described

> an atmosphere of unreality in the White House that prevailed to the very end. If you said it often enough, it would become true. When the press learned of the wiretaps on newsmen and White House staffers, for example, and flat denials failed, it was claimed that this was a national security matter. I'm sure many people believed the taps were for national security, but they weren't. That was concocted as a justification after the fact. But when they said it, you understood, they really believed it.[23]

The difference in recent years has been that this distortion has spread to the press corps who also believed what they were told. Because of the 9/11 attacks, journalists were more willing to give the president the benefit of the doubt. Reporters largely accepted the contention that some things were being kept secret for "national security" reasons.

ARE YOU WITH US OR AGAINST US?

Bush made it clear to the world that he was not interested in discussion or debate when he said on September 20, 2001: "Either you are with us or you are with the terrorists." While his ultimatum was directed at other countries, the line he drew compounded the problem for journalists, who did not want to be "with the terrorists."[24]

Members of Congress who disagreed with the president were publicly chastised. Members of the press who asked difficult questions lost their access to top
officials.

As a result, government warnings about another terrorist attack were amplified by journalists who reported information without pausing for reflection or
asking relevant questions. These stories increased the public's fear.

During one orange terror alert, the news media widely reported warnings by
Homeland Security officials about impending chemical attacks and their advice
to buy duct tape to insulate houses. The stories caused a run on duct tape as
Americans rushed to follow instructions and guard their homes against hazardous
chemicals. Embarrassed government officials later admitted that tape offers little
protection against chemical weapons.

Geraldo Rivera described the atmosphere on CNBC on September 13, 2001:

> New York and Washington are rattled, shaken, edgy. Police action and perverse
> false bomb threats are causing frequent closings of institutions of various kinds from
> the private school across the street from my girls' home in Manhattan to the Capitol
> building, the White House itself in D.C. Buildings are opened, only to be closed.
> Commercial flights are started, only to be stopped. Sirens pierce air still filled with
> the dust of disaster, and our anger brims at the bastards who have wrought this awful
> travail.[25]

News reports made more terrorist attacks seem inevitable, and the question
was not whether the country would be attacked but when. It was a climate in
which paranoia thrived, and reporters were not immune to its influence. Paranoia blocks out rational thought and makes it difficult if not impossible to dis-
criminate between real and imagined or escalated threats.[26]

On September 17, 2001, CNN began a report with the question:

> Are we ready for this frightening and potentially even more deadly threat: chemical
> and biological weapons in the hands of terrorists?... The most likely biological
> killer terrorists might use, experts say, is anthrax. It can easily be found in cow pas-
> tures. Agents made from it produce fever, stomach pain, then a horrible death....
> Still more terrifying, though much harder for terrorists to get their hands on, [is] a
> disease that was eradicated in the 1970s, smallpox...[which killed an estimated]
> 120 million people in the 20th century.[27]

A few weeks later, the first death from anthrax inhalation was reported in the
United States, causing more panic and chaos. Manhattan subway trains were
stopped in tunnels while white substances on platforms and tracks were investigated. Sugar and powdery substances were banned from airplanes after a sweet-
ener caused panic on a plane. Congressional offices were closed. Bomb threats
continued to disrupt life throughout the country.

A sense of chaos had overtaken even day-to-day activities, so much so that even commuting to work or opening mail caused anxiety, paranoia, and fear. Caught up in this just as the public was, the media simply recorded what the administration said. It did not explore the issues that were raised in any depth.

For example, in an action reminiscent of the detention of Japanese-Americans after Pearl Harbor, a massive roundup of about 1,200 Arab men followed the terrorist attacks. It was a major story that was largely ignored by the media. If it was noted at all, it was mentioned within larger stories discussing how the Justice Department was protecting the country. Few if any articles in major media outlets provided historical context about U.S. responses to perceived threats during times of crisis, or reminded the public about the Japanese internment camps during World War II.

A report from the Migration Policy Institute, a nonpartisan, nonprofit think tank that has two former Immigration and Naturalization Service leaders on its board, later found that none of the men arrested was charged with terrorist activities. The only charges brought against them were for routine immigration violations or petty crimes. The report said that the roundup "provided ammunition to some of the fiery imams who encourage young people [to sacrifice] themselves."[28]

PARANOIA AND PUBLIC REACTIONS

There are many examples of fear-induced paranoia shaping societal opinions. In the aftermath of the 1995 Oklahoma City bombing, the media immediately latched onto a rumor that three men of "Middle Eastern heritage" were seen fleeing from the area. Police chased the Arab ghosts around the country before realizing their mistake.

Investigative journalist Steven Emerson told CBS Evening News shortly after the tragedy: "Oklahoma City, I can tell you, is probably considered one of the largest centers of Islamic radical activity outside the Middle East.... This bombing was done with the intent to inflict as many casualties as possible. This is a Middle Eastern trait."[29] A New York Times story about the bombing called Oklahoma City "the home to at least three mosques" without explaining why the number of mosques in the city was relevant. Columnist Mike Royko called for the immediate bombing of civilian infrastructures abroad: "If it happens to be the wrong country, well, too bad."[30]

Ron Noble, who was the Treasury undersecretary for enforcement at the time, said about the confused reports: "What happens is the media is so intent on investigating our investigation [that] any kind of lead that's being followed [by us is] being followed [and reported by the media]. So there are a lot of false reports."[31]

It is an important observation. Often, journalists spend so much time trying to understand the motives of government officials and worrying about what their competitors are filing that they lose sight of the story itself and report rumors and speculation as fact. The result is a dizzying array of information that is reported and then often taken back. It leaves the public confused and promotes a sense of instability and paranoia.

While reporting on September 11, the late broadcast journalist Peter Jennings recalled his initial reaction to the Oklahoma City bombing: "I remember sitting in this exact same chair at the time of the Oklahoma City bombing, and we all thought it was a Middle East attack. We all thought it was the Arabs attacking the United States, and that's where much of the violence is these days, but it was sort of a knee-jerk reaction, then it turned out to be one of our own."[32] Jennings seemed to be reminding himself to retain his objectivity and to keep his eye on the ball in the face of a national crisis.

As time passed, however, it became increasingly difficult for the media to maintain its focus. Attention was often diverted by terror alerts or press conferences about the arrest of alleged terrorists. It took a long time for journalists to understand their failures and to acknowledge that they had spent too much time trying to understand what the administration was thinking and too little time examining the facts, chasing down leads, and reporting the news. By the time journalists did realize their mistakes, the United States was deep into the war in Iraq.

It was not until late 2004, when it was clear that no WMD had been found in Iraq, that editors on major newspapers acknowledged that they had allowed themselves to be deceived.

EXPLANATIONS

After 9/11 the media experienced a surge in popularity. Polls shortly after the attacks showed that for the first time in 16 years, the American public felt journalists were doing a good job and were acting responsibly. It is possible that after years of scorn, journalists were enjoying their newfound popularity and did not want to appear to be too aggressive in dealing with a well-liked president.

Their decision, however, allowed the administration to ignore some potentially awkward reasons for the attacks. Violence is never an acceptable response, and the perpetrators of the 9/11 attacks were misguided and wrong. Still, it is important to explore the reasons why they said they attacked. Osama bin Laden did not say he attacked the United States because he hated its freedom and democracy. He said it was because of U.S. policy in the Middle East—in particular, the country's strong ties to Israel and the thousands of U.S. troops left in Saudi Arabia after the first Gulf war.

For devoted Muslims, Saudi Arabia is considered to be *the* holy land. The presence of the U.S. military, and especially female American soldiers who do not follow the country's strict dress code, is considered a "sinful crime against Islam." Freedom and democracy were discussed by the administration and in American media reports but were never mentioned by the enemies of the United States.

In an open "Letter to the American People" released on November 24, 2002, bin Laden said:

> Why are we fighting and opposing you? The answer is very simple: because you attacked us and continue to attack us....You attacked us in Palestine....You attacked us in Somalia; you supported the Russian atrocities against us in Chechnya, the Indian oppression against us in Kashmir, and the Jewish aggression against us in Lebanon. Under your supervision, consent, and orders, the governments of our countries, which act as your agents, attack us on a daily basis. These governments prevent our people from establishing the Islamic Shariah, using violence and lies to do so. These governments give us a taste of humiliation and place us in a large prison of fear and subdual.[33]

The letter continued: "The American Government and press still refuses to answer the question: Why did they attack us in New York and Washington?"

The letter was printed in several publications in Europe, Australia, and elsewhere, but an extensive LexisNexis search did not turn up any references in publications in the United States. Americans were denied another chance to better understand their enemy.

In the early days after the 9/11 attacks, a handful of reporters did ask the "why" question and were persistent enough to push administration officials for a response. CNN's online web site ran a comprehensive article about bin Laden's grievances on September 26, 2001. In a September 12, 2001, interview with Paul Wolfowitz, Fox News reporter Brit Hume said, "it is a kind of conventional wisdom that it is U.S. support for Israel that occasions the hatred of us in parts of the Arab world, and that is really, at bottom, what this all about."[34]

In time, however, this "conventional wisdom" was overwhelmed by the administration's more persistent claims about being attacked because of the country's freedom and democracy.

According to the psychological theory of cognitive dissonance, people have a basic need for their beliefs, attitudes, and actions to be consistent. When they are not, it becomes extremely uncomfortable. Naturally, people avoid information that increases this distress and search for ways to relieve the discomfort. The terrorist attacks in the United States opened a whole host of issues that had rarely been explored by most Americans. While most observers outside the United States pinpointed the country's foreign policy as the reason for the attack, most Americans had never considered the implications of their government's actions abroad.

Thus, questions such as who attacked us and why caused great distress and confusion among the general population. In his September 20 speech to Congress, Bush helped calm this discomfort when he said:

> Americans are asking, why do they hate us? They hate what we see right here in this chamber: a democratically elected government. Their leaders are

self-appointed. They hate our freedoms: our freedom of religion, our freedom of speech, our freedom to vote and assemble and disagree with each other.[35]

The president's words comforted Americans; they could relieve some of the dissonance they were experiencing.

How could Americans be so blind to such a growing hatred?

It is hard not to place much of the blame on the American media. Throughout the years, international news was edged out by "infotainment" in the United States. A study of newspapers by the University of California at San Diego found that international news accounted for a mere 2 percent of total newspaper coverage in 1998, down from 10 percent in 1983. A Harvard University project found that in 1970, 45 percent of total network coverage was devoted to international news; by 1995, that number had plummeted to 13.5 percent. That is a decline of 70 percent. Another study found that in 2000, the three major networks—ABC, CBS, and NBC—had a combined total of 1,382 minutes of news from their foreign bureaus, down more than 65 percent from 1989.[36]

This is another example of the media's misinterpreting what the public wanted. Polls showed that the public did not want its international news cut. "When the Pew Research Center for the People and the Press asked Americans in 1996 what kinds of stories they regularly followed, 15 percent named international news; that was 1 percentage point below Washington politics and just ahead of consumer news (14 percent) and celebrity news (13 percent)."[37]

When asked why the media had failed to track the events that led to the 9/11 attacks or to provide any sort of warning to the American public, journalist Mike Wallace responded: "Like the rest of America, we were fat, happy, and arrogant." He added that to his 60 Minutes viewers, a story about bin Laden or al Qaeda would have looked like "Arab extremists in some godforsaken country raving on about loathing America." That, he said, would not make the cut on the competitive program.[38]

Infotainment edged out hard news and continues to do so. Celebrity break-ups or sensational crimes still beat out news about the war in Iraq.

An Obedient Press

For many people, obedience is a deeply ingrained behavior tendency, indeed a potent impulse overriding training in ethics, sympathy, and moral conduct.
                                        —Stanley Milgram, social psychologist[1]

Obedience to authority is such an integral component of a productive society that some would say it is a necessary element in a civilized world. Drivers obey traffic laws and pull over when signaled to do so by a police officer. Employees do their bosses' bidding during the course of the workday. Soldiers obey their commanding officers.

But just how far will people go when it comes to obeying authority? A world history polluted with genocide suggests that many will go as far as requested.

To understand this tendency to obedience, social psychologist Stanley Milgram created an experiment at Yale University that pit "stark authority" against the subjects' "strongest moral imperatives against hurting others."[2]

Milgram found that ordinary people—homemakers, construction workers, social workers, office workers—would yield to authority and administer what they believed were painful, potentially fatal electric shocks to a middle-aged man in another room rather than submit to their own nagging concerns about their actions. Participants' apprehension was so real that it manifested physically with stuttering, profuse sweating, and trembling. But despite their obvious discomfort, and with their "ears ringing with the screams of the victims [whom they believed they were shocking in the next room], authority won more often than not."[3]

Milgram noted:

> I observed a mature and initially poised businessman enter the laboratory smiling and confident. Within 20 minutes, he was reduced to a twitching, stuttering wreck who was approaching nervous collapse. He constantly pulled at his ear lobe and twisted his hands. At one point, he pushed his fist to his forehead and muttered "Oh God, let's stop it." And yet he continued to respond to every word of the experimenter and obeyed to the end.[4]

Milgram concluded that the experiment's results

> raise the possibility that human nature, or—more specifically—the kind of character produced in American society, cannot be counted on to insulate the citizens from brutality and inhumane treatment at the direction of malevolent authority. Ordinary people, simply doing their jobs, and without any particular hostility on their part, can become agents in a terrible destructive process. Moreover, even when the destructive effects of their work become patently clear, and they are asked to carry out actions incompatible with fundamental standards of morality, relatively few people have the resources needed to resist authority.[5]

Milgram's experiment was duplicated repeatedly around the world, and the findings remained consistent.

Imagine his experiments in an environment loaded with the tension of real-world dangers like the ones that followed the 9/11 attacks. If people cannot resist authority during times of relative calm, how can they resist during a terrorist attack when fear is well-founded and obedience may very well save lives? With thousands dead from suicide attack missions, fatal biological agents arriving in the mail, and authority figures telling people to obey or risk further attacks, the urge to comply may be overwhelming. It certainly was for journalists.

While members of the press like to consider themselves immune to pressure from authority, the fact is that most are not. During times of uncertainty, like a buildup to war, reporters tend to be more subservient than objective. Additionally, administrations are not adverse to using "national security" as a chit that they call in from time to time.

History shows that a call by a president claiming risk to national security can squelch a news story even in times of relative calm.

In 1961, *New York Times* reporter Tad Szulc uncovered a government plan to use CIA-trained Cuban exiles to invade Cuba in an attempt to overthrow Communist leader Fidel Castro. He wrote a story describing how anti-Castro Cuban defectors had trained in Florida and Guatemala since 1960, with financial support and direction from the CIA. It was set to run on page A1, with a four-column headline, when President John F. Kennedy learned about the story and called the paper's Washington bureau chief. Kennedy said running the story would threaten national security and asked editors to use restraint. The next day, a short, single-column story ran down the side of the front page. Reference to a planned coup attempt in Cuba was eliminated, as was any mention of CIA involvement. The story received little attention and was soon forgotten.

Ten days later, 1,500 Cuban exiles landed at Cuba's Bay of Pigs and attempted to overthrow Castro. Within three days, 114 of them were dead, and more than 1,000 were captured and imprisoned. The disastrous mission drew international attention and resulted in harsh criticism of the United States and Kennedy. It was one of the low points in Kennedy's term as president and provoked anti-American protests in Europe and Latin America.

Kennedy later told the *Times* Managing Editor Turner Catledge, "if you had printed more about the operation, you could have saved us from a colossal mistake."[6]

Journalists, however, did not learn the history lesson. After the 9/11 attacks, members of the media were again approached by the White House with requests to self-censor the news. Again, they complied.

During a conference call with network television news executives in October 2001, National Security Adviser Condoleezza Rice urged them to stop airing bin Laden's statements in their entirety. Rice argued that bin Laden could be sending coded messages to his followers, which could threaten national security and open the United States to further attacks.[7]

Broadcasting bin Laden's messages, she told the executives, could increase anti-American sentiment among Muslims in the United States and other countries that aired CNN, Fox News, NBC, ABC, and CBS.

Rice offered no evidence that secret messages were being embedded into statements and ignored the fact that anyone, anywhere could easily access bin Laden's proclamations online, on the radio, and via satellite television. If he were so inclined, bin Laden could reach his followers in any number of other ways—through individuals with tapes or letters, by sending messages through the mail, by creating a coded web site, or by sending coded e-mails. Despite this, all the major U.S. networks agreed to censor their news. Why? They said they wanted to be "patriotic."

"In deciding what to air, CNN will consider guidance from appropriate authorities," CNN's official statement read. CNN chief Walter Isaacson added, "after hearing Dr. Rice, we're not going to step on the land mines she was talking about." CBS News President Andrew Heyward told the *Washington Post*: "We are giving the government the benefit of the doubt." News Corporation chief Rupert Murdoch agreed: "We'll do whatever is our patriotic duty."[8]

Network executives were rewarded for their compliance when the president sent word that Americans were safer because of their actions.

Ari Fleischer told reporters: "The president is pleased by the reaction of the network executives....The same request that was made yesterday of the network executives will also be made to other media because of the same principle."[9]

Noam Chomsky once said, "Any dictator would admire the uniformity and obedience of the [U.S.] media." Here's why: When the next tape from bin Laden spokesman Suleiman Abu Gheith aired on Al-Jazeera a few days later, Fox News Channel and MSNBC did not show any of the footage. The other networks either paraphrased the statement or showed part of the tape followed by dismissive statements from U.S. officials that the remarks were propaganda.[10]

A similar request by the British government that the nation's press corps ban bin Laden from broadcasts was met with a definitive no. No such request was made to Canada's media, and television and radio programming there provided comprehensive coverage that included bin Laden's messages and analysis of their meaning and context. Osama bin Laden's messages were broadcast worldwide, with everyone but Americans gaining important knowledge about their enemy.[11]

Many journalists in the United States would say this interpretation of events is simplistic and naive. They would claim that during times of war, the media has a responsibility to cooperate with the government to protect the public.

It is true that journalists should use caution when reporting details such as the specifics of military strategy or operations. But statements by groups or organizations opposing the U.S. government's actions are news and should be broadcast, debated, and, when warranted, discredited. Instead, virtually every uncomfortable dialogue or anti-American opinion was ignored or mocked by the media after September 11.

The networks chose to present pro-administration views and promote a sense of nationalism. Erik Sorenson, president of MSNBC, told the *New York Times* that there was not enough dissent about the government's actions to warrant coverage. "There has not been a lot of debate, period....Most of the dissent we've had on the air is the opposite—conservatives like John McCain and Bill Bennett saying we should bomb more or attack Iraq."[12]

Studies have shown that it is human nature to seek conformity and to acquiesce to authority figures and group pressure. Psychologist Irving Janis popularized the phrase "groupthink" to describe how group pressure often limits open discussions about issues and creates a mindset that minimizes options. Janis found that those working within a cohesive group often become so focused on presenting a united front that they block out alternative viewpoints and limit discussion of different options. "Concurrence thinking becomes so dominant in a cohesive ingroup that it tends to override realistic appraisal of alternative courses of action," Janis said.[13]

He found that groupthink often leads to self-censorship, illusions of morality, stereotyping (in which dissenters are considered weak, stupid, or dangerous), and direct pressure on dissenters to conform. Those who succumb to groupthink are selective in the information they gather and avoid data that contradict or cast doubt on the group's decision.

The comments by MSNBC's Sorenson about dissent against the Bush administration's actions reflect groupthink. He said there was not enough disagreement with the government's policies to warrant coverage, then, to back his claims, pointed to "on air" discussions in which conservatives called for the administration to more aggressively pursue its chosen course of action. The problem with this logic is that those who strongly objected to the government's actions were not given air time to discuss their perspective or to voice their dissent. Sorenson, like other members of the media, was of the mindset that because he did not hear dissent in the media, there was none.

Washington, D.C., is a self-contained, bubble world of politics, and members of Congress have often been accused of being out of touch with the reality of average Americans. Journalists who cover the nation's capital live in an even smaller world depending on their beat: the White House, the Pentagon, or an agency. Some cover Washington from the perspective of a specific state or city, and information is filtered down to fit that particular looking glass.

Journalists on these beats could certainly be considered what Janis called "ingroups." They read and listen to each other's reports and compare and contrast the information in them. They note the presentation and the play of their peers' stories and compare them with their own. They often socialize together and sometimes with the politicians they cover. White House and Pentagon reporters often share their perspective through "pool" reports, in which one reporter is given access to information and is expected to summarize it for others on the beat. As such, they are susceptible to groupthink and appear to have succumbed to it in the aftermath of the 9/11 attacks.

Journalists later said they believed administration officials' claims about Iraq's weapons capabilities, partly because everybody was saying the same thing. ABC's Ted Koppel said: "Did I believe at the time that there were weapons of mass destruction? Absolutely, I did."[14]

CNN's Wolf Blitzer explained it this way during an appearance on *The Daily Show with Jon Stewart*: "It's groupthink....You know, when you're told repeatedly—everybody said the same thing—there is no doubt, there are stockpiles of chemical and biological weapons, and it's only a matter of time before he has a nuclear bomb. Condoleezza Rice said on my show...'We can't wait for a smoking gun to be a mushroom cloud.' You remember that?" Blitzer added, "We should have been more skeptical."[15]

Groupthink has been attributed to everything from the Vietnam War to the Challenger space shuttle explosion and the media's handling of the information about Saddam Hussein's weapons capabilities. It can be avoided by using simple techniques that should be second nature to journalists: playing devil's advocate (even in one's own thinking) and seeking outside opinions.

Social psychologist Solomon Asch designed an experiment that looked at the tendency of individuals to conform to group pressure and found that when presented with the choice of agreeing with a group's obvious error or standing alone with the correct answer, individuals tended to go along with the group. Asch's studies are different from Janis's in that they focus on how strangers, rather than colleagues or acquaintances, influence individual decisions. In the experiment, one person was placed in a group of six to eight others who were secretly collaborating with Asch. They were shown a straight line and told that their responsibility was to pick the one in a group of three that was the closest to it in length.

One of the lines was obviously longer, another obviously shorter, making the correct answer clear. When the subject of the experiment was able to choose the answer first, the correct line was always chosen. However, when placed in the middle or at the end of a group in which everyone else chose an incorrect answer, six in ten participants also gave that answer.[16] Unlike the pressures on journalists to conform in the aftermath of the terrorist attacks, there was no punishment or reward for providing the correct or incorrect answer in Asch's experiment. There was simply the internal conflict between an individual's desire to be right and his desire to fit in with the group.

It is interesting to note that polls found seven in ten Americans (similar to Asch's finding of six in ten) supported the war in Iraq after hearing the administration's arguments and the media's interpretation of the government's information.

Social psychologist Philip Zimbardo's prison experiment at Stanford University demonstrated just how vulnerable people are to pressures to conform and obey. In an experiment that was scheduled to last two weeks but was stopped after six days because of the dramatic results, students were randomly chosen to work as either guards or prisoners for the duration of the study and immediately assumed the assigned role. Prisoners were deloused, given an uncomfortable uniform to wear, and forced to follow guards' orders. Guards wore reflective glasses and a khaki uniform, and were told to keep order within the prison. After six days, the transformation of the students was astounding—they became so involved in their roles that they believed they were guards and prisoners in a real jail, not participants in a study at a university. Guards were abusing prisoners, and prisoners were demoralized and desperate. A few inmates were removed from the experiment on the verge of a breakdown. The results explain, in part, how human nature led to the horrific Abu Ghraib prison scandal.

But it also illustrates how easy it is to lose sight of reality when role-playing. Once a pattern of obedience, groupthink, or conformity has been established, it gains momentum and becomes difficult to stop.

Zimbardo explained, an outsider "strongly objected when she saw our prisoners being marched on a toilet run, bags over their heads, legs chained together, hands on each other's shoulders. Filled with outrage, she said, 'It's terrible what you are doing to these boys!' Out of 50 or more outsiders who had seen our prison, she was the only one who ever questioned its morality."[17]

It is very telling, and another example of obedience to authority (Zimbardo was a prestigious university professor), that of the more than 50 people who passed through the fictional prison, only one complained about the treatment of the student prisoners.

Zimbardo had the advantage of being a psychologist and recognizing his errors once they were pointed out to him—members of the media did not. Voices of dissent and concern could not permeate journalists' groupthink or slow the momentum of their self-censorship.

Shortly after Rice's request that the networks ban bin Laden's statements, CNN took the policy further and initiated a rule that any reporter writing a "negative" story, such as the accidental bombing of a civilian village by U.S. forces in Afghanistan, must include at least a sentence reminding viewers that terrorists had killed thousands of Americans on September 11. Isaacson told his staff that it "seems perverse to focus too much on the casualties or hardship in Afghanistan....We must talk about how the Taliban are using civilian shields and how the Taliban have harbored the terrorists responsible for killing close to 5,000 innocent people [on September 11]."[18] Essentially, CNN was doing public relations work for the Pentagon. Years later, such qualifying sentences could still be found in CNN stories about the conflict in Iraq.

The *Los Angeles Times* joined the self-censoring ranks a year later with an order that its reporters stop describing anti-American forces in Iraq as "resistance fighters." The term was accurate but was too romantic, editors of the paper said. It evoked images of World War II and specifically of the French Resistance or Jews who fought the Nazis in the Warsaw ghetto, an editor was quoted as saying. Reporters were told to use the terms "insurgents" or "guerillas" instead. The editors said the decision was prompted not by readers' comments or a request from the government but by a discussion among the paper's top editors.[19]

Nightline's Ted Koppel told a group of scientists that advances in technology,

> means, paradoxically, that Americans are likely to know less about this war than any other. You should expect to be more in the dark about what is really happening [in Iraq] than ever before. I say that in the hope that we'll be able to *sit down with our friends at the Pentagon* and reach an arrangement that will serve both of our interests. ...I don't like censorship any more than anyone else, but if we don't have some kind of formalized censorship policy in effect prior to the start of this war, I'm afraid all we're going to get out of this one are briefings.[20] (emphasis added)

What about questioning soldiers? Asking locals what happened? Actually going out onto the battlefield or the streets of Iraq as reporters—not as embedded reporters but as independent news gatherers—and recording history?

Dozens of foreign journalists (and a handful of Americans) do report on the war from the field as they did in Vietnam, risking their lives on a daily basis to report the news. Many have been killed in Iraq and Afghanistan. Unfortunately, few of their reports are seen in the United States.

MEDIA LABELED "DANGEROUS"

After the September 11 attacks, President Bush and his administration rein-
forced the need for cooperation from the media at every opportunity. Journalists
were constantly reminded that the war was, as Bush put it, "a black-and-white
choice with no grays," and that there was a right side and a wrong side of the
line. Those on the wrong side of the line included journalists who asked too
many difficult questions or who broadcast bin Laden's messages. These journalists were labeled dangerous and unpatriotic because they refused to obey and purportedly caused divisions that left the country vulnerable to another attack.

"I accuse the media in the United States of treason," began a *Washington Post*
opinion piece by Dennis Pluchinsky, a senior intelligence analyst with the State
Department.

> It seems reasonable to me that a process should be established where such articles
> [about potential terrorist attacks at chemical plants or on water and food supply
> sources] are filtered through a government agency such as the proposed Department
> of Homeland Security. A skeptic would call this censorship; a patriot would call it
> cooperation....If there were an "Osama bin Laden" award given out by al-Qaeda,
> I believe that it would be awarded to the U.S. news media for their investigative
> reporting.[21]

While most journalists succumbed to groupthink, a handful remained skeptical. These reporters with "prolific pens" were locked out of the White House or
had their access minimized. Sarah McClendon, a tough investigative reporter,
had had a White House press pass from Franklin Delano Roosevelt through Bill
Clinton and spent decades asking uncomfortable questions of presidents. The
Bush administration rejected her request for a White House press pass, citing
"national security concerns." She was unable to attend White House briefings
or to question Bush (McClendon died in 2003).

Reporters Warren Strobel and Jonathan Landay of Knight Ridder's Washington bureau were among the very few who persistently pursued leads that questioned the information provided by the administration. When the *New York
Times* and *Washington Post* were publishing articles saying the case against Hussein was strong, Strobel and Landay were writing articles saying it was not. Both
papers later praised Strobel's and Landay's work.

The White House response to the stories was to try to block Knight Ridder
from briefings. Landay said he believes the tactic frightened a lot of Washington
reporters. "I think this administration may have a fairly punitive policy when it
comes to journalists who get in their face. And if you talk to some White House
reporters, there is a fear of losing access."[22]

Losing access was a valid concern. Consider the access *Washington Post* editor
Bob Woodward had to White House officials vs. that of his colleague, Dana
Milbank. Woodward wrote very positive stories about the administration after

the terrorist attacks, including an eight-part series that made the president and his advisers seem strong and decisive. According to anecdotes from the series, the attacks were met with calm demeanors and positive, rational responses by Bush and his staff. Woodward was rewarded with more access. The result was his book, *Plan of Attack*, which contained more complimentary anecdotes about the administration.

Milbank, on the other hand, was a constant source of annoyance for members of the administration. He dug up several embarrassing pieces of information that made the administration look bad. He was the first to write about the vice president's secret energy task force meetings, which led to calls for more openness and demands for access to minutes of the meetings. A stream of lawsuits against the vice president followed—including one from Congress's watchdog, the GAO (Government Accountability Office)—and well-publicized refusals by Cheney to hand over documents.[23]

Milbank was also one of the few who wrote articles that disputed Bush's claims about WMD in Iraq. As a result, he was regularly attacked by the administration, his access was limited, and complaints about him were made to his editors.

Most of Milbank's articles ran on the back pages of the *Post*, where they received little notice. Woodward's stories usually ran on page A1.

After no WMD were found in Iraq, Woodward acknowledged that he had suppressed information that would have refuted the administration's claims before the war, saying, "I think I was part of the groupthink."[24]

Some skeptical journalists also had trouble with their own editors and publishers, many of whom felt the pressure to support the administration during wartime.

Columnist Dan Guthrie says he was fired by the *Oregon Daily Courier* for writing a column that criticized Bush for "hiding in a Nebraska hole" after the September 11 attacks. His publisher denies that was the reason but did write an apology for the column, saying it was not "responsible or appropriate." The city editor of the *Texas City Sun*, Tom Gutting, was also fired after writing a column critical of Bush's actions on the day of the attacks. His column was also the subject of an apology from the paper's publisher, who wrote an accompanying op-ed column, "Bush's Leadership Has Been Superb."[25]

Officials used fear and intimidation to urge journalists to help protect the country from another attack. As a result, reporting government policies without question or debate became standard practice for the press.

After briefings at the White House, Press Secretary Fleischer told reporters to "be careful what you say." Those who were not "careful" enough suffered the consequences in a public arena.

Bill Maher, host of the irreverent television program *Politically Incorrect*, took exception to the use of the word "cowards" to describe the 9/11 hijackers and said so on his program: "We have been the cowards, lobbing cruise missiles from 2,000 miles away. That's cowardly. Staying in the airplane when it hits the building, say what you want about it, it's not cowardly."[26]

Fleischer's response: "All Americans...need to watch what they say, watch what they do."[27] It was reminiscent of some of the country's darker moments, such as the McCarthy Communist hunt and Japanese internments during World War II.

After Maher's remarks and Fleischer's response, major companies pulled their advertising from *Politically Incorrect,* and the program lost an estimated $10 million in revenue. Maher was trashed by radio jocks throughout the country and belittled in newspaper editorials. The program never fully recovered and was off the air less than nine months later.

A Washington newspaper editor later said that the furor that followed Maher's comment "was a lesson to all of us."[28]

When the administration began building its case for war in Iraq, MSNBC canceled a talk show hosted by Phil Donahue. The network said low ratings were responsible, but Donahue had more viewers than *Hardball with Chris Matthews,* another MSNBC program that continued to be broadcast. It was later revealed that the network deemed Donahue's antiwar spin problematic. A study commissioned by the network found that Donahue presented a "difficult public face for NBC in a time of war....He seems to delight in presenting guests who are antiwar, anti-Bush, and skeptical of the administration's motives. [Donahue could become] a home for the liberal antiwar agenda at the same time that our competitors are waving the flag at every opportunity."[29]

Donahue's replacement was controversial radio talk show host Michael Savage, who said the government should "arrest the leaders of the antiwar movement." The network also hired former Texas Republican Congressman Dick Armey, as a commentator.

The broadcast industry chose to keep a low profile and wave the flag as much as possible. Journalists explained at the time that they were simply giving the public what it wanted.

On November 9, 2001, *New York Times* television critic Alessandra Stanley began an article:

> It is not true that antiwar speakers are unwelcome on television news and talk shows.... [But] just as television news programs are careful to filter Taliban propaganda and omit the most wrenching images of bombing victims, they do not dwell on criticism of the United States' effort; mostly, the small pools of dissent are absent from American television. Most viewers, still aching over the attacks of September 11, are in no mood to listen to views they dismiss as either loopy or treasonous. And network executives are particularly attentive to the national mood these days. "In this environment, it feels slightly different," Walter Isaacson, the president of CNN, said...."If you get on the wrong side of public opinion, you are going to get into trouble."

Isaacson and others were basing their assessment on perceptions that were not backed up by fact.

Andrew Kohut, director of the Pew Research Center for the People and the Press, explained the results of a comprehensive survey in November 2001:

> The public finds a solid majority favoring war coverage that is neutral rather than pro-American, and an even larger 73 percent margin favoring coverage that portrays all points of view, including those of countries that are unfriendly to the United States, over pro-American news reports. And by a 52 to 40 percent margin, the public says the press should dig hard to get news and not trust government and military officials. Finally, there continues to be support for the press's watchdog role even in a time of national crisis. Half of the public thinks press scrutiny of the military keeps the nation prepared compared to 37 percent who think it weakens its defense. There was an even bigger margin of support for press criticism of political leaders at this time.[30]

Network executives who said the public was not interested in unfiltered news coverage should have read a *New York Times* story that ran the same day as Stanley's piece. The article, "British Take Blunter Approach to War Reporting," noted that ratings had increased by 50 percent for International Television Network's "World News for Public Television," a daily, hard-hitting 30-minute news program produced in England for an American audience. ITN, carried by 92 stations in the United States, did not focus on the American perspective but provided a more international approach to the news that included a more realistic picture of the fighting in Afghanistan.[31]

However, in the aftermath of the September 11 attacks, most criticism of the administration or its policy was labeled unpatriotic. This labeling was so successful that it continued to be used years after the attacks.

Here are a few examples:

- When opponents spoke out against provisions of the USA Patriot Act—the most dramatic, far-reaching law enacted in decades—Attorney General John Ashcroft said on December 6, 2001: "Your tactics only aid terrorists, for they erode our national unity and diminish our resolve. They give ammunition to America's enemies, and pause to America's friends."[32]

- When reporters questioned whether the president's aircraft carrier speech—the one with the now infamous "Mission Accomplished" sign—was appropriate while battles continued in Iraq, White House spokesman Fleischer said on May 7, 2003: "It does a disservice to the men and women of our military to suggest that the president, or the manner in which the president visited the military, would be anything other than the exact appropriate thing to do."[33]

- Defense Secretary Donald Rumsfeld told *Newsday* on September 9, 2003, that critics of the Bush administration's Iraq policy are "encouraging terrorists and complicating the ongoing U.S. war on terrorism." Rather than questioning the comment, the paper emphasized it with the headline "Rumsfeld: Critics Give Terrorists Hope."

- In response to U.S. Senator Ted Kennedy's statement that "Iraq is George Bush's Vietnam," Colin Powell said on April 7, 2004, that Kennedy "should be a little more restrained and careful in his comments because we are at war."[34]

DICTATING TERMINOLOGY

The media assisted the administration further by allowing government officials to largely dictate the terminology it used in its reports.

This practice became more obvious with time as war was launched in Afghanistan and Iraq. Those who supported U.S. actions were not "allies," they were "the coalition of the willing." Before the conflict in Iraq, reporters were simply assigned to military units during wartime. Now journalists are "embedded" with troops. Journalists who were not embedded were not favored by the administration and in turn were called "unilaterals." The tag implies that they are not team players like the "embeds."

The war in Iraq began with a "shock and awe" campaign in Baghdad, similar in tactic and connotation to the German "blitzkrieg" during World War II. Bombs dropped by planes were "smart bombs" used during "surgical air strikes" and "strike packages."

Troops went after "targets of opportunity" in assaults in which "collateral damage" would be minimized.

"Collateral damage," of course, means the death of civilians who happen to be in the way and are killed when the U.S. military or its allies drop bombs or fire weapons.

The United States and its allies were not "occupiers"; they were "liberators."

The military terminology was found in nearly every news report and became even more common after "embeds" began filing from Iraq. Military jargon became part of the embedded journalists' vernacular and in turn a part of their reports. The problem is that military terms are designed to disguise the very horrors of war that journalists are supposed to expose.

The most obvious example of members of the media obediently echoing the administration's claims can be found in the reports about Iraq's receiving "partial sovereignty." Sovereignty, by definition, means freedom from a controlling influence. The media often discussed a June 30, 2004, deadline by which "Iraq would return to self-rule" while noting in the same story that the administration was imposing restrictions that in fact made "self-rule" unlikely. A front-page *New York Times* story 10 weeks before the handover date began: "The Bush administration's plans for a new caretaker government in Iraq would place severe limits on its sovereignty, including only partial command over its armed forces and no authority to enact new laws."[35] What self-ruling nation has "partial command over its armed forces and no authority to enact new laws"?

The *Times* did periodically address this issue, but it simultaneously ran stories that ignored the obvious conflict.

It is natural for military phrases to pepper ordinary conversation during times of war and conflict. During the Vietnam War, the term "friendly fire" was popularized. However, the aftermath of the 9/11 terrorist attacks led to an unprecedented acceptance of not only the terms used by the administration but also the limited, militaristic definitions.

William Lutz, a professor of English at Rutgers University, said, "warfare has always generated linguistic Novocaine—it's designed to numb. Language works best when it paints a mental picture for us, when it palpably and vividly creates a reality in our minds. When you want it to do the exact opposite, you create a new language for that."[36]

Other examples of recent linguistic anesthesia: "asymmetric warfare," the more palatable term for guerrilla warfare; "military-age males" in war zones, all boys and men in the country; "detainees" or "enemy combatants," those apprehended in conflict zones—certainly not prisoners of war; "operational pauses," halts in a campaign because the military is strategizing, not "bogged down" as occurred in past wars.[37] The conflict switched from a "war with Iraq" to a "battle for Iraq" to a "struggle in Iraq." This type of terminology encouraged the environment that made the torture and abuse at Abu Ghraib possible. The American mission and troops were glorified, and Iraqis who opposed the foreign military presence were labeled terrorists or Saddam loyalists. Most Iraqis imprisoned at Abu Ghraib were "military-age males," which made their innocence questionable. All were treated as potential enemies rather than possible innocent civilians.

Veteran journalist Jim Lehrer said reporters were so enamored with the government after the September 11 attacks that they did not consider second-guessing officials. In a May 12, 2004, interview on MSNBC's *Hardball with Chris Matthews*, Matthews asked why journalists had not explored the issue of how Americans would be received by Iraqis once the war was over. Lehrer responded: "The word 'occupation,' keep in mind, Chris, was never mentioned in the run-up to the war. It was 'liberation.' This was a war of liberation, not a war of occupation. So as a consequence, those of us in journalism never even looked at the issue of occupation." Matthews asked why reporters were not able to go beyond the Bush administration's perspective that the war was one of "liberation." Lehrer replied: "It just didn't occur to us. We weren't smart enough to do it."

A more likely explanation is that to raise the issue of Americans' being "occupiers" rather than "liberators" after the war seemed like biased reporting. If nobody was discussing or debating the issue openly, then journalists considered exploring the possibility to be exhibiting bias rather than "objectively" reporting the news. Objective reporting was perceived as repeating what government officials said and echoing the terms they used. Analyzing what was said and the implications of the statements was considered exhibiting bias.

Very few news reports questioned the whys behind the administration's declared need to curb debate and stifle free speech. Few editorials questioned how silence protected national security. If the press had put more pressure on the administration, and asked for clarification of conflicting information about Iraq's weapons capabilities, the efforts to thwart terrorism might have taken a different turn.

And while groupthink and obedience tendencies explain why the media may have done such a bad job, it does not excuse the practitioners. Journalists need to take responsibility for their actions and work to ensure that they do not repeat the same errors over and over again. They have acknowledged their mistakes. Some journalists and media organizations have apologized, but few have explained how they will avoid those mistakes the next time. Instead, they have minimized their errors and placed the blame elsewhere—it was Iraqi dissidents' fault, the administration's failure, and groupthink. Their response does not instill confidence that journalists will not fall victim to the same pressures in the future.

CHAPTER 3

Civil Liberties, Security, and Silence

The people can always be brought to the bidding of the leaders. That is easy. All you have to do is tell them they are being attacked and denounce the pacifists for lack of patriotism and exposing the country to danger. It works the same way in any country.

—Hermann Goering, Hitler's propagandist[1]

To those who scare peace-loving people with phantoms of lost liberty, my message is this: Your tactics only aid terrorists, for they erode our national unity and diminish our resolve. They give ammunition to America's enemies and pause to America's friends. They encourage people of good will to remain silent in the face of evil.

—U.S. Attorney General John Ashcroft, defending the USA Patriot Act[2]

Six weeks after the September 11 attacks, Congress passed the USA Patriot Act —the title stands for Uniting and Strengthening America by Providing Appropriate Tools Required to Intercept and Obstruct Terrorism. It is by all measures one of the most sweeping pieces of legislation in U.S. history. President Bush signed the bill on October 26, 2001.

The new law intended to dramatically increase government powers of investigation and enforcement—many would argue at the expense of individual liberties—was reported only superficially when it was introduced and shot its way through Congress.

Although portions of the law resembled the Antiterrorism Act of 1996, passed after the Oklahoma City bombing and later ruled unconstitutional by federal courts, there were no public hearings before the Patriot Act became law. Very few editorials—none in the major mainstream newspapers—referred to the similarities between the Patriot Act and the Antiterrorism Act. In fact, the Patriot Act goes far beyond the Antiterrorism Act, which legal critics called "one of the worst assaults on the Constitution in decades."[3]

Attorney General John Ashcroft pushed hard for passage of the legislation, claiming that delays, debates, and questions endangered the country. He introduced the brilliantly named Patriot Act by saying: "The danger that darkened the United States of America and the civilized world on September 11 did not pass with the atrocities committed that day. It requires that we provide law enforcement with the tools necessary to identify, dismantle, disrupt, and punish terrorist organizations before they strike again."[4]

Ashcroft then asked that it be fast-tracked through Congress and be ready for the president's signature within a week. Approval took longer than a week, but the measure did make it through the process at lightning speed.

Years after the Patriot Act became law, members of Congress complained that they had been intimidated into approving it during a time when dialogue was discouraged and action to safeguard the nation encouraged.

"The final version of the Patriot Act that was passed into law was rewritten between midnight and 8 o'clock in the morning behind closed doors by a few unknown people, and it was presented to Congress for a one-hour debate and an up-or-down vote," U.S. Representative Peter DeFazio said in 2003. "It was hundreds of pages long, and no member of Congress can tell you they knew what they were voting for in its entirety. It was time to be stampeded, and who wanted to be against the USA Patriot Act at a time like that?"[5]

The Patriot Act's lone dissenter in the Senate, Russell D. Feingold, urged his colleagues to consider history before casting their votes:

> There have been periods in our nation's history when civil liberties have taken a back seat to what appeared at the time to be the legitimate exigencies of war. Our national consciousness still bears the stain and the scars of those events: The Alien and Sedition Acts, the suspension of habeas corpus during the Civil War, the internment of Japanese-Americans, German-Americans, and Italian-Americans during World War II, the blacklisting of supposed Communist sympathizers during the McCarthy era, and the surveillance and harassment of antiwar protesters, including Dr. Martin Luther King Jr.[6]

The act concentrates increased new powers in the executive branch of government, while decreasing judicial oversight. Briefly, these measures include the following:

- Creation of the new federal crime of "domestic terrorism," which includes any dangerous acts that "appear to be intended...to influence the policy of a government by intimidation or coercion." Broadly applied, this could be (and has been) used to silence any political dissent critical of government policies, including antiwar protestors.

- Diminished due process for immigrants, who can be detained or deported with little or no judicial review.

- Broadening the grounds for increased surveillance and wiretap authority (including roving wiretaps), sneak-and-peek searches, tracking of Internet use, and monitoring of financial transactions. It lets the FBI track library books checked out by individuals and place a gag order on librarians. The same goes for bookstore owners and their customers. Student records that were confidential—including classes taken, grades obtained, medical records, and family information—are now available to the FBI upon request. These records were made confidential in 1974 after it was discovered that the government had used student records to spy on Vietnam War protestors.

- Lowering standards of probable cause and allowing the FBI to obtain personal records by certifying that they are sought for an investigation to prevent terrorism. It need not suspect the person of any wrongdoing to obtain the information.

These are sweeping reforms that were passed with little public debate or media analysis.

Before the bill became law, reporters described the legislation in terms of its being a necessary tool to protect the country from another attack. The concerns of civil liberties experts were mentioned but were largely minimized by stronger quotes from administration officials, who warned that without the law, the country was vulnerable to terrorist attacks.

A *Washington Post* news story on September 16, 2001, noted that members of Congress were wrestling with difficult decisions, such as whether to give the president undivided support or to monitor and safeguard the balance of power among the branches of government.

> The rush by lawmakers to give rhetorical support, money, and broad war-making authority to President Bush to respond to terrorism was a display of bipartisan unity and deference to the executive branch that is without precedent in Washington in recent decades. But lurking beneath the surface of this united front is a more complicated reality....Democrats, and even some Republicans, have expressed concern that the necessity to give broad powers to the White House could go too far, robbing what they said was Congress's constitutional authority to appropriate money and hold the administration accountable for policy decisions it makes to meet the crisis. ...These so-far muted notes of dissension suggest Bush cannot for much longer expect a reprieve from opposition during a war against terrorism. Democrats said this is especially so because—despite the unanimous desire to respond and the unanimous outrage at events—many of the specific choices he faces are inherently controversial: Should there be a ground war to evict Middle Eastern regimes that

support terrorism? How much must Americans' freedoms be curtailed to protect security?[7]

Balancing patriotism and skepticism was "agony" for lawmakers who worried that asking questions would make them look unpatriotic. "The most dangerous time for any democracy is at times of crisis," said U.S. Representative David R. Obey. "Asking even the most innocent and basic questions is seen as being non-supportive. In the heat of the moment, everyone wants to rally around the flag, and sometimes they do that to the great benefit of the country, and sometimes to the great detriment."[8]

The *Post*'s prediction that Bush's bipartisan support would be short-lived was not realized. In the years after the attacks, Republicans, Democrats, and members of the media largely responded with agreement and consensus to calls for a united front in the war against terrorism. Any dissent that was expressed by members of Congress about the Patriot Act was done without vigor, and ultimately dissolved amid more enthusiastic concerns expressed about national security. This was reflected in the media coverage.

For example, an October 3, 2001, *Washington Post* article carried quotes from Ashcroft's saying, "talk won't prevent terrorism" and that he was "deeply concerned about the rather slow pace of the legislation" as it wound its way through Congress.[9]

Democrats' concerns about the lack of FBI oversight provided by the Patriot Act were summarized in the story, but no party member was quoted by name. An anonymous Democrat complained not about provisions of the bill but about Republican tactics: "Right off the bat, they said they wanted to pull back from the language agreed to on Sunday night. It was the last major issue."[10]

Republican Senator Orin Hatch was quoted as saying the Democrats' questions were "a very dangerous thing. It's time to get off our duffs and do what's right."[11]

The article made the Democrats' complaints sound like partisan bickering and effectively minimized their primary concern: that without the FBI's having to obtain search warrants, the agency would be free to operate without a system of checks and balances. This left the potential for abuse of power, the primary reason Congress took away the FBI's freedom to work independently 25 years ago.

Additionally, the story neglected to mention that the bill had been introduced 11 days earlier—it is very rare for a bill of that size to make it through the congressional process at such speed. The legislation was not bogged down, as Ashcroft claimed, but was actually moving rapidly through the process.

During times of crisis and war, legislation can be expedited, such as a vote to allow the president to declare war or a decision to allocate more funds for military equipment. This law, however, reversed the result of years of debate in the country; some legal experts say it breached the Constitution. For instance, under the new law, U.S. citizens can be detained indefinitely (and have been) without being charged with a crime, without the right to a trial, and without the right to speak with an attorney. American citizens who have not committed a crime but have expressed support for the country's "enemies" can be arrested and held indefinitely. Discussion, debate, and media analysis of these types of issues seem warranted.

It may be true that the Justice Department needed better law enforcement tools to combat terrorism and that the Patriot Act helped protect the nation. But the logic that was behind the push for the bill was flawed and should have been explored further.

The 9/11 attacks obviously revealed major security problems in the United States, and the Attorney General pointed to them as proof that the Justice Department needed more freedom to pursue terrorists than existing law allowed. But were the successful attacks the result of laws that hampered the FBI's ability to track potential terrorists, or was the agency negligent in implementing existing laws?

A few probing questions could have brought some clarity: Was information shared among counterterrorism units before the attacks? If not, how will this problem be resolved? Was there negligence by any agency or division within the Justice Department? If so, how will the system be improved? How will the provisions of the Patriot Act improve the system for information sharing? How was information received about potential terrorists handled before the attacks, and how will this differ under the Patriot Act? What checks-and-balances system will be in place to ensure that the act's provisions are not abused?

These are not unpatriotic questions, but practical ones. Information obtained years after the attacks shows that many problems that led to the attacks were preventable with the laws in place at that time.

For example, the FBI's Phoenix, Arizona, counterterrorism unit sent a memo dated April 17, 2000, to the New York counterterrorism office saying:

> The purpose of this memo is to inform the bureau of New York of a coordinated effort of Usama Bin Laden [UBL] to send students to the United States to attend civil aviation universities and colleges. Phoenix has observed an inordinate number of individuals of investigative interest who are attending or who have attended civil aviation colleges and universities in the State of Arizona.

They recommended that FBIHQ (FBI headquarters) inform other counterterrorism units of a possible bin Laden plot and ask them to share any information they found. "FBIHQ should consider seeking the necessary authority to obtain visa information from the USDOS [U.S. Department of State] on individuals obtaining visas to attend these types of schools and notify the appropriate FBI field office when these individuals are scheduled to arrive in area of responsibility."[12]

The Justice Department had no trouble accurately pinpointing what turned out to be an essential element of the terrorists' plot. It had trouble coordinating efforts and following up the warnings. Information on these students, and perhaps the 9/11 hijackers, could have been obtained by asking the State Department for it. It just was not done.

Similarly, controversial FBI whistle-blower Sibel Edmonds, who was hired by the language translation department after the attacks, claims that incompetence, security breaches, and management's deliberate efforts to slow the pace of translators' work continue to thwart attempts to capture terrorists.

In August 2004, she wrote a letter to 9/11 Commission Chairman Thomas Kean:

> To this date, the public has not been told of intentional blocking of intelligence, and has not been told that certain information, despite its direct links, impacts, and ties to terrorist-related activities, is not given to or shared with counterterrorism units, their investigations, and countering terrorism-related activities. This was the case prior to 9/11, and remains in effect after 9/11. If counterintelligence receives information that contains money laundering, illegal arms sale, and illegal drug activities, directly linked to terrorist activities; and if that information involves certain nations, certain semi-legit organizations, and ties to certain lucrative or political relations in this country, then that information is not shared with counterterrorism, regardless of the possible severe consequences.[13]

Republican Senator Charles Grassley, chairman of the Judiciary Committee, which has direct oversight of the FBI, said of Edmonds, "she's credible. And the reason I feel she's very credible is because people within the FBI have corroborated a lot of her story."[14]

Edmonds was fired from her job, and the Justice Department classified the previously unclassified documents that she had used to prove her case. She is no longer able to discuss the issue without facing arrest.

In June 2005, the Justice Department inspector general released a report saying that the FBI had missed at least five opportunities to capture two of the 9/11 hijackers as they prepared for the attacks. The report also found that communication between field offices and FBIHQ was terrible, and information sharing between the FBI and the CIA even worse; the FBI's computer system was cumbersome and ineffective, and bureaucracy prevented the agency from stopping the terrorist attacks.[15]

The FBI says it has made significant improvements since 2001, but in 2005 it scrapped a $170 million "virtual case file" computer system that it had been working on since the attacks. The agency announced a new plan the same week the critical Justice Department report was released.

Senator Grassley said the report shows that "even when there were eyes and ears before 9/11 that told the FBI things that needed to be known, they ignored it, and they just didn't have the capability to connect the dots." Kristen Breitweiser, whose husband died in the attacks, called the report "a long time coming" and asked, "How much ineptitude are we going to tolerate?"[16]

In 2006, right before Congress had to decide whether to extend portions of the Patriot Act that were about to expire, there was a flurry of activity by the Justice Department and a sudden surge in the number of alleged terrorists arrested in the United States. President Bush and Justice Department officials attributed the arrests to provisions of the Patriot Act and called for its renewal. The media did not question the timing of the arrests or ask officials to be specific about how the act has helped protect the country. Congress responded by renewing the act.

DON'T ASK

Of course, the administration did not make it easy for reporters to obtain information. When journalists did ask questions that the officials did not like, they were warned that they were jeopardizing the safety of American citizens. White House spokesman Ari Fleischer told reporters shortly after the attacks that probing questions were not in the best interests of the country. "The press is asking a lot of questions that I suspect the American people would prefer not to be asked, or answered."[17]

With Ashcroft warning that without the legislation, terrorists would run rampant through the country reporters said they felt pressured to keep their questions in check.

"Trade Civil Liberties for Security," said a *Washington Times* editorial. "The media should be falling in line. The danger is great enough for us to cut back now on civil liberties. It is all a question of balance. I have been a civil libertarian and will be again in a couple of years. The terrorists will win when they kill us, and we will win when we kill them."[18]

As a result of this pressure, the Patriot Act, despite being such a major piece of legislation, received scant attention from the media. The implications of the legislation were not thoroughly reported until many months after it became law. And then they were explored in response to complaints from bookstores, libraries, and universities.

Thomas Kunkel, dean of the University of Maryland in College Park's journalism school, said in December 2001:

> Editors and editorial dictators have taken it upon themselves to downplay the issue, and what coverage we have seen has been largely sympathetic toward the expansion of law-enforcement powers. I have the sense the Bush administration has been given a lot of rope and that it is not getting enough criticism. I think [members of the media] feel they have to tread carefully, partly because the public is mobilized behind the war effort and they don't want to appear unpatriotic.[19]

The deconstruction of a document titled the USA Patriot Act so soon after such a horrendous attack on American soil must have seemed unthinkable.

"The new anti-terrorism measures will make the kind of broad changes to current law that would normally take months, if not years, to achieve," reported the *Houston Chronicle* on the day Bush signed the legislation. "But with national leaders anxious to apprehend Osama bin Laden's associates—*many of whom are living in the United States*— lawmakers set aside their disagreements and finalized, in less than six weeks, much of what the Bush administration had requested" (emphasis added). The story carried Ashcroft's ominous warning: "Today's terrorists enjoy the benefits of our free society, even as they commit themselves to our destruction. They live in our communities, plotting, planning, waiting to kill Americans again."[20]

Reporters took a hard look at the new law after banks, libraries, and universities complained about the type of information they had to give government officials. The media reported possible breaches of civil liberties based on those complaints. These stories also provided insight into how Americans guarded against the prospect of too much governmental infringement long before it became a media topic.[21]

Officials visited at least 545 libraries seeking patrons' records, according to a University of Illinois study. In 209 of them, staffers cooperated without requesting a court order. The rest resisted, some going so far as to implement new policies mandating that borrowing records be deleted upon return of the books.[22]

An NPR (National Public Radio) story in November 2002 revealed how some people had chosen to fight the infringement of individual privacy early on. The story focused on how the FBI had confiscated computers at a library in Paterson, New Jersey, shortly after September 11, 2001. The most telling aspect of the report was the librarians' response to the FBI's visit: "[FBI agents] had partitioned a hard drive, and you can do that and sort of, like track things more easily, but we undid that. I mean we have people who have the expertise who could say, 'Well, wait a second. What did they do to this hard drive?'"

Rather than waiting for the media to catch up and report the reversal of years of closely guarded privacy—in this case, it took 14 months—librarians did what they felt was necessary to safeguard the rights of their patrons.

In the summer of 2002, city councils throughout the country began saying that they would not comply with the Patriot Act's provisions and would not help the federal government enforce them. Conservative media outlets clung to the patriotism theme when discussing municipalities' rejection of the act.

Sean Hannity of the radio program, *Hannity and Colmes*, ridiculed Hope Marston, a member of the city council of Eugene, Oregon, the 15th city to reject the Patriot Act. After she explained that "people . . . are concerned about liberty and protecting our Bill of Rights," Hannity replied: "Hope, you know, you may have forgotten, but America got attacked on September 11. . . . There are people plotting and planning and scheming right now in America."[23]

This discussion took place on a talk radio, but it illustrates the fact that a year after the attacks, open dialogue was still labeled dangerous and un-American.

THE PATRIOT II

Not long after municipalities began complaining about the Patriot Act's provisions, another version of the law was secretly drafted by the Justice Department. Titled the Domestic Security Enhancement Act of 2003 and dubbed the Patriot II, it was leaked to a few members of Congress and allegedly given to the vice president in January 2003. A concerned anonymous federal worker passed it on to members of the media. Stories about the "Patriot II" appeared in major publications, and public opinion was squarely against it.

Grassroots organizations were formed to fight the "son of the Patriot Act." Papers of record, including the *New York Times* and the *Washington Post*, editorialized against the proposal. According to the *Times*:

> The most troubling part of the new plan is the call for expanding government access to private data, allowing federal agents to issue subpoenas for private medical, financial, and other records, without a court order. The lack of judicial oversight removes an important check on government misconduct. Record holders would be required to comply, or face prison, and would be barred from telling anyone about the subpoena.[24]

The Justice Department denied the existence of the Patriot II and stories about it disappeared from print.

What the media failed to notice, until it was too late, was that key elements of the Patriot II—including the one the *Times* said was "the most troubling"—were incorporated piecemeal into other pieces of legislation and stealthily passed into law.

On Saturday, December 13, 2003, the day the Pentagon announced Hussein's capture, the president signed the Intelligence Authorization Act for Fiscal Year 2004. This hefty piece of legislation, which funded all the government's intelligence activities for the year, contained provisions that expanded the powers of the FBI and reduced congressional oversight.

The Patriot Act gave the FBI the ability to obtain some financial information from a limited number of places, such as banks and credit unions, without a court order or subpoena if it had the approval of a senior government official. The Intelligence Authorization Act expanded the definition of "financial institution" from banks and similar entities to include the post office, real estate agents, insurance companies, libraries, car dealerships, casinos, jewelry stores, pawn shops—even eBay purchase records are open for inspection by FBI agents without a court order or permission from their superior officer. Agents simply need to find any senior government official to give them the okay. There is no longer any oversight of the agency when it comes to accessing personal information from places where "cash transactions have a high degree of usefulness in criminal, tax, or regulatory matters."[25]

The day Bush signed the bill, Americans were flooded with images of a disheveled Hussein being checked for lice and receiving a dental examination. Bush's landmark signature went virtually unnoticed that day.

Weeks later, editorials appeared in newspapers criticizing the provision and the "sneaky" manner in which it had been made into law. A *Washington Post* editorial on January 4, 2003, titled "Too Much Power" condemned the manner in which the provision was made law. The editorial did not take to task members of Congress who had voted for the legislation despite the fact that public opinion was squarely against it. The paper simply said that the authorization bill contained "a little-noticed and dangerous expansion of a peculiar and unaccountable FBI investigative power. Last-minute efforts to modify the provision in conference committee failed, unfortunately, so the bureau now has more power to compel the production of certain business records in national security investigations, with no court oversight and in nearly total secrecy."

In defense of the media, intelligence authorization acts are classified, and journalists never know their full details. No government official or politician is going to send out a press release about a provision he or she believes is necessary but knows is controversial. However, even a "little-noticed" provision or "last-minute efforts" to modify the bill should have been picked up by reporters, whose editors should have given it the front-page, top-of-the-news attention it deserved. The public had left no doubt about its feelings about the Patriot II. Journalists should have sources who tip them off early to proposals that create major changes in the balance of power.

In the case of the authorization bill, journalists should have seen it coming—the administration had already tried to expand the powers of the CIA in the same bill. In May 2003, when the Senate Intelligence Committee was debating the measure behind closed doors, a staffer leaked information about a provision enabling the CIA to search Americans' private records without warrants, permission, or reasonable cause. The CIA had never had such authority before, yet this attempt to expand its powers failed to receive front-page play in major newspapers.

The *New York Times* ran a story about the provision on page A21 that began:

> The Bush administration and leading Senate Republicans sought today to give the Central Intelligence Agency and the Pentagon far-reaching new powers to demand personal and financial records on people in the United States as part of foreign intelligence and terrorism operations.... The surprise proposal was tucked into a broader intelligence authorization bill now pending before Congress.[26]

These sorts of tactics should have tipped off journalists and members of Congress that other unpopular proposals could be hidden within large bills. But rather than emphasize the deception with critical, bold, front-page headlines and editorials, newspapers relegated the stories to back pages. And instead of becoming fired up to fight for access or outraged that the administration had slipped a major piece of legislation past them, journalists simply shrugged it off.

Newsday columnist Jimmy Breslin complained about the media's passivity in general: "The big thing in the press is total absence of anger. They're the best-educated people we've ever had, but there's nothing inside them to get mad. They're sheep. There's a famous saying you don't hear in this country much anymore. 'The hottest place in hell is reserved for those who pursue neutrality in times of crisis.' That goes for the fucking press, too."[27]

USE OF THE PATRIOT ACT

The law's stated purpose is to extend the powers of the Justice Department in its quest to thwart terrorism. However, as many immigration and civil liberties attorneys feared, it has since been used in criminal cases that are unrelated to terrorism.

In November 2003, the Justice Department acknowledged it had used the Patriot Act to investigate a corruption case involving a Las Vegas strip club owner and several politicians. The Act's provisions enabled the Justice Department to obtain financial information on the club owner, his lobbyist, and the politicians.[28]

It is one of more than a dozen cases in which federal investigators have relied on the Patriot Act for purposes unrelated to homeland security.[29]

Additionally, the FBI used the Act to recruit police officers from around the country to track and monitor activists. Police were ordered to report all antiwar activities to the FBI's counterterrorism squads and were given detailed instructions on how to target and monitor lawful, peaceful political demonstrations in an attempt to stop them and their participants, according to a classified FBI memo leaked to the *New York Times*. The *Times* described it as "the first corroboration of a coordinated, nationwide effort to collect intelligence regarding demonstrations."[30]

Sometimes police officers videotaped war protestors as an intimidation technique, claiming participants were potential terrorists.[31]

The use of similar tactics was the reason Congress limited the FBI's powers 25 years ago. Then, the agency was tracking Vietnam War protestors.

The actions of the law enforcement officers should have resulted in steady stream of scathing editorials and searing questions by journalists. At the very least, they should have sparked questions about the need to monitor activists. The agency seems to have spent a lot of time on such activities.

Drake University was issued a subpoena by the U.S. attorney in Iowa, a member of the joint FBI terrorism task force, and ordered to turn over attendance records from a November 5, 2003, forum on the use of civil disobedience to protest the war in Iraq. In addition, four activists who had attended the seminar were ordered to appear before a grand jury, and the university was ordered to provide all records relating to the local chapter of the National Lawyers Guild, a New York-based legal activist organization that had sponsored the forum.[32]

In California, a group of antiwar activists was pulled over by a police officer accompanied by six cars and a helicopter hovering overhead. Citing seatbelt violations, police handcuffed the group and led them to separate cars for interrogation. Police searched their car without consent and confiscated a guitar. The activists were booked, fingerprinted, and questioned about their activities—all legal actions under the provisions of the Patriot Act.[33]

Activists have since wondered whether simply issuing the subpoenas accomplished the goal of quieting dissent.

"This reminds me of the old Nixon times and the enemies list," U.S. Senator Edward Kennedy said after learning about the harassment of antiwar protestors. "How could we be fighting abroad to defend our freedoms and diminishing those freedoms here at home?"[34]

No individuals involved in any of these investigations have any terrorist ties, nor does the Justice Department claim that they do. Few journalists asked Ashcroft the difficult questions about how using agents to catch common criminals has helped protect the country from another terrorist attack or how monitoring peace activists has helped track members of al Qaeda. Reporters have yet to investigate how many bin Laden associates "living in the United States," as the Houston Chronicle put it, have been apprehended because of the Patriot Act.

A look at the Justice Department's record on terrorist arrests does not instill confidence. Most cases in which the department sought prosecution of purported terrorists were botched—so much so that either the terrorism charges were dismissed or the defendants were found guilty only of minor offenses unrelated to terrorism. On September 17, 2001, Ashcroft announced the arrest of members of a "terrorist sleeper cell" in Detroit. Justice Department officials claimed the men were a "sleeper operation combat cell" with plans to secure weapons and launch terrorist attacks on targets in the United States and abroad. Government officials said the arrests represented a significant step in securing the United States and fighting the war on terrorism.

In June 2003, three of the men were convicted of conspiring to provide material support to terrorists and of document fraud. A fourth was convicted of document fraud. Ashcroft said: "Today's convictions send a clear message: The Department of Justice will work diligently to detect, disrupt, and dismantle the activities of terrorist cells in the United States and abroad." The men were kept in solitary confinement for two years.[35]

More than a year after their conviction, the Justice Department's case fell apart and the terrorism charges were dropped. The Washington Post wrote in September 2004: "Prosecutors failed to turn over dozens of pieces of evidence to defense attorneys in the first major terrorism trial after the September 11, 2001, attacks, and [a review of the case] chronicles 'a pattern of mistakes and oversights' so egregious that the government has agreed to abandon the terrorism portion of the case altogether."[36]

U.S. District Judge Gerald E. Rosen, who presided over the case, said that the government had "materially misled the court, the jury, and the defense [about] critical evidence that provided important foundations for the prosecution's case. . . .[the lead prosecutor] simply ignored or avoided any evidence or information which contradicted or undermined" his case.[37]

The behavior of Justice Department lawyers did not improve during the trial of Zacarias Moussaoui, the only person arrested in connection with the 9/11 attacks. In March 2006, it was discovered that they had coached six of their witnesses. The judge said "in all the years I've been on the bench, I have never seen such an egregious violation of a rule on witnesses."[38] She added "There are a number of errors so serious that that portion of the government's case has been seriously eroded."[39]

A week before these revelations Congress voted to renew the Patriot Act. Senator Jon Kyl, an Arizona Republican said, "It's about time. It will make America more secure, and that's the bottom line."[40]

The questions that remain unanswered are: How does it make America more secure? Why did the Justice Department taint evidence and coach witnesses if the Act provided them with the tools necessary to catch real terrorists?

Using the Patriot Act, the Justice Department sought the prosecution of 6,400 people in the United States from 2001 to 2003 either for committing terrorist acts or to prevent or to disrupt potential or actual terrorist threats that these people might commit if they were not jailed. Most of the cases were dropped without action. The average median prison term for those who were convicted was 14 days. In many cases, defendants received no jail sentence at all and were released without charge and/or were deported, according to a study by Syracuse University's Transactional Records Access Clearinghouse. Only five—tagged as "the Lackawanna five" by the press—have been sentenced to 20 years or more.[41]

The arrest of the Lackawanna five was hailed as a major victory in the war against terrorism. However, when asked about the arrests, Buffalo FBI officials said they occurred after administration officials asked: "'Can you guarantee to me that these people won't do something?' And the answer [was] we think we can. We are probably 99 percent sure that we can make sure that these guys don't do something—if they are planning to do something. And under the rules that we were playing under at the time, that's not acceptable."[42]

Put that way the case does not seem as strong as administration officials—or the press—made it out to be.

In a speech that marked the first high-profile criticism of the administration in the aftermath of the terrorist attack, Al Gore noted in November 2003 that "simply piling up more raw data that is almost entirely irrelevant is not only not going to help [track terrorists but] the mass collecting of personal data on hundreds of millions of people actually makes it more difficult to protect the nation against terrorists, so they ought to cut most of it out. . . .I believe the Patriot Act has turned out to be, on balance, a terrible mistake."[43]

In April 2006, the Justice Department acknowledged that the FBI had secretly obtained information on 3,501 American citizens or legal residents in 2005 without court approval. The information was obtained from individuals' banks and credit card, and telephone and Internet companies. Additionally, the FBI examined the records of 155 businesses and secretly collected the phone records of millions of Americans.

The Patriot Act and its expansion dramatically altered the legal system in the United States without a critical examination of its contents or implications. It demonstrates that without careful scrutiny from the media, the Constitution is vulnerable to being seriously diminished.

CHAPTER 4

The Buildup to War

The truth is that for reasons that have a lot to do with the U.S. government bureaucracy, we settled on the one issue that everyone could agree on, which was weapons of mass destruction as the core reason [for the need to go to war with Iraq].

—Paul Wolfowitz, deputy defense secretary[1]

For the United States to go to war with Iraq, two things needed to happen: Congress had to give its approval, and the American public had to be convinced that it was necessary. As this chapter will make clear, the American media played a dominant role in boosting the case for war and was largely responsible for swaying public opinion.

Members of the media say that placing the responsibility on them is unfair because they do not have political power; their role in politics is to follow those with power and report what they say and do. The problem with this view is that it allows journalists to avoid taking ownership of their work, which is what occurred after no WMD were found in Iraq and errors were discovered in broadcast and print stories. The mistakes were blamed on government officials, Iraqi dissidents, and groupthink; not on their decisions to omit alternative perspectives and to deliver one-sided stories.

An example of how journalists influenced public perspectives is found in the work of Judith Miller, a *New York Times* reporter who wrote many of the paper's front-page articles about Iraq's WMD in the 18-month buildup to war. Most of those stories contained information that was false or exaggerated.

She later defended her coverage by saying, "My job was not to collect information and analyze it independently as an intelligence agency; my job was to tell readers of the *New York Times*, as best as I could figure out, what people inside the government...were saying to one another about what they thought Iraq had and did not have in the area of weapons of mass destruction."[2]

Many would disagree with this assessment. However, it is difficult to disagree that balanced coverage would also tell readers of the *Times* what those *outside* the U.S. government thought about Iraq's arsenal. Does soliciting additional opinions make journalists independent intelligence analysts or pursuers of information?

The *Washington Post*'s Karen DeYoung made a similar statement: "We are inevitably the mouthpiece for whatever administration is in power. If the president stands up and says something, we report what the president said." Opposing opinions are easily missed because they are often placed "in the eighth paragraph, where they're not on the front page; a lot of people don't read that far."[3]

DeYoung is correct in her assertion that journalists must report what the president says, but opposing opinions should be high in the story, and analysis of what the president's statements mean should be part of the coverage. These job descriptions by top journalists are disturbing because they illustrate that balanced coverage is no longer a consideration.

Headlines reflecting some of Miller's pre-war stories include: "An Iraqi Defector Tells of Work on at Least 20 Hidden Weapons Sites," "U.S. Says Hussein Intensified Quest for A-Bomb Parts," "Iraq Said to Try to Buy Antidote Against Nerve Gas," and "CIA Hunts Iraq Tie to Soviet Smallpox." None of these stories have withstood the test of time.

Journalists on major papers did more than any member of Congress could to persuade the American public that Iraq posed a threat to the United States. In the months before the war, papers carried articles based on information from pro-war Iraqi "defectors" and administration officials (many of them unnamed) proclaiming that Saddam Hussein was developing nuclear, biological, and chemical weapons and was prepared to use them. Missing from most of the articles were opinions that disagreed with the administration's assessment of Hussein's weapons capabilities and the need to go to war. After the war began journalists continued the practice, often justifying the administration's position or claiming WMD had been found. WMD were never found in Iraq nor were any active chemical weapons found.

However, the public could be forgiven for not knowing this since they were repeatedly told otherwise by reporters. In one front-page story by Miller shortly after the war began she says:

A scientist who claims to have worked in Iraq's chemical weapons program for more than a decade...led Americans to a supply of material *that proved to be the building blocks of illegal weapons*....Finding and destroying illegal weapons was a major justification for the war. The [U.S. military] officials' account of the scientist's assertions and the discovery of the buried material, which they described as the most important discovery to date in the hunt for illegal weapons, *supports the Bush administration's charges that Iraq continued to develop those weapons and lied to the United Nations about it.* [These] accounts also *provided an explanation for why United States' forces had not yet turned up banned weapons in Iraq.* The failure to find such weapons has become a political issue in Washington.[4] (emphasis added)

The army did not allow Miller to interview the Iraqi scientist and "declined to identify him," but she told readers she had watched "from a distance" as a man "clad in nondescript clothes and a baseball cap pointed to several spots in the sand where he said chemical precursors and other weapons material were buried."

The day after her story appeared, she went on PBS's *The NewsHour with Jim Lehrer* and contradicted a statement by U.N. weapons inspector Hans Blix that "shaky" intelligence had been used to convince the U.N. that Iraq had WMD. Miller said Americans had discovered "more than a smoking gun"; they had found "a silver bullet in the form of an Iraqi individual, a scientist, as we've called him" who said Hussein had an active weapons program. The "we" she is referring to is the American forces that she was embedded with. "What's become clear is the extent to which Iraq and this regime was able to pull the wool over the eyes of the international inspectors," Miller said.[5]

She obviously became too involved with the story. Miller not only analyzed the information independently but also presented herself as an authority on the authenticity of the U.S. weapons' claims, presented the information given to her by officials as fact, and contradicted outside experts who criticized the U.S. evidence.

The story fell apart a few weeks later when the same Iraqi "scientist" described himself as an "official of military intelligence" in another article by Miller.[6] A year later the *Times*'s editors acknowledged that the article gave the false impression that the "scientist" "had provided the justification the Americans sought for the invasion."[7]

Somehow, policy and the media became inextricably intertwined in the buildup to war. Journalists, including those on the papers of record—the *New York Times* and the *Washington Post*—became a tool that was manipulated to rally support for U.S. policy. Miller continues to defend her coverage, although many of her articles were filled with false information.

"The fact that the United States so far hasn't found WMD in Iraq is deeply disturbing," she said in 2004. "It raises real questions about how good our intelligence was. To beat up on the messenger is to miss the point."[8]

Is it? Skepticism is an important part of a journalist's job. Should journalists on the *New York Times* and the *Washington Post* be exempt from responsibility when they so egregiously lacked skepticism? Are journalists simply messengers or mouthpieces for the administration, as Miller and DeYoung believe?

STORY PLACEMENT

Reporters' alarmist "messenger" stories gained credibility with the public because they were often placed on the front page. There are several reasons Miller's editors ran her stories on page A1, despite gaping holes and obvious unanswered questions. A simple explanation is that she was providing the paper with scoops, and the paper's editors needed them—it was in their interests to run them. Philosopher Thomas Hobbes made the case that self-interest is the primary human motivation in 1660 when he published *Leviathan*. Human motives have been much debated, but the consensus is that acting out of self-interest is normal human behavior. When people have to decide whether to pursue a course that others would not take—when the action would be solitary and could provoke suspicion and criticism—self-interest is often a motivating factor.[9] As Solomon Asch's line-length experiment demonstrated (described in Chapter 2), few individuals are courageous enough to stand alone with the truth when the crowd chooses an incorrect answer.

American journalists determined that in the highly charged environment that followed the 9/11 attacks, believing the administration's claims and keeping their questions in check best served their interests. To do otherwise could have led to ostracism by the administration and the general public, and possible harm to their careers. Columnist Mary McGrory wrote: "Ask any journalist who raised questions about [Bush's] early handling of the crisis: They have been inundated with furious calls calling them a disgrace to their profession and even traitors."[10]

Washington Post Pentagon correspondent Thomas Ricks said of his paper's coverage, "There was an attitude among editors: Look, we're going to war, why do we even worry about all this contrary stuff?"[11]

Journalists chose to protect their self-interests (their jobs, their reputations) by focusing on what the government's next move would be, not what it should be or whether officials' allegations about Iraq's arsenal were on target.

People generally pursue their self-interest in a narrowly defined manner that maximizes positive emotions such as pride and minimizes negative ones such as guilt or culpability.[12] Motivation comes from material profit, such as additional readers or a Pulitzer Prize. People pursue self-interest more when they perceive similar behavior in others and fear that to do otherwise could lead to exploitation.[13]

Major publications thrive on winning awards, and events such as the terrorist attacks provide opportunities for journalists to shine and for newspapers to pick up prestigious prizes. The hijackings occurred during a period of transition at the *Times*; Howell Raines had become executive editor just a few days before.

September 11 gave Raines and the *Times* the opportunity to go after the big prize
—some reports say Raines told Miller to "go get a Pulitzer."

To win the prize, editors had to consistently highlight the paper's strengths,
such as reporters' access to inside sources, and beat other major publications to
stories. The paper was largely successful in its quest—in April 2002, the *Times*
won a record seven Pulitzer Prizes, six for its coverage of the attacks and the
war on terror.

Another explanation for the play Miller's stories received is the fact that editors must trust their reporters. Editors depend on their star reporters—their
experts—to tell them what information is valid and what is not.[14] If a reporter
becomes too involved with a story and does not pursue alternative viewpoints,
which appears to have happened with Miller, editors may not know until it is
too late. In Miller's case, she was scooping the competition, which gave her some
leverage with her editors. Some reports claim she often had no high-level editorial supervision.

When outrage about Miller's work began to mount in March 2004, the *Times*
executive editor, Bill Keller, decided against reviewing the validity of the complaints: "The brief against the coverage was that it was insufficiently skeptical,
but that is an easier claim to make in hindsight than in context....Like many
aggressive reporters...[Miller] has sometimes stepped on toes, but that is hardly
grounds for rebuke."[15]

The comments by Miller and *Times* editors show a lack of concern or remorse
about egregious errors. This should be a source of concern for those in the profession and readers of the paper—if reporters and editors refuse to take responsibility for such serious errors in stories, how can anyone be confident that the same
thing will not happen again?

Journalists have a responsibility to the public to fight for access to information
and to search for the truth. Ideally, it would be in the journalists' self-interest to
do so. During times of crisis, it takes steady editorial leadership and persistent
reporting to maintain focus and provide the public with the information it needs
to make informed decisions.

Howard Kurtz, the *Washington Post*'s media editor, reported in late 2004 that
from "August 2002 through the March 19, 2003 launch of the war, the *Post* ran
more than 140 front-page stories that focused heavily on administration rhetoric
against Iraq."[16]

In a sense, American journalists created a self-fulfilling prophecy: They highlighted alarmist viewpoints, minimized alternative perspectives, convinced the
American public that the need to go to war in Iraq was urgent, and then gathered
their Pulitzers and justified their work. As reporters put it, "to beat up the messenger is to miss the point" because they are simply "the mouthpiece for whatever administration is in power."

According to sociologist R.K. Merton, "The self-fulfilling prophecy is a basic
sociological tenet whereby public definitions of a situation [prophecies or predic-
tions] become an integral part of the situation and thus affect subsequent

developments."[17] Journalists made the administration's claims viable by high-lighting officials' unchallenged perspectives with front-page play. The result was a public that largely supported the call to war.

JOURNALISM 101

A study by the CISSM (Center for International and Security Studies at Mary-land) at the University of Maryland found that journalists did not fully under-stand the debate about WMD and were often led astray by officials.

> Many stories stenographically reported the Bush administration's perspectives on WMD giving too little critical examination of the way officials framed the events, issues, threats, and policy options. The American media did not play the role of checking and balancing the exercise of power that the standard theory of democracy requires.[18]

The study concluded that by taking advantage of the journalists' "inverted pyramid" style of writing, the administration was able to direct the manner in which the WMD debate took place.

Journalism 101 teaches that the most important or most jarring piece of infor-mation said becomes the lead paragraph. Thus, the media gave alarmist presiden-tial statements about Iraq's having WMD and purported connections with al Qaeda front-page treatment in an inverted pyramid format, effectively magnify-ing their validity and minimizing alternative views. Other opinions, if presented at all, were usually buried on inside pages near the end of the articles. "The net effect was both to disseminate as well as to validate the administration's mes-sage," the study found.[19] This occurred both before and after the war with Iraq began.

In May 2003, the *Washington Post* ran an A1-page story that gave the impres-sion that justification for the war had been found, this time in the form of bio-logical weapons labs. "Bush: 'We Found' Banned Weapons; President Cites Trailers in Iraq as Proof," said the headline. The story stated:

> President Bush, citing two trailers that U.S. intelligence agencies have said were probably used as mobile biological weapons labs, said U.S. forces in Iraq have "found the weapons of mass destruction" that were the United States' primary justification for going to war..."You remember when Colin Powell stood up in front of the world, and he said Iraq has got laboratories, mobile labs to build biological weapons? ...We found them.[20]

Seven paragraphs down, however, the article noted: "U.S. authorities have to date made no claim of a confirmed finding of an actual nuclear, biological, or chemical weapon." The story's bias was obvious. The seven sources in it were Tony Blair (a strong Bush ally), Donald Rumsfeld, the CIA, Colin Powell, "Bush administration officials," "U.S. authorities," and "a senior administration official." There were no rebuttals or opposing viewpoints in the story.[21]

An AP story the same day had information that should have been in the *Post*'s story: "There is no evidence the two trailers were ever actually used to make biological weapons....Captured Iraqi scientists have said the vehicles were for producing hydrogen for weather balloons in support of artillery."[22]

In other words, the story did not belong on page A1 in the *Post*; the president should have been challenged when he said the weapons had been found, and the headline should have noted that there were doubts about whether the trailers were weapons labs.

According to the CISSM study,

> even by May 1, 2003 [after Bush declared an end to major combat operations in Iraq], when many journalists actively questioned White House and Pentagon pronouncements, they continued to accept the administration's set of priorities. If the White House acted as if a WMD story was important, so, too, did the media. If the White House ignored a story [or an angle on a story], the media were likely to as well.[23]

An October 2003 study by the Program on International Policy Attitudes found that "increased attention [to media reports] did not reduce the likelihood of misperceptions. Most striking, in the case of those who primarily watched Fox News, greater attention to news modestly increases the likelihood of misperceptions."[24]

These misperceptions included a belief that WMD not only had been found in Iraq but also had been used against U.S. troops, that world opinion was in favor of the war, that Iraq was directly involved in the September 11 attacks, and that links had been found between Iraq and al Qaeda.

The misperceptions were largely due to journalists who dutifully relayed the Pentagon's messages without providing clarity. Even reporters in Iraq relied heavily on U.S. officials for information—very few went out into the field to talk to Iraqis or to investigate an area after a firefight. Here are a few examples of media reporting about WMD before and after U.S. troops landed in Iraq:

"U.S. Suspects al-Qaeda Got Nerve Agents from Iraqis," was the headline of a page A1 *Washington Post* article on December 12, 2002.

"Sources Say Intercepts Prove Iraq has WMDs," said a UPI headline on December 18, 2002. The story said: "U.S. officials say they have convincing evidence of Iraq's continued efforts to build WMDs in the form of communications intercepts that depict transactions with foreign suppliers of Baghdad's secret program...."[25]

On February 6, 2003, the *New York Times* reported on page A1 that Powell had "set forth the first evidence of what he said was a well-developed cell of al-Qaeda operating out of Baghdad...."[26]

CBS News correspondent David Martin reported from Iraq on March 25, 2003: "Iraqis have drawn a red line on the map around Baghdad, and once American troops cross it, the Republican Guards are authorized to use chemical weapons. The Iraqi Republican Guard controls the bulk of Iraq's chemical weaponry, most of which can be fired from artillery guns or short-range rocket launchers, according to U.S. officials."[27]

Fox News said on April 4, 2003: "U.S. troops found thousands of boxes of white powder, nerve agent antidote, and documents in Arabic on how to engage in chemical warfare at an industrial site south of Baghdad."[28]

Looking at the news reports, it is no wonder that Americans had misconceptions. We now know that none of those stories were true. More than a year after the war began, Congress concluded that there was no link between Hussein and al Qaeda. It is unclear where the information about the "red line on the map around Baghdad" came from, but chemical weapons were never used on any American troops in Iraq. Members of the administration backed away from its claims that they had "rock solid" proof that Iraq had WMD and stopped searching for them.[29] The follow-up reports that cast doubt on the administration's claims were either short mentions in larger stories about the progress in the search for the weapons or articles that were buried on back pages. Broadcasts rarely mentioned the stories after first reporting them. The public was left with the impression that the original reports were correct.

Dependency on official sources blocked out journalists' independent analysis, and dissenting views were all but eliminated from coverage, even as the war progressed.

EDITORIALS

The news stories about the buildup to the war in Iraq were accompanied by pro-war editorials that added to the growing sense of urgency.

According to an analysis by the *Columbia Journalism Review*, editorials in the country's six leading papers during the six-week period between Powell's U.N. speech on February 5, 2003, and the beginning of the war on March 19, 2003,

> ranged from hawkish without a shade of doubt (the *Wall Street Journal* and, to a lesser extent, the *Chicago Tribune*) to pro-war but conflicted (the *Washington Post* and *USA Today*) to antiwar without United Nations approval (the *New York Times* and *Los Angeles Times*). None of these six unconditionally opposed war. Neither did any of them throw their weight behind intellectually appealing, but nevertheless unofficial, pro-war arguments. . . .[30]

The *Washington Post* editorialized in favor of ousting Hussein nine times in February 2003, the month before the invasion. One of the editorials was a long and unusual piece addressing complaints by readers that the paper was irrationally and consistently promoting the war.[31]

"Our editorials in favor of disarming the dictator have prompted a torrent of letters, many approving and many critical," read the *Post*'s February 27, 2003, editorial, "'Drumbeat' on Iraq? A Response to Readers."

> They are for the most part thoughtful and serious; the antiwar letters in particular are often angry and anguished as well. "It is truly depressing to witness the depths *Washington Post* editors have reached in their jingoistic rush to war," [a] reader writes. It's a serious charge, and it deserves a serious response.... What of our "jingoism," our "drumbeating"? Probably no editorial page sin could be more grievous than whipping up war fever for some political or trivial purpose. And we do not take lightly the risks of war—to American and Iraqi soldiers and civilians first of all. The right question, though, is not "Is war risky?" but "Is inaction less so?".... We respect our readers who believe that war is the worst option. But we believe that, in this case, long-term peace will be better served by strength than by concessions.[32]

The disturbing realization that years of economic sanctions had been largely successful in Iraq and that there was probably never any WMD threat is exacerbated by reports about misinformation campaigns by the Pentagon and the Iraqi "defectors" that the news media depended upon for its stories.

These campaigns should not have come as a surprise to journalists covering the Pentagon—the administration was straightforward about its plans from the beginning.[33]

One month after the 9/11 attacks, the Department of Defense hired the Rendon Group, a public relations firm, "to help it explain U.S. military strikes in Afghanistan to global audiences."[34]

The Rendon Group was awarded a no-bid, 120-day, $397,000 contract with an option to extend the contract for another year. The *New York Times* wrote in February 2002, "the firm is well known for running propaganda campaigns in Arab countries, including one denouncing atrocities by Iraq during its 1990 invasion of Kuwait."[35] Knight Ridder's Washington office filed a story that said the company

> has worked in the past for U.S. government agencies, including the CIA, which paid it to boost the image of the Iraqi National Congress, a U.S.-backed group of Iraqis opposed to the rule of President Saddam Hussein. That effort in the mid-'90s ended with an investigation by the CIA's inspector general over how a reported $23 million was spent on behalf of the Iraqi National Congress and its leader, Ahmed Chalabi.[36]

No news outlets noted that the cost was pretty high for a no-bid contract or explored what the Pentagon's hiring of the Rendon Group might mean. Rumsfeld said simply: "We need to do a better job to make sure that people are not confused as to what this is about."[37] Knight Ridder was more specific when it noted, "the choice of the Rendon Group to advise the Pentagon may not be a coincidence, given its past work on behalf of the Iraqi opposition."[38]

Four months later, the *New York Times* reported a Department of Defense plan "to provide news items, possibly even false ones, to foreign media organizations as part of a new effort to influence public sentiment and policy makers in both friendly and unfriendly countries." The Defense Department, the *Times* reported,

> recently created the Office of Strategic Influence, which is proposing to broaden that mission into allied nations in the Middle East, Asia, and even Western Europe. The small but well-financed Pentagon office, which was established shortly after the September 11 terrorist attacks, was a response to concerns in the administration that the United States was losing public support overseas for its war on terrorism, particularly in Islamic countries. . . . "Saddam Hussein has a charm offensive going on, and we haven't done anything to counteract it," a senior military official said.[39]

The Rendon Group was assigned to the Office of Strategic Information, the story noted.

The foreign press expressed immediate outrage:

> "Pentagon Plans Propaganda War," the BBC said. "The Pentagon is toying with the idea of black propaganda. As part of George Bush's war on terrorism, the military is thinking of planting propaganda and misleading stories in the international media. A new department has been set up inside the Pentagon with the Orwellian title of the Office of Strategic Influence. It is well funded, is being run by a general, and its aim is to influence public opinion abroad."[40]

In the days after the announcement, media both within the United States and outside reacted with indignation, negative editorials, and a slew of political cartoons that rattled Rumsfeld. Eventually, he told reporters that the office was being closed. "Notwithstanding the fact that much of the thrust of the criticism and the cartoons and the editorial comment has been off the mark, the office has clearly been so damaged. . .it's pretty clear to me that it could not function effectively. So it's being closed down."[41]

Journalists patted themselves on the back for stopping a propaganda campaign. But they were premature and lazy. Few journalists noted that the Rendon Group had retained its contract.[42]

Douglas Feith, then the undersecretary of defense for policy, hinted to reporters that nothing had changed shortly after Rumsfeld announced the office was being closed. When asked if the Pentagon would distribute false information, Feith answered: "We are not going to have Defense Department officials lying to the public, neither the foreign public, nor the domestic public, nor to the press."[43] But the *New York Times* then noted that, "Mr. Feith declined to rule out the possibility that the Pentagon might hire an outside firm that would be authorized to spread disinformation overseas. 'We are going to preserve our ability to mislead an enemy,' he said."[44]

Rumsfeld mentioned the office again in conversation with reporters nine months later:

> And then there was the Office of Strategic Influence. You may recall that. And "oh my goodness gracious, isn't that terrible, Henny Penny, the sky is going to fall." *I went down that next day and said fine, if you want to savage this thing, fine, I'll give you the corpse. There's the name. You can have the name, but I'm gonna keep doing every single thing that needs to be done, and I have.*[45] (emphasis added)

No reporters caught the importance of this statement and reported it. A transcript of the statement may still be available on the Department of Defense web site. Certainly there are times when the government must lie to protect the country's national security interest. For example, the U.S. military strength in a conflict zone may be exaggerated, its troop movements disguised, and its knowledge of the enemy or of enemy intelligence concealed. However, lying routinely or for political purposes is unacceptable.

The administration was so sure of itself that it did not even try to disguise what it was doing. And yet the media continued to passively report what it was told. Worse, it never followed up on controversial stories.

Sam Gardiner, a retired Air Force colonel who taught strategy and military operations at the National War College, Air War College, and Naval War College, analyzed the Pentagon's campaign and determined that it was extremely effective:

> There were over 50 stories manufactured or at least engineered that distorted the picture of Gulf II for the American and British people. What becomes important is not each story taken individually. If that were the case, it would probably seem only more of the same. If you were to look at them one at a time, you could conclude, "Okay, we sort of knew that was happening." It is the pattern that becomes important. It's the summary of everything. To use a phrase often heard during the war, it's the mosaic.[46]

According to Gardiner, the "manufactured" stories appeared thousands of times in a variety of forms in different publications and covered everything from large doomsday stories such as Iraq's ability to detonate chemical and biological warheads within 45 minutes and its purchase of uranium from Niger, to humanitarian propaganda such as reports of vast improvements in Afghan women's lives. The stories even included "punishment" rumors for countries that disagreed with the United States. "The evidence points to the French being the focus of punishment in the strategic influence campaign," Gardiner said. "There are at least eight times when false stories or engineered stories were aimed at them, the majority appearing after their lack of support in the U.N. for U.S. and U.K. actions...."[47]

The coverage of the so-called Iraqi "defectors" was even worse. Members of the American media have admitted that they relied heavily on stories and sources provided primarily by Ahmad Chalabi or his group, the INC (Iraqi National Congress).

A handful of journalists were able to maintain their focus throughout the buildup to the war and resisted the pressures of groupthink. The *New Yorker's* Hersh, the *Washington Post's* Walter Pincus, and Knight Ridder's Washington, D.C. bureau reporters are examples of this. They consistently doubted rumors and asked difficult questions of officials, but their reports were overwhelmed by the majority and barely noticed.

An investigation by Knight Ridder found that the *Times* was only one of dozens of publications that were fed false information by Chalabi and the INC. Other publications include the *Washington Post*, *Vanity Fair*, the *Atlantic Monthly*, the *Kansas City Star*, and the *Philadelphia Daily News*. Chalabi's group claims to have influenced 108 articles in 2002. Some of this false information included purported links between Saddam Hussein and Osama bin Laden, the existence of mobile weapons labs in Iraq disguised as yogurt and milk trucks, and that Iraq had trained terrorists in the same hijacking techniques that were used in the 9/11 attacks.[48]

"Many of the articles relied on interviews with the same defectors, who appeared to change facts with each telling," Knight Ridder reported. "For instance, one defector first appeared in several stories as an Iraqi army former captain, but a later story said he was a major."[49]

Astute editors should have picked up on clues that stories throughout the nation were riddled with inconsistencies and gaping holes. Why didn't any of them ask for clarifications or follow-up stories?

As the evidence mounted, the *New York Times* editors reconsidered their position about self-examination and took a hard look at the paper's pre-war coverage. Their conclusion, published on May 26, 2004:

> We have found a number of instances of coverage that was not as rigorous as it should have been. In some cases, information that was controversial then, and seems questionable now, was insufficiently qualified or allowed to stand unchallenged. Looking back, we wish we had been more aggressive in re-examining the claims as new evidence emerged—or failed to emerge. . . . The problematic stories. . .depended at least in part on information from a circle of Iraqi informants, defectors, and exiles bent on "regime change" in Iraq. . . .Editors at several levels who should have been challenging reporters and pressing for more skepticism were perhaps too intent on rushing scoops into the paper. Accounts of Iraqi defectors were not always weighed against their strong desire to have Saddam Hussein ousted. Articles based on dire claims about Iraq tended to get prominent display, while follow-up articles that called the original ones into question were sometimes buried. In some cases, there was no follow-up at all.[50]

The paper then listed 28 dubious stories (including the one by Miller highlighted at the beginning of the chapter) in which false information planted by administration officials or Iraqi defectors was presented as fact or where alternative viewpoints were not adequately represented. The editors noted that in at least one case, a follow-up story that reversed the claims of a major front-page article was buried on page A10, when it "might well have belonged on page A1."

The piece that appeared in the *Times* was not an apology, executive editor Bill Keller told his staff in a memo. "The purpose of the note is to acknowledge that we, like many of our competitors...were misled on a number of stories by Iraqi informants dealing in misinformation."[51]

Rather than take responsibility for the errors, members of the media claimed they had been duped, much like the public, and should be excused for their mistakes. While this may be true, the media are more culpable because papers such as the *New York Times* and the *Washington Post* are resources that people trust to provide them with the information they use to form their opinions.

It is telling that instead of reprimanding their correspondents for poorly reported, factually false stories and demanding that they do better next time, editors chose to relieve them of responsibility for their mistakes. How will this be avoided in the future if members of the media do not take responsibility for their errors?

The *Times* admission was quietly placed in the paper's back pages—the lower left corner of A10—with no front-page alert to readers. No reporters were named or chastised by the paper.

It was hypocritical of the paper to claim it had learned its lesson about story placement and the importance of alerting its readers to its errors and then to bury the admission.

The *Times* supplies stories to dozens of newspapers across the country and its pseudo-apology sent editors of those papers scrambling to come up with explanations for their readers. Most placed the acknowledgement of the mistakes more prominently than the *Times* did.[52] After all, the stories had been prominently displayed on their pages, too, effectively making them pawns in the political attempt to sway public opinion.

"We are trying to be as transparent as possible," explained Robert J. Rosenthal, the managing editor of the *San Francisco Chronicle*, about the 18-inch article about the *Times* admission that ran on page A2 of the paper. "We wanted to make readers aware." The *Chronicle*'s explanation described in detail how the four stories it ran from the *Times* were flawed.[53]

The good news is that the *Times* admission of its poor reporting must have hit a nerve with reporters and editors there. The next time the administration sounded the terrorist alarm with a claim that al Qaeda would attempt to disrupt the U.S. elections with a large terrorist attack in the summer of 2004, the paper ran a story whose headline noted some skepticism about the claims. "As

Ashcroft Warns of Attack, Some Question Threat and Its Timing."[54] The headline is a far cry from the alarmist WMD headlines that were common in the
buildup to war.

Nearly three months after the *Times* explanation, the *Washington Post* published an article about its pre-war coverage by media critic Howard Kurtz on its
front page. The story concluded that editors had buried anti-administration
claims on back pages and highlighted the need for war on the front page. "The
result," Kurtz said, "was coverage that, despite flashes of groundbreaking reporting, in hindsight looks strikingly one-sided at times."[55] None of the *Post*'s editors
felt the need to apologize for their errors. None explained any changes they had
made to ensure that the same mistakes would not occur again.

In a sad testament to the state of today's newspapers, Leonard Downie Jr.,
executive editor of the *Post*—the paper that uncovered the information that
led to the exposure of the Watergate scandal and the resignation of President
Richard Nixon—now says his paper has no influence: "People who were opposed
to the war from the beginning and have been critical of the media's coverage in
the period before the war have this belief that somehow the media should have
crusaded against the war. They have the mistaken impression that somehow if
the media's coverage had been different, there wouldn't have been a war."

Downie missed the point—reporters and editors for the paper should not have
crusaded against the war or for it, they should have exhibited skepticism about
what they were told. They should have dug for the facts and provided a more
global perspective on the issues. His statement is another example of how journalists chose to justify pursuing their self-interest after the case for war fell apart.

It is unfortunate that on the 30th anniversary of Watergate, the *Post* claimed
that its journalistic value is insignificant. Facts presented to the public by ambi-
tious journalists can certainly change the course of history. Editors and reporters
at the *Post* should know that better than most.

Studies have found that television broadcasts were just as uneven when it
came to presenting both sides of the war issue. *60 Minutes* journalist Leslie Stahl
revisited a story she had aired based on information from Chalabi before the war
and found that almost all of it was incorrect.

Still, many big-name broadcast journalists insist that they do not owe anybody
an apology for their work. ABC's Ted Koppel said he believed the administration's claims about WMD and did not work hard to disprove them, but he did
not feel the need to apologize.

"I don't think an apology is due," he said. "If what you are saying is could we
all have been more critical, I think the answer is yes....Did I believe at the time
that there were weapons of mass destruction? Absolutely, I did."[56]

Koppel may have believed the claims, but it was still his job to present all sides
of the story to the American public so it could formulate its own opinion based
on all the facts.

David Albright, a physicist who heads the Institute for Science and
International Security, said he often felt pressured by newscasters to agree with

the administration's arguments about the need for war. "I felt a lot of pressure [from journalists] to stick to the subject, which was Iraq's bad behavior," he said. "I always felt the administration was setting the agenda for what stories should be covered, and the news media bought into that, rather than take a critical look at the administration's underlying reasons for war." He said a cable news host once "got really mad and chastised me" during a commercial break after he said he thought U.N. inspections should continue.[57]

A study by Fairness and Accuracy in Reporting found that 76 percent of the guests on network talk shows in late January and early February 2003 were current or former government officials. Antiwar sources accounted for less than 1 percent.

THE DEFINING MOMENT

Nowhere was the American media's passive acceptance of information from the administration more obvious than in the stories and editorials that followed Powell's United Nations speech outlining U.S. evidence against Iraq on February 5, 2003. The divide between coverage in the foreign press and the American media was enormous.

The speech, hailed as a success by the American media, was immediately called "unconvincing" by the international media. In fact, the day Powell presented his evidence, the BBC ran a story casting doubt on U.S. claims that al Qaeda and Hussein were working together. In his speech, Powell asserted that there was a "sinister nexus between Iraq and the al Qaeda terrorist network, a nexus that combines classic terrorist organizations and modern methods of murder."[58]

The BBC reported on its web site: "There are no current links between the Iraqi regime and the al-Qaeda network, according to an official British intelligence report seen by BBC News....That conclusion flatly contradicts one of the main charges laid against Iraqi leader Saddam Hussein by the United States and Britain—that he has cultivated contacts with the group blamed for the 11 September attacks."[59]

In a presentation that lasted almost 90 minutes, Powell provided U.N. representatives with intercepted audiotape recordings purportedly of Iraqi officials discussing how to hide WMD from U.N. inspectors, satellite photos of buildings surrounded by large trucks that he claimed was proof that Iraq was cleaning out a weapons facility before a U.N. inspectors' visit, and intelligence reports from human sources verifying the existence of mobile weapons units that in a matter of months "can produce a quantity of biological poison equal to the entire amount that Iraq claimed to have produced in the years prior to the Gulf war." Powell produced drawings of these mobile weapons that he said were based on descriptions from defectors who "have risked their lives to let the world know what Saddam Hussein is really up to."[60]

Powell mentioned aluminum tubes that the administration believed had been purchased to produce nuclear weapons and sites where he believed banned weapons were being developed.

The speech was met with rousing applause on the pages of American papers. The *Columbia Journalism Review* later noted, "without appearing to weigh...contrary evidence, the U.S. papers all essentially pronounced Powell right, though they couldn't possibly know for sure that he was. In short, they trusted him. And in so doing, they failed to bring even an elementary skepticism to the Bush case for war."[61]

The *New York Times* ran an analysis piece on page A1 that said: "The secretary offered much evidence that Iraq has weapons programs to hide....It will be difficult for the skeptics to argue that Washington's case against Iraq is based on groundless suspicions and not intelligence information."[62]

An editorial in the paper said: "Mr. Powell's presentation...may not have produced a 'smoking gun,' but it left little question that Mr. Hussein had tried hard to conceal one."[63]

The *Washington Post*'s editorial was headlined "Irrefutable." It said: "...it is hard to imagine how anyone could doubt that Iraq possesses weapons of mass destruction. Mr. Powell left no room to argue seriously that Iraq has accepted the Security Council's offer of a 'final opportunity' to disarm."[64]

The *Wall Street Journal* went even further, dismissing Powell's own claims that his evidence was not as strong as some may need to support a war. "Powell's Smoking Gun: His Presentation Persuades All but Saddam's Diehard Backers," was the headline on its editorial. The editorial said:

> ...Colin Powell warned that his U.N. presentation yesterday would contain no "smoking gun." He was too modest. The array of evidence he presented amounts to a smoking fusillade of Saddam Hussein's efforts to resist and confound the U.N. order that he disarm. The Powell brief contained reconnaissance photos, communications intercepts as well as information from human sources. Some of it probably shouldn't have been made public, since it no doubt tipped off Iraqis about U.S. intelligence sources and methods. But there can be no further doubt that Iraq is in material breach of U.N. Resolution 1441—at least not among anyone still open to the facts....The secretary of state had to provide this smoking proof because some people still refuse to believe what they see with their own eyes. An example is the way many, including U.N. inspector [Mohamed] El Baradei, have accepted Iraq's explanation that its import of high-strength aluminum tubes was for conventional rocketry, not uranium enrichment.[65]

The *Chicago Tribune* wrote:

> Secretary of State Colin Powell's strong, plainspoken indictment of the Saddam Hussein regime before the U.N. Security Council Wednesday embodies something truly great about the United States. When in history has a government so carefully outlined and documented grievances against another government, or given that

government so many chances to mend its ways before resorting to war? Those around the world who demanded proof must now be satisfied, or else admit that no satisfaction is possible for them.

The American media was clearly taken with Powell's presentation. Journalism professors and cranky editors working with novice reporters have been known to quip: "If your mother says she loves you, check it out." In other words, never take anything at face value, go and find out if it is true.

The foreign press did just that. Journalists abroad were immediately suspicious of the information presented by Powell and spent more time analyzing the data. The British daily newspaper the *Guardian* did an exceptional reporting job, printing several articles questioning the reliability of Powell's information the day after his speech.

"U.S. Recycles Human Test Claims; Iraq Accused of Using Prisoners as Guinea Pigs" said the headline on an article exploring one of Powell's assertions. The paper wrote:

> Colin Powell highlighted the claim that Saddam Hussein had used 1,600 prisoners on death row as guinea pigs for his biological and chemical weapons program as an indication of how the Iraqi dictator's "inhumanity" had no limits. But last night, it emerged that this part of Mr. Powell's testimony to the Security Council was old news....A spokeswoman for Amnesty International said it had no recent reports of such experiments: "We are aware that that did happen, but it happened in the 1980s. Prisoners were being experimented on, but as far as we know, it's not something that is actually happening currently."...A spokeswoman for the Foreign Office said it had no records of such experiments on its file of Iraqi human rights abuses.[66]

Another story focused on the human sources of Powell's information. "All Too Human Failings of 'Human Intelligence'; Information From Defectors, Spies and Prisoners May be Unreliable, Say Experts," said a *Guardian* headline. "Defectors are tempted to inflate their stories, Joseph Cirincione, senior associate of the Carnegie Endowment for International Peace, warned yesterday. 'We should never go to war based on a defector's tale. There's a long history of defectors' tales being erroneous. It is a problem that detectives have all the time; somebody comes to them hoping to get something in exchange.'"[67]

Both stories are excellent examples of how journalists are supposed to do their jobs. A fact is presented; calls are made to verify the information; the findings appear in the paper. The *Guardian* also mentioned that Powell's findings were at odds with information provided to the U.N. by weapons inspector Blix and Mohamed El Baradei, director of the IAEA (International Atomic Energy Agency). None of this information made it into major mainstream American publications and broadcast reports.

A British tabloid newspaper, the *Daily Mirror*, asked on its front page: "Dodgy tapes, grainy videos, great rhetoric, but where's the proof Colin?"[68]

Other foreign papers highlighted what was missing in U.S. discussions. Though few disputed that Hussein was a brutal dictator, the question Europeans wanted answered was, Is war the best solution?

The French paper *Le Figaro* noted: "[Powell] may have convinced the Minnesota rancher, but the European farmer will certainly continue to have doubts.... Almost no one disputes that Saddam is brutal and dangerous. Controversy flares up rather over the issue of whether the costs of a war, including civilian deaths and the burden of years of occupation, are proportionate to its usefulness."

A dialogue between Katie Couric and three international journalists on February 6, 2003, revealed the American perspective and highlighted different interpretations of the speech. Note the bias in Couric's questions (all emphasis added).

> Couric to Gordon Corera, a foreign affairs correspondent for BBC Radio:
> Do they want—many people in Great Britain *still, despite Colin Powell's presentation, still want to give the inspectors more time?* And what about the al-Qaeda/Iraq connection that—that was put forth during Colin Powell's presentation yesterday, the intelligence that was gleaned from—from some terrorist cells, and—and *the fact that there have been al-Qaeda operations going on for eight months in Iraq* and the danger that poses. Did that cause any shift in the mood there?

> Corera:
> Eighty percent of people [in Great Britain] believe that Iraq does have weapons of mass destruction, it does have biological and chemical weapons. But what the public is divided over is whether that's a threat and whether that justifies war.... There is a feeling here that trying to make the Iraq/al-Qaeda link is a miscalculation on the part of the American administration because people just aren't convinced by it.

After learning from journalist Patrice De Beer of the French daily paper *Le Monde* that "not a single French newspaper—left, right, or center—has appeared convinced by Colin Powell's arguments and evidence," Couric seemed incredulous.

> She responded:
> So Patrice, all these satellite photos, these intercepts, and various other pieces of evidence that Colin Powell used in his presentation, couldn't they be interpreted by some people in France as the so-called smoking gun?

> De Beer:
> No, they are suspicions. These are a pattern, a web of suspicion that nobody, as far as I can see, has considered sufficient evidence for preemptive war.

Couric:
And do they believe in France, Patrice, that if given more time, the weapons inspectors *suddenly will have access to many more of these materials, that
the Iraqis will stop hiding them and cooperate fully,* or do they just want to basi-
cally give the inspectors a chance to see if that would happen? *Because, as
Colin Powell said yesterday, this has been a pattern of behavior by the Iraqis for
12 years now.* Do the French people really think this will change if the
inspectors are given more time?[69]

Couric clearly believed Powell. Her reasoning illustrates why most journalists
did not pursue the types of stories the foreign media did. If journalists believed
the administration, as many later said they did, there was no reason to pursue
information that contradicted its viewpoint—doing so was perceived as a waste
of time. The story then became the inevitable war and the issues surrounding
it: when the attack would occur, what the troops might encounter, who would
join with the United States.

Had Couric or any other journalist exhibited even a passing curiosity, she or
he would have approached Powell with some relevant questions about statements he had made about Iraq's capabilities before the 9/11 attacks.

In February 2001, Powell said at a press conference in Cairo that, "Frankly,
[sanctions against Iraq] have worked. [Saddam Hussein] has not developed any
significant capabilities with respect to weapons of mass destruction. He is unable
to project conventional power against his neighbors." Powell made the statement on camera; it was not made in a secret meeting.[70]

On May 15, 2001, Powell told a Senate Appropriations subcommittee:

The sanctions, as they are called, have succeeded over the last 10 years. . . . The Iraqi
regime militarily remains fairly weak. It doesn't have the capacity it had 10 or 12
years ago. It has been contained. And even though we have no doubt in our mind
that the Iraqi regime is pursuing programs to develop weapons of mass destruction
—chemical, biological, and nuclear—I think the best intelligence estimates suggest
that they have not been terribly successful. There's no question that they have some
stockpiles of some of these sorts of weapons still under their control, but they have
not been able to break out, they have not been able to come out with the capacity
to deliver these kinds of systems or to actually have these kinds of systems that is
much beyond where they were 10 years ago. So containment, using this arms control
sanctions regime, I think has been reasonably successful.[71]

Similarly, in July 2001 Condoleezza Rice said on CNN *Late Edition with Wolf
Blitzer:* "In terms of Saddam Hussein being there, let's remember that his country
is divided, in effect. He does not control the northern part of his country. We are
able to keep arms from him. His military forces have not been rebuilt. This has
been a successful period."[72]

Nobody was asked to clarify why Powell presented completely different information to the U.N.

Joseph Wilson, who was the deputy chief of mission at the U.S. Embassy in Baghdad from 1988 to 1991 and clashed with the Bush administration over the intelligence used to justify the war, asked at a conference: "Did anybody bother to go out and ask an inspector his interpretation of what Powell said? Did anybody go out and ask an expert on disarmament about the meaning of what Powell said? If they did, I certainly didn't see it in any newspapers."[73]

It was not until the war in Iraq was well under way that the American media began to closely examine Powell's assertions.

Editor & Publisher, a magazine that covers the newspaper industry, noted:

> Simply put, the Powell charade was the turning point in the march to war, and the media, in almost universally declaring that he had "made the case," fell for it, hook, line, and sinker, thereby making the invasion (which some of the same newspapers now question) inevitable.
>
> It's a depressing case study of journalistic shirking of responsibility. The press essentially acted like a jury that is ready, willing, and (in this case) able to deliver a verdict—after the prosecution has spoken and before anyone else is heard or the evidence studied. A hanging jury, at that.[74]

Six months after Powell's speech, the AP took a close look at his claims. The conclusion: Powell's information was almost all wrong.[75]

While it is praiseworthy that the AP took a hard look at the evidence and did the reporting necessary to uncover the facts, one wonders what took it so long? Much of the evidence disputing his claims, as the AP story pointed out, was available at the time of the speech. U.N. inspectors Blix and Baradei repeatedly said they did not believe Iraq had revived its weapons program.

More than a year after his speech and the invasion of Iraq, Powell admitted to reporters that perhaps he had been wrong.

"It turned out that the sourcing was inaccurate and wrong, and, in some cases, deliberately misleading. And for that, I am disappointed, and I regret it," he told reporters.

The *Washington Post* later reported:

> CIA officials reviewing the bioweapons intelligence say that the engineer who provided the original tip [about the mobile labs] never dealt directly with U.S. intelligence agencies, and that he passed along the information through a foreign intelligence service, which they refuse to name. U.S. intelligence analysts did not know his name before the war, relying entirely on foreign officials to vouch for his credibility.[76]

Unlike the pre-war buildup stories that dominated the paper's front page, the story ran on page A20.

The *Los Angeles Time* discovered that the source of the information on the labs was the brother of a senior aide to Chalabi. "U.S. officials never had direct access to the defector and didn't even know his real name until after the war," the paper reported.[77]

As skepticism began to build and Chalabi's information was questioned, he told the *Daily Telegraph* in London: "We are heroes in error. As far as we're concerned, we've been entirely successful. That tyrant Saddam is gone, and the Americans are in Baghdad. What was said before is not important."[78]

The administration seemed to agree. Bush backed away from his original assertions that Iraq was an "imminent threat" to the world and said instead that Hussein was a bad guy who needed to be removed.

"There is no doubt in my mind the world is a better place without Saddam Hussein. America is more secure. The world is safer, and the people of Iraq are free," Bush told reporters when they questioned him about the lack of WMD in Iraq.[79]

It is a refrain that has been repeated in the media, even by reporters questioning the president.

Listen to a journalist's question to the president at a White House press conference:

> It's impossible to deny that the world is a better place in the region, certainly a better place without Saddam Hussein. But there's a sense here in this country, and a feeling around the world, that the U.S. has lost credibility by building the case for Iraq upon sometimes flimsy or, some people have complained, nonexistent evidence. And I'm just wondering, sir, why did you choose to take the world to war in that way?[80]

When he finally gets to his question, he makes a good point.

CHAPTER 5

Embedded Reporters: Was Objectivity Sacrificed for Access?

The reason we embedded so many journalists is that we wanted to dominate the information environment. We wanted to beat any kind of disinformation or propaganda by beating them at their own game.
—Lieutenant Colonel Rick Long, a Marine Corps spokesman[1]

More than 600 American and foreign journalists were embedded with allied troops as they marched through Iraq toward Baghdad. The cost to their news organizations totaled more than $100 million.

Embedding reporters with troops is not a new concept. Famous war journalist Ernie Pyle spent much of his time during World War II following U.S. troops into battle and sending heart-warming stories about their heroics to readers in America. What was different, however, is that Pyle was free to hopscotch around the war, visiting troops and battle scenes; the Pentagon did not place him there. More importantly, dozens of other reporters were covering different aspects of the war: the civilian casualties, the bloody battles, and the troops' wins and losses. This type of reporting provided a balanced perspective that gave Americans a broad picture of the war.

This was not the case with the war in Iraq, where journalists signed a contract with the Pentagon and were assigned to various allied units. Among other things, embedded reporters could not travel independently, their reports could be delayed or censored by officers, and all interviews had to be conducted "on the record." In addition, they agreed to "follow the direction and orders of the Government related to [embedding]"—and to "follow Government regulations." A reporter who disobeyed any "direction order, regulation, or ground rule" could be kicked out of the war. One who left his or her battalion for any reason—even to explore a story further—would not be allowed to return.[2]

Many reporters went to a Pentagon-organized boot camp and were palpably excited about the prospect of the adventure.

The enthusiastic reports from journalists began even before the war did. Mark Mazzetti, the defense correspondent for *U.S. News & World Report*, wrote a column about his time at boot camp for *Slate*, an online news site:

> It doesn't take long for the six-foot swells off the North Carolina coast to have their way with 20 reporters sandwiched in a hovercraft heading out to sea. Sitting in jump seats normally occupied by marines in full combat gear, we watch each others' faces turn unnatural shades, and the whole group fights the urge to toss up the ham-bologna-and-cheese sandwich served on the bus.[3]

Mazzetti notes that the reporters on the hovercraft "will likely end up on CNN, since other members of the media have been invited on base for the day to watch us suffer. So not only do we get to lug our packs up and down the hills of Quantico but we get to do it in front of members of our profession who dodged media boot camp. The pansies."

Certainly, Mazzetti is having harmless fun with the column. But it illustrates two things: The reporters in the camp are beginning to feel a sense of camaraderie with the soldiers, and the Pentagon has successfully turned attention away from the impending war and all its implications and toward the reporters themselves. Journalists became a large part of the story, and that continued when they reported from Iraq.

The *Los Angeles Times* noted,

> Grunting under the load of full packs, the journalists carried out a live landing drill, alternately crawling and running across an open field while under mock fire.... Reporters and photographers participated in military briefings, rode small amphibious craft through rough seas, visited the amphibious assault ship *Iwo Jima*, toured three other Navy ships, and accompanied marines on a rigorous training mission at Quantico, Va.[4]

They were, in a sense, "one of the troops." In their excitement, journalists missed hints that would have helped explain why the Pentagon had organized the boot camps. More than a few times the Pentagon let slip the fact that in addition to helping reporters become better prepared for the battlefield, it hoped the experience would "give news people a better appreciation for how the military operates."[5]

It apparently did. CBS News correspondent Byron Pitts said that he had bonded with members of the military before the war.

> Whether you're a hawk or a dove, once you deal with people who do it, there's a new level of appreciation for them. It was valuable to spend time with the young men and women who may have to do this very difficult job. It's one thing to view a victory or a mistake by the military from a distance. It's another when you can give some context to it, when you understand how it came about.[6]

The time Pitts spent in boot camp did not provide him with context about a military victory or mistake. It provided him with a limited opportunity to better understand how new soldiers are trained for battle.

Journalists were taught at the camp that war is incredibly dangerous and unpredictable. Fear was an important element of the training.

Mazzetti described coffee-drinking, donut-eating journalists being startled one early morning in a lecture hall by a marine instructor who suddenly shouted, "Gas! Gas! Gas!" and began counting down from nine as they stumbled for their gas masks. "As the count hits zero," he wrote, "a quarter of the room is still breathing Saddam's chemicals, and 15 of our group have become battlefield casualties. One scribe, clearly frustrated by the quick countdown, asks why only nine seconds. 'Because at 10 seconds you die,' answers the instructor. Got it."[7]

Journalists were told that land mines are abundant in Iraq and that if they found themselves in the middle of a minefield, they were probably going to die. They learned that the Kevlar flak vest body armor they would wear in Iraq was not very effective after marines fired a few rounds and "blew the stuffing out of them." Even the toilets were not safe: "Don't smoke while using a military latrine. The smoke could mix with the chemicals used to decompose human waste, and you might blow up."[8]

Carol Williams, a Los Angeles Times foreign correspondent who participated in the media boot camp, said she sometimes felt as though she was being primed for protection by the troops. "It could all have been a charade," she said. "We were constantly being told, 'If this were live fire, you'd be dead now.'"[9]

A month before troops went into Iraq, a reporter for the Army Times wrote that a general involved in organizing the "initial stages of Operation Enduring Freedom suggested in an internal memo that the Pentagon pursue a more offensive press strategy: 'Reactive [public affairs] posture [in Afghanistan] inhibited managing regional/global perceptions to U.S. advantage.'"[10] The war in Iraq would be different, officials decided.

"The military wants positive stories about the grit and resolve of its troops," the Army Times reporter noted.[11]

Minneapolis Star Tribune reporter Paul McEnroe, a "unilateral" journalist who was not embedded in Iraq, said that a sergeant in a foxhole outside Baghdad told him, in a "surprisingly frank conversation," that there was another reason the Pentagon agreed to allow journalists to follow soldiers. The sergeant explained: "You know the reason why there's embedding? The United States wants to counter all the coverage that Al Jazeera gets to the West now."[12]

KICKOFF TO WAR

As the nation prepared for the inevitable war, the media took steps to ensure maximum use of its resources. Television networks began tagging coverage with dramatic, patriotic logos, such as NBC's "Operation Iraqi Freedom." The discussions about whether the United States would invade turned to predictions about when it would happen. The concept of "shock and awe"—a massive bombing campaign—was introduced to the world. As soon as journalists arrived in Iraq, they began filing stories and dominating the news on network television.

The Pentagon had a tight grip on reporters in the first few days in Iraq. MSNBC's Brian Williams complained that the United States was censoring everything. Many journalists reported news blackouts; others found their satellite phones inexplicably blocked. An *Army Times* reporter said that some embeds were being "hounded by military public affairs officers who follow their every move and look over their shoulders as they interview aviators, sailors, and maintainers for their stories. Strict ground rules and monitoring have put a chill on reporting any worthwhile news from these locations."[13]

That is one obvious downside to the embed's contract requirement that all interviews be on the record with all sources quoted by name. In Washington, politicians and government officials are given many opportunities to speak anonymously without having to worry about the consequences. It is a luxury that should have been afforded to the troops as they went off to war. As the situation in Iraq became more unstable, many wondered why few negative comments were being made by soldiers in the field. The prospect of negative consequences for speaking frankly could certainly be the reason.

In time, positive stories were sent back to the United States, bonds between soldiers and journalists were forged, and official censoring lessened.

Journalists struggled visibly with the conflicts they encountered in the embedding process. NBC's David Bloom, who tagged along with the 3rd Infantry Division, told viewers,

> As a journalist, obviously we're trying to maintain our objectivity and report factually what we see and hear here and not to become one with the force, if you will, because we still have to maintain that appropriate journalistic distance....As a person, I can tell you that these soldiers have been amazing to us. They have done anything and everything that we could ask of them, and we in turn are trying to return

the favor. . . . As far as the relationship is concerned, we are about as one with this force as you could possibly be.

Here, Bloom described the major problem that embeds inevitably faced. The question he could not seem to answer is, is he "one with the force" or has he remained an unbiased journalist. (Bloom later died in Iraq from a blood clot in a lung.)

Many journalists recounted their experiences after they had left the war zone not in terms of the stories filed or the battles witnessed, but by referring to the admiration they gained for the soldiers they were with. The bonds forged between journalists and soldiers created an added benefit for the Department of Defense.

ABC News' Ted Koppel, who was embedded with the 3rd Infantry Division, said he made some lasting friendships. "It really did enable you to establish a level of trust in both directions, and I must say that the afterglow of that has lasted. I now feel that I have a number of, if not close personal friends, then at least good friends, from Gen. [Buford] Blount on down."[14]

NBC correspondent Chip Reid said he had expected to be "scared senseless" when he first encountered gunfire but was calmed by "the marines who surrounded me [who] seemed so focused, so utterly confident." He noted: "It's hard to believe that, as someone with no military background, I was virtually 'adopted' by the marines and lived like one of them."[15]

After returning to the United States, Reid went to Camp Pendleton "for my battalion's homecoming (Third Battalion, Fifth Marines). My cameraman, Joe Klimovitz, went, too. We were treated like royalty. I can't tell you how many mothers, fathers, wives, sons, and daughters thanked us profusely for helping them to keep track of their marines during those difficult early days of the war. They gave me a large scrapbook filled with dozens of beautifully written thank-you notes, which is now one of my earthly treasures."[16]

The embed experience had obviously affected journalists; they became very involved with the soldiers. The faces of the soldiers they befriended in Iraq will likely follow them into any future wars or even any stories about the military that they cover. This, of course, is very human. But it is also precisely the problem. How can you write negative stories about friends and protectors? It is easy to say that the professional responsibilities come first and that nothing affects objective reporting. However, it is more difficult for journalists to adhere to those principles while reporting from a dangerous situation, surrounded by "brave" men and women who protect them. Even subconsciously, journalists could censor their own stories.

CBS's Jim Axelrod told the *Washington Post*:

This will sound like I've drunk the Kool-Aid, but I found embedding to be an extremely positive experience. There was some initial mistrust and suspicion: "Who are you guys and what are you gonna do to harm us?" But we got great stories and they got very positive coverage—in large part because there were some very compelling stories to tell about the military.[17]

Washington Post media critic Howard Kurtz noted however that, "even some journalists conceded it would be hard to write critically about their units because, as ABC's John Donvan put it, 'they're my protectors.'"[18]

The embeds let it be known in their reports that they admired the soldiers they were with and felt safer with them than without them.

A discussion between *Christian Science Monitor* correspondent Scott Peterson, embedded in the 1st Marine Expeditionary Unit in Fallujah, and CNN's Paula Zahn exemplifies the potential problem of admiration clouding objectivity. CNN's introduction said that "the violent standoff between Iraqi insurgents and U.S. Marines in Fallujah has created an atmosphere of unpredictable danger. [Peterson] spoke with CNN's Paula Zahn by phone about why the military chose to stand back and why the strength of the insurgency has been a surprise." The report began well, with Peterson explaining that military leaders were focusing on pinpoint attacks rather than "having to actually roll into the entire city" of Fallujah. But it almost immediately drifted off topic into a story about the dangers for journalists and the bravery of members of the military.

> Peterson:
> I think that this conflict is one that is incredibly dangerous, not only for the marines themselves, because this is...an urban environment, but also I think for the journalists who are covering it. In many cases, we are embedded with marines who are right there on the front line, along with troops who are on the front line....We get to see what's going on. But it also means that we are right there with them. We have...a feeling for the kind of stresses and the kind of dangers that that front line brings with it.

> Zahn:
> ...There have been so many marines wounded in Fallujah that there is actually a backlog of Purple Hearts. What does that do to the morale of troops?

> Peterson:
> Well, it's surprising, to be honest....I was in one of the combat surgical rooms where they were working on a couple of these guys. There were two that had gunshot wounds. And they pulled a huge slug, a bullet, out of the leg of one of the marines. And another one had a bullet wound right through the back. And, amazingly, they were trying to convince their commanders that they were ready to go and go back out. I have been really surprised at...the high degree of morale that these marines have shown.

...The marines that are here certainly appear to be geared up for whatever the future holds.[19]

Peterson's words paint a compelling image of the determined young men and women fighting in Fallujah, and his admiration of the marines is evident. What is not so evident is the purported reason for the interview: Why was the strength of the insurgency a surprise? What was happening in Fallujah? How many marines had been injured? How many insurgents were there? Who were they? There are dozens of questions that could have been asked.

In a similar exchange on the CBS *The Early Show*, Pitts sounded like a proud father when he recalled a battle scene with tears in his eyes: "To me, one of the great moments was [watching] the captain in charge of Lima company, 31 years old from Harrisburg, Pa., who remained so calm in such a difficult situation. ...People were, marines were on their stomachs. I was laying on my back and this guy sat up, ankles crossed, and very calmly made decisions."[20] His "worst day," Pitts said, was the day Baghdad fell.

> All of a sudden, the gunfire got closer and the cement behind us started to flake and fall to the ground and we realized, "Oh my God, they're shooting at us." So we're running, and there's videotape where you see me running, and at one point, I fell down and this young marine came over and straddled me and he said, "Mr. Pitts, you OK?" And I said, "Yeah, yeah, I'm OK." He says, "You sure?" I said, "Yeah, yeah, I'm fine." He said, "Well, Mr. Pitts, don't worry. You won't die here, and you certainly won't die alone."[21]

It was this type of dependence that led NPR reporter John Burnett to conclude that it was "a flawed experiment that served the purposes of the military more than it served the cause of balanced journalism. During my travels with the marines, I couldn't shake the sense that we were cheerleaders on the team bus. ...The inability of embedded journalists to verify the military's version of the war in Iraq made for one-sided reporting."[22]

Burnett left the safety of the marines and happened upon a small village called Al-Taniya, where he learned that 31 civilians had been killed in their sleep by American bombs that accidentally rained down on them. "A distraught local man named Salem Abda said, 'We ask Bush, why did he bomb us? Are there weapons, tanks, soldiers, fedayeen? No. There is nothing here, not even food.'" A U.S. spokesperson confirmed for Burnett that American forces had dropped 500-pound "precision bombs" that morning "on tanks and tracked vehicles in the area" but said there had been "no mention of missed targets." Burnett said the story illustrated the "disconnect" he experienced between what he saw as an embed and what he saw when he traveled on his own. "For the U.S. military, the accidental bombardment of Al-Taniya village had simply not occurred," he said.[23]

Al-Taniya and stories like it are exactly why some reporters need to remain independent, even if it involves more personal danger, said CBS's Lara Logan, who was embedded in Afghanistan for a short time but chose to remain independent during the war in Iraq. "Undoubtedly, the embeds were a huge success, particularly from the U.S. military point of view," she said.

> When you're embedded with troops, you bond with those soldiers on the ground and gain respect for what they do, [and] that undoubtedly affects the way you report. It's hugely important that there are independent outside witnesses to what happened in a situation so that you don't just have the U.S. military or the Iraqis putting out their own side.[24]

Many embedded journalists vehemently disagree and point out the benefits.

"We had total freedom to cover virtually anything we wanted to cover," said NBC's Reid.

Washington Post editor Phil Bennett agreed. "There was a real interest among people in the field. They wanted the story told the way it was happening. They didn't want reporters to sugarcoat it or cover it up."[25]

Others acknowledge that the exchange was mutually beneficial.

As CBS's John Roberts put it: "Mind you, you've got to remember that this worked brilliantly for the Defense Department. They had their story told in real time, which is exactly what they wanted to have happen. But for us as well, we've crossed the Rubicon into the realm where you took us with you in Iraq. Now if you go anywhere else, you've got to take us with you as well."[26]

REPORTING FROM THE FRONT LINES

Reporting on a war is never easy. It is dangerous. Information is often unavailable or propagandized from all sides. Getting from place to place can be dangerous and exhausting. Reporting on a war while traveling in a forward direction with troops, which is what the embeds did, is next to impossible. One on-air reporter called it a "drive-by war."

George Wilson, who covered the Vietnam war for the *Washington Post* and now writes for the *National Journal,* said: "We would see a shell go downrange, but we had no way to find out what it hit or who was killed. In Vietnam, you could really find out what we'd done and not done. Here, I felt like the second dog in a dogsled. All you saw was the dog in front of you, and if you broke out of the traces, you lost your place."[27]

The public was, as one reporter put it, seeing the war through a soda straw. The picture that emerged depended largely on the journalist holding the straw. In some cases, viewers who monitored international news and U.S. reports were left wondering whether the journalists were covering the same conflict.

BBC's world affairs editor, John Simpson, was with a convoy of U.S. Special Forces and Kurdish fighters when it was hit by a bomb dropped by a U.S. plane. The BBC's camera, splattered with blood at first, recorded what Simpson described as "a scene from hell." It was a remarkable piece of reporting and one of the few instances in which the raw brutality of war was recorded. Simpson, himself injured and bleeding on camera, was visibly shaken as he described the scene: "All the vehicles are on fire. There are bodies burning around me, there are bodies lying around, there are bits of bodies on the ground. This is a really bad own-goal by the Americans. We don't really know how many Americans are dead."

Later, Simpson more calmly described what had happened. An American officer had called in an air strike to take out an Iraqi tank about a mile away. "I saw two F-15 American planes circling quite low overhead....As I was looking at them...I saw the bomb coming out of one of the planes—and I saw it as it came down beside me." He said that at least 10 people were killed, later reporting that 18 were dead.[28]

CNN did not mention the incident until 10 hours later, when it simply noted that a "friendly fire" incident had been reported. Anchor Leon Harris told viewers: "No word yet on U.S. casualties." Certainly, CNN had had time to investigate the report that a friendly fire incident had, in fact, killed more than a dozen Americans. All it had to do was tune in to BBC to see the footage.[29]

Interestingly enough, different studies on stories by embedded reporters reach different conclusions about whether they show bias. The Pentagon and its British counterpart consider the program a success. "We're seeing most importantly how well-equipped, well-trained, and how well-led U.S. forces are; we see how careful they are in carrying out their duty," said Bryan Whitman, a Pentagon public affairs official.[30]

A military analysis comparing print media stories written in the first five days after ground landings in the 1991 Gulf War, the 2002 war in Afghanistan, and the 2003 war in Iraq found "that, as journalists are absorbed into military organizations—by meeting and congregating with troops, learning about their service culture and establishing similarity—the more positive the reporting will be."[31]

Conversely, a study done for the BBC found that British embeds remained objective. If British journalists could maintain objectivity, there is no reason to assume that U.S. reporters were unable to do the same. The study did find some downsides to the embed reports:

> On certain key issues, broadcasters tended to assume what they had been told by the government was true. Nine out of 10 references to WMDs during the war assumed that Iraq possessed them. While reporters on the ground found a very mixed response, broadcasters were twice as likely to show Iraqis enthusiastic about the invasion than as suspicious or hostile.[32]

According to Tom Rosenstiel, director of the Project for Excellence in Journalism, the big problem with television coverage of the war was the fact that it did not "take all of the soda straws together and give some sort of perspective, particularly on morning news and cable news. You would get one person's embedded report, and what you didn't see was someone taking the elements of three reports and putting together a nuanced and multitiered look at the day's events." [33]

Without this step back being taken, the American public was not getting a very comprehensive picture. Access is an important element to reporting, but access alone does not produce the whole story. With only one side available in a fast-paced environment, mistakes are inevitable.

Editor & Publisher noted that during the first week of the war 15 stories were widely misreported by journalists in Iraq. They included rumors that Hussein may have been killed in the first night's surprise attack, that Iraqi soldiers were surrendering by the hundreds, that Americans were being greeted as liberators, and that an entire division of 8,000 Iraqi soldiers had surrendered. [34] The information obviously came from U.S. military officials.

The television embeds also spent a lot of time declaring that they were presenting "historic war coverage," and focusing on the fact that they were right beside U.S. troops. While it was true that viewers were getting real-time images from Iraq, not much of the reportage could be considered "historic."

CNN's Walter Rodgers excitedly told viewers:

> The pictures you're seeing are absolutely phenomenal. These are live pictures of the Seventh Cavalry racing across the deserts in southern Iraq....If you ride inside that tank, it is like riding in the bowels of a dragon. They roar. They screech. You can see them slowing now. We've got to be careful not to get in front of them. But what you're watching here...is truly historic television and journalism. [35]

It may have been historic television, but historic journalism it definitely was not.

The Project for Excellence in Journalism found that 80 percent of the television stories by embeds featured the reporters alone, not interviewing anyone. Journalists became a large part of the story and chronicled some of their own difficulties—from breaking a division's coffee pot to running from gunfire. Television embeds also began slipping "we" and "us" into their reports, blurring the line between their subjects and themselves.

CBS News's Axelrod reported that he had just come from a military intelligence briefing, where "we've been given orders." He quickly corrected himself and said "soldiers have been given orders," but his slip demonstrated the change in reporters' attitudes. [36]

Embedded reporters were never "off duty," which created a strange work environment that further blurred the lines between the soldiers and the journalists. NBC's Bloom, for example, did 13 live reports in a 19-hour period. As combat raged around them, journalists increasingly became engaged in the action. A *Boston Herald* reporter pointed out snipers that soldiers in his unit killed. An *Atlanta Journal-Constitution* photographer held an intravenous drip over an injured Iraqi. An armed bodyguard with CNN's Brent Sandler returned Iraqi fire near Tikrit. Most dramatically, CNN correspondent and doctor Sanjay Gupta operated on a 2-year-old Iraqi boy.[37] "It was a heroic attempt to try to save the child's life," he declared after the boy died of the injuries he suffered when a taxi he was riding in was riddled with bullets by allied forces.[38]

Some anchors romanticized the war with long-winded monologues.

Koppel dramatically concluded a March 23, 2003, *Nightline* program by saying:

> Forget the easy victories of the last twenty years; this war is more like the ones we knew before. The president has determined that U.S. security and national interests are at stake. Such determinations always carry with them a high cost in blood and treasure. Watching that unfold on your television screens, sometimes watching it live, as it's happening, will not be easy for you. Telling you if and when things are going badly for U.S. troops, enabling you to bear witness to the high cost of war, is the hard part of our job. In a famous couple of lines from the movie "A Few Good Men," Jack Nicholson, playing a marine colonel, snarls: "You want the truth? You can't handle the truth." Well, this is no movie. We'll do our very best to give you the truth in the hope and the belief that you can handle it.

Some of the ugly truths about the war were reported by embedded journalists who contradicted Pentagon statements, and some showed the less-than-rosy image of frightened soldiers making horrifying mistakes.

On March 31, 2003, 10 members of a family were killed by American troops at a checkpoint outside the town of Naja. MSNBC's Carl Rochelle reported the event as the Pentagon explained it: "What happened there, the van with a number of individuals in it...approached the checkpoint. They were told to stop by the members of the 3rd Infantry Division. They did not stop. Warning shots were fired. Still, they came on. They fired into the engine of the van. Still it came on, so they began opening fire on the van itself."[39]

However, William Branigin, who was traveling with the infantry, witnessed the event and reported it differently. His *Washington Post* article said that U.S. Army Captain Ronny Johnson ordered soldiers at the checkpoint to "fire a warning shot" at the approaching vehicle.

> Then, with increasing urgency, he told the platoon to shoot a 7.62-mm machine gun round into its radiator. "Stop [expletive] around!" Johnson yelled into the company radio network when he still saw no action being taken. Finally, he shouted at the top of his voice, "Stop him, Red 1, stop him!" That order was immediately followed by the loud reports of 25-mm cannon fire from one or more of the platoon's Bradleys. About half a dozen shots were heard in all.

Johnson ordered a cease fire and, as he "peered into his binoculars from the intersection on Highway 9, he roared at the platoon leader, 'You just [expletive] killed a family because you didn't fire a warning shot soon enough!'" Of the 15 Iraqi civilians in the car, 10 died instantly; five of them were under the age of five.[40]

Many papers, including the *New York Daily News*, *Boston Globe*, *Chicago Tribune* and *San Francisco Chronicle*, incorporated Branigin's information into the stories they ran, giving readers both the official account and the embed's eyewitness account. Others, including the *New York Times*, ran the official account without Branigin's information.[41]

Less dramatically, NPR's Burnett also managed to bring some balance to one-sided Pentagon reports. He told viewers that the battalion he was riding with was down to one meal a day because supply trucks had been unable to reach them for days, contradicting official reports that there were no delays. The two examples illustrate the value of having reporters in the field with troops.[42]

For the most part, those covering the front lines did not send back pictures of the horrors of war. Even the obvious reality of war—that innocent civilians die —was often cushioned for Americans by the media.

NBC's Jim Miklaszewski explained the U.S. "shock-and-awe" campaign in Baghdad this way (emphasis added):

> 500 to 600 cruise missiles from U.S. warships and Air Force B-52s, followed by waves of B-2 stealth bombers and stealth fighters dropping 2,000-pound bunker buster bombs. More than 1,000 weapons pounded Baghdad today, three times the total number during the entire Gulf War. *And every weapon is precision guided, deadly accuracy designed to kill only the targets, not innocent civilians.*[43]

Very reassuring indeed, but shouldn't there have been some skepticism on the part of the journalist?

Most studies show that the war was sanitized for public consumption. A study by the Project for Excellence in Journalism found that in the first three to six days of the war, not a single television story showed people being hit by a weapon.[44]

War photographer Peter Howe said the media projected

> an extremely sanitized version of the war. There are very few images of Iraq casualties, let alone American casualties, and it's a real problem because as a nation, we are consistently unprepared for the reality of war. Unless we understand the full implication of our actions, as a democracy, we can't make a reasonable assessment of when it's the right time to go to war. If war is divorced from daily life, as a video game [is], we can't make judgments, and we find ourselves mired in something we did not expect.[45]

Even as their reporters experienced the horrors of war, news organizations made conscious decisions to spare American viewers the images of war.

CBS News correspondent Pitts said:

> I quickly discovered that war is not simple; it is not clean. I remember hearing a young Iraqi girl. Her legs had been blown off, and these marines were trying to save her life. And you could hear her cry. I worry that we still failed to get across to the

American people just how awful and how violent war can be...I never thought I did
a story that portrayed fully what I saw or what I felt.[46]

The words echo those of journalists in nearly every war that has occurred. It is
difficult to capture the brutal savagery of limbs being snapped like twigs, bombs
tearing bodies to pieces, or soldiers desperately trying to convince their dying
friends that everything will be fine. But unlike the situation in past conflicts,
there were plenty of cameras in Iraq.

The images that would have provided a better understanding of both the dangers of the conflict and the terror experienced by U.S. troops and Iraqi civilians
were available. There were also plenty of images that shed light on the growing
disillusionment of Iraqis and the consequential growing danger for U.S. troops.
They are now popping up in documentaries about the war.

An example of the difference between what was portrayed by embeds and
what was happening in Iraq is the arrest of Iraqi General Taha Hassan Abbas
on November 17, 2003. In a larger story about U.S. troops working in Baghdad,
the AP included a few paragraphs noting that Abbas had been arrested "for
alleged involvement in mortar attacks on police stations" in Baquoba. A day
later, AFP (Agence France-Presse) reported that a U.S. spokesman said Abbas
had "resisted when an assault force approached his house," and "engaged [in]
fire," which was returned by U.S. troops who then captured Abbas and two
others and took them to Abu Ghraib prison.[47]

No U.S. papers picked up the story, probably because it was one of dozens of
similar accounts of "uncomplicated" arrests. But Abbas's arrest was far from
uncomplicated, as footage shot by the Associated Press Television News reveals.
The vivid images did not make it into any news program but were included in a
documentary called "Iraq—On the Brink," by Ross Coulthart. The footage
shows U.S. soldiers approaching Abbas's house at night. They kick open a garden
gate and chaos ensues. Abbas's son goes to the roof of the house with a gun.
Coulthart explains: "The officer's son—thinking the soldiers are thieves—goes
to the roof of the house and fires into the air to scare them away." The film shows
U.S. soldiers responding: "We've got a shooter on the roof!" and firing round
after round of bullets at the house. The camera follows the soldiers inside and
shows Abbas, a middle-aged man in pajamas, holding his hands above his head,
as six or seven U.S. soldiers point guns at him. Abbas repeats the only English
he appears to know: "Welcome! Welcome!" One soldier yells: "Want me to
shoot him in the leg? I might shoot you!"

Coulthart tells filmgoers: "The Iraqi officer, thinking he's about to die can now
be heard praying." The American soldiers do not understand what he is saying
and have no translator with them. "Who the fuck are you talking to? Who the
fuck are you talking to? Shut the fuck up! Shut the fuck up!" One of the soldiers
hurls Abbas across the room and onto the floor. A soldier kicks him. He can be
seen on his back, hands in the air. "Welcome! Welcome!" he tells the soldiers.

Three soldiers put their guns to his face one can be heard saying repeatedly, "Shoot him!"

The last shot is of Abbas leaving his house under arrest. His arms are restrained behind his back, his face is battered and bruised, his shirt is stained with blood.

Coulthart summarized the scene: "No one here was killed. But it's raids like this that can only fuel the resentment against coalition forces."[48]

In another documentary, "Feels Like War," raw footage of U.S. troops being bombarded by bullets and mortars in Baghdad is striking because it is not something that was shown on U.S. news programs. A Polish reporter who was not embedded with the troops says "it doesn't look good," and adds that a marine had told him "too many people still have weapons."

Much of this may be deemed too graphic for prime time television news. But there are alternative news programs, such as 60 Minutes, that could have explored pieces of the footage coming out of Iraq and provided a better understanding of the conflict.

Peter Turnley, who photographed the war for the Denver Post, said there were dozens of images Americans should have seen but were denied. He recalled watching doctors working on a girl in a Baghdad hospital five days after allied troops had liberated the city.

> I saw this beautiful little girl on the bed—yellow socks, white shirt—and I noticed two doctors were doing cardiac massage on her chest, and that I was watching the life of this little girl evaporating. I thought I saw her chest exhale, and I had this leap of joy. I thought she was coming back to life—and one of the doctors had this look of disgust and put a towel over her face and walked out.

The girl died of treatable pneumonia, but rioting crowds prevented her father from getting to the hospital before it was too late. Meaningless death is the reality of war that most Americans never saw, Turnley said.[49]

During a lecture in Kansas, MSNBC reporter Ashleigh Banfield said viewers were not getting the real story from embeds in Iraq.

> There were horrors completely left out of this war. Is this journalism, or is this coverage? I am not so sure that we in America are hesitant to do this again, to fight another war, because it looked like a glorious and courageous, and so successful, terrific endeavor. We got rid of horrible leadership, got rid of a dictator, got rid of a monster, but we didn't hear the civilians' opinions. We didn't see the bodies.[50]

The American public did not see the pain of war on the home front either. The media was banned from soldiers' funerals and was unable to record caskets returning to the United States. No tears for the fallen were shed on camera.

The ban on photos of soldiers' coffins was first implemented by George H. W. Bush in 1991 during the first Gulf War, purportedly to protect the privacy of the victims' families. More than a year after the war in Iraq began, on April 27, 2004, the *Seattle Times* published a picture of flag-draped coffins on a cargo plane in Kuwait. The picture was striking in several ways, including the obvious care and respect the military took to prepare the bodies for the trip back to the United States. The coffins were perfectly aligned, were hugged by American flags that were smooth on the surface, all wrinkles patted down by men and women in uniform who could be seen working in the cargo plane.

The images quickly became among the most controversial of the conflict. The paper ran an article explaining the procedure for sending the dead home, noting that "few such photographs have been published during the conflict in Iraq."[51]

Tom Jarriel, former correspondent for ABC News, said the media should have fought to get more of these types of vivid pictures that illustrate the consequences of war.

This was an effort by the Pentagon to do what they have so often done, which was try to control the media. They try to prevent Americans from seeing the toll that the war is taking in terms of graphic pictures, so that they don't lose public support for the war. I am totally convinced that [censorship] was not for the men who have died and their families. It was entirely to control public opinion from going against the war.[52]

The publication of the pictures brought mixed reviews from family members and the American public. "The image of dead Americans, especially the dead American soldier, is probably the most powerful image of war for Americans," David Perlmutter, a professor at Louisiana State University said. "It's the one that immediately strikes us in the gut, because we hate to see it but we recognize we may need to see it."[53]

The media also minimized the death toll in other ways. For eight months after the war began, newspapers printed the Pentagon-dictated numbers of members of the military killed in combat action, which did not include all of those who died in Iraq and Afghanistan. Members of the military who were killed in traffic accidents, who became chronically ill and died, or who committed suicide were not counted among the dead.[54] Injuries were also downplayed by the press. *San Francisco Chronicle* columnist Harley Sorensen wondered what happened to those thousands of U.S. soldiers after they are transported out of Iraq. "Judging from press reports, none of these wounded ever dies," he said.

Maybe I don't know where to look, but I haven't been able to find one single report of a soldier who died later of his or her injuries....I wonder how many limbs have been blown off or later amputated?... So far, the press has shown an amazing lack of curiosity about the fate of Americans wounded in Iraq. The modern U.S. press seems to have adopted as its mantra: "See no evil, hear no evil, speak no evil."[55]

TARGETING JOURNALISTS

This lack of curiosity extended to the fate of their fellow journalists who were
not embedded with troops. Labeled "unilaterals" by the Pentagon, a phrase
repeated by the press in its stories, these independent reporters had trouble from
the beginning of the war. Where embeds were welcomed by the military, "unilaterals" were seen as a nuisance.

"I was told by a senior officer in the Pentagon that if uplinks—that is the television signals...—were detected by any planes...above Baghdad...they'd be
fired down on. Even if they were journalists," BBC war correspondent Kate Adie
told Irish public radio. When she expressed concern, her source's response was:
"They've been warned."[56]

There were several incidents involving the U.S. military and non-embedded
journalists in Iraq. On April 8, 2003, a U.S. tank outside the Palestine Hotel,
where most of the non-embedded international journalists were staying, fired a
single shot directly into the building. Two journalists were killed and three
others injured. The Pentagon said the tank was responding to shots fired from
inside the hotel, a charge that was denied by the journalists who witnessed the
events. The denials were backed by footage they provided that showed quiet in
the area immediately before the attack.

David Chater of British Sky TV said he was on a balcony of the hotel right
before the attack.

> I never heard a single shot coming from any of the area around here, certainly not
> from the hotel. I noticed one of the tanks had its barrel pointed up at the building.
> We went inside and there was an almighty crash. That tank shell, if it was indeed
> an American tank shell, was aimed directly at this hotel and directly at journalists.
> This wasn't an accident; it seems to be a very accurate shot.[57]

U.S. officials responded

> commanders on the ground reported that coalition forces received significant enemy
> fire from the Palestine Hotel and, consistent with the inherent right of self-defense,
> coalition forces returned fire. Sadly, a Reuters and a Tele 5 (Spain) journalist were
> killed in this exchange. These tragic incidents appear to be the latest example of
> the Iraqi regime's continued strategy of using civilian facilities for regime military
> purposes.[58]

In a letter to Spain's foreign minister, Colin Powell explained: "Our review of
the April 8 incident indicates that the use of force was justified, and the amount
of force was proportionate to the threat against United States forces."[59]

Two other news organizations were hit by U.S. forces that day. Al-Jazeera's
Baghdad office was hit and destroyed by two bombs during a U.S. air raid. One
reporter was killed and another injured. Almost simultaneously, Abu Dhabi
TV, another Arab television station, was hit by small arms fire. Both stations

had given allied forces information about their locations. American forces again said they were returning fire.[60]

The journalist advocacy group Reporters Without Borders said in a statement: "We can only conclude that the U.S. Army deliberately and without warning targeted journalists." The Committee to Protect Journalists said in a letter to Rumsfeld: "We believe these attacks violate the Geneva Conventions." British journalist Robert Fisk said that the attacks on journalists "look very much like murder."[61]

The Pentagon's response was reminiscent of what the BBC's Adie claimed to have heard before the war began. Pentagon spokeswoman Victoria Clarke told the AP, "We've had conversations over the last couple of days [with] news organizations eager to get their people unilaterally into Baghdad. We are saying it is not a safe place; you should not be there."[62] At least one news organization pulled its journalists out of the capital city after the attacks.

Award-winning Reuters cameraman Mazen Dana was killed outside Abu Ghraib prison when a U.S. tank crew shot him. The military said the TV camera on his shoulder looked like a missile launcher. Soundman Nael al-Shyoukhi, who was with Dana, said the U.S. soldiers "saw us and they knew about our identities and our mission," yet they shot anyway.[63] Reuters said distinguishing a television camera from a missile launcher was very easy at the distance at which the tank fired at Dana. Additionally, "it clearly was not 'reasonable' for the U.S. troops as a whole to have allowed the shooter to be unaware of the significant media presence around the prison," the news agency concluded in a report.[64]

Independent journalists also reported that their film was confiscated by U.S. troops and that they were threatened and detained by allied forces.

The animosity from allied forces was not what reporters were expecting. Most news organizations had planned on having half of their news correspondents embedded and the other half reporting independently from inside Iraq and from the million-dollar press center at Central Command headquarters in Doha, Qatar. When the "unilaterals" arrived, however, they were corralled and told that they would be escorted in and out of Iraq.

"Nobody I know is asking for armed protection, simply the right to be able to cross over on a daily basis, make our reports, and then return to Kuwait before nightfall. Even that's been denied," complained Canadian journalist Paul Workman. "I didn't expect...that embedded journalists would be given exclusive access to the war, leaving the rest of us shut out of the battlefield, or even the near-battlefield....We were allowed to cover the war from the sanctuary of our hotel rooms and little more." In one supervised day trip, he said, British escorts took him to the port of Umm Qasr and displayed an electric generator that the Royal Engineers had repaired. "We heard how grateful the people of the town were to have power, how safe the streets had become since the invasion, how well the British were doing at winning the hearts and minds of ordinary Iraqis, but when we asked to actually see an Iraqi turning on his lights or his television, we were told that was impossible."[65]

When Workman's producer complained, a U.S. spokesperson replied: "I don't give a damn about the unilateral journalists. We've fulfilled our obligation to the media, and if you don't like it, you can go home."[66]

Turnley, the *Denver Post* photographer, said he watched reporters race into towns, escorted by military officials, spend a few minutes looking around, and race out again.

> It took me literally five seconds of entering into Iraq and looking into the eyes of people whose eyes showed mistrust, open hostility at the worst. There were towns that troops had just flown through, not staying to create any law and order. People showed me leaflets the Americans had dropped from the sky saying they should be embraced with joy and welcomed because we were bringing liberation and food and water and power, and they'd scream at me, "Where's the water? Where are the medical supplies? In the hospital we have nothing."[67]

Those who did travel deep into Iraq encountered resistance from both sides.

A Portuguese television team made it to the city of Najaf, where, they say, members of the U.S. military police seized their vehicle, used the crews' satellite phones to call family members back in the United States, and then handcuffed them and brought them back to Kuwait City. "I believe the reason we were detained is because we are not embedded," one of the journalists was quoted as saying. "Embedded journalists are escorted by military minders, and what they write is controlled, and through them, the military feeds its own version of the facts to the world."

Rather than fight for a more balanced perspective through the use of independents, other members of the media ignored them. As CNN chief news executive Easton Jordon put it simply, some independent journalists "obviously had a bad war."

EMBEDS ARE HERE TO STAY

For better or for worse, the embedded experiment has been labeled a success by the Department of Defense and is likely to remain in place during the next conflict. Members of the media, while acknowledging the drawbacks to the embedding system, say it is far better to be embedded with the troops than to be banned from the battlefields, which occurred in past conflicts. But if embedding is here to stay, journalists must learn to work the system better to provide a more comprehensive view of a conflict. Lessons learned from Iraq should be applied to the next conflict.

Media outlets should fight for more non-embedded journalists to be allowed into the conflict zone unhindered by the U.S. military. The Pentagon has acknowledged that embedded journalists enabled them to get their message out. Media managers should fight for the same right. Embedded and non-embedded journalists should work in tandem, remaining in contact as the war progresses. By working together, the embeds and the "unilaterals" can provide an accurate picture of a war's ups and downs.

Additionally, facts that cannot be verified by those in a war zone should be pursued by journalists on the home front. Historically, many stories about U.S. actions during wars were broken by journalists covering the Pentagon. Some of the biggest war stories in history—including the secret bombing of Cambodia and the My Lai massacre during the Vietnam war—were uncovered by Washington journalists working their sources.[68]

Finally, journalists who gained a better understanding of how the military operates during their embedding should take that information with them when they return to their regular beats. They should challenge obvious false statements by military officials.

As one major put it: "When these reporters go to a Pentagon press conference and a general stands up and gives them a bullshit answer, maybe now, they'll know to say, 'Hey, wait a minute.'"[69]

CHAPTER 6

An Indifferent Press

Why should we hear about body bags and deaths....It's not relevant. So why should I waste my beautiful mind on something like that?
—Barbara Bush, former first lady, just before the war in Iraq began[1]

On December 1, 2001, a small village near the Tora Bora mountain range on the Afghanistan/Pakistan border was destroyed by bombs dropped by American B-52s searching for bin Laden. Of the 300 people who lived in Kama Ado, as many as 115 were reportedly killed when twenty-five 1,000-pound bombs fell on their homes in four passes by the planes.

When asked about the village bombing, a U.S. Marine Corps spokesman, Major Brad Lowell said: "It just didn't happen." News reports in the American media either labeled the allegations of civilian casualties as suspect or minimized the human toll and emphasized the search for bin Laden. Kama Ado and several other villages that reportedly were bombed were just a few miles from the mountain range, which was carpet-bombed by U.S. planes sent to flush bin Laden from what was believed to be his cave hideout.

The day Kama Ado was hit, CNN's Brent Sandler reported that local security forces said "550 Afghan villagers were killed in [U.S.] bombings [of villages near Tora Bora] within the last 24 hours." Sandler explained:

> The warlords in this area are still sticking by their story that they believe there's a good chance—60, 70, 80 percent chance, they say, that Osama bin Laden himself may well be in this Tora Bora area, where there's a remote mountain complex of caves and tunnels....[Local security officials will] take journalists into that remote area as soon as they can to show us what's been happening in terms of damage to crops, livestock, and property as a result of the military effort from the air to get bin Laden or his associates.[2]

The vastly different versions of the Tora Bora bombings by U.S. and local officials illustrate the difficulty journalists have when reporting in combat zones where it is physically impossible to verify the facts. Ideally, journalists would impartially report what both sides say and explain that they will visit the area as soon as possible to determine what actually happened. In the aftermath of the traumatic 9/11 attacks, American journalists frequently gave the benefit of the doubt to U.S. officials, often ignoring obvious signs that they were being misled.

Fox News' Brit Hume provided a potential explanation about the choices journalists made when he told the *New York Times* in November 2001: "Look, neutrality as a general principle is an appropriate concept for journalists who are covering institutions of some comparable quality. This is a conflict between the United States and murdering barbarians."[3]

Hume's contempt for those he is covering is obvious. Studies about hatred and stereotypes have shown that the use of stereotypes, such as Hume's "murdering barbarians" comment, triggers a reaction in the amygdala, the part of the brain that is associated with anger and fear.[4] As discussed earlier, anger and fear are emotions that cloud judgment and block rational thought.

Psychologist Robert J. Sternberg wrote about the theory of hate, saying,

> individuals explain and interpret their violence toward others as a response to the actions, intentions, or character of their victims. As their aggressive actions continue, they are likely to increasingly devalue their victims. At the extreme, they may engage in a kind of "moral exclusion" whereby the moral standards and values that they believe apply to everyone else are seen as no longer applying in behavior toward their victims....[they are] somehow "other," on the opposite side of a sturdy wall that separates good from bad. Even worse, as people begin to engage in acts based on their hate, they and their society can progress along a continuum of destruction whereby the perpetrators, the institutions to which they belong, and, ultimately, the society as a whole can change in ways that facilitate even more hateful and harmful acts.[5]

Journalists did not perpetrate violent acts. But as Hume's comments demonstrate, some of them did consider those in Afghanistan and Iraq on "the opposite side of a sturdy wall"—they were "murdering barbarians," who deserved whatever retaliation the United States delivered. In the Tora Bora mountain range, the United States used massive firepower in an attempt to find bin Laden. Those who happened to be in the way were not considered newsworthy.

It is difficult to know where to draw the line when it comes to reporting about civilian deaths during wartime. It is impossible for journalists to write about every civilian death. But it is very possible to chronicle patterns of widespread violence against civilians and to question officials about them.

For example, civilians have been shot at checkpoints in Afghanistan and Iraq and continue to lose their lives needlessly. Reporters should ask officials what they are doing to prevent civilian deaths at checkpoints, what the U.S. policy is toward civilians approaching checkpoints, and how civilians are made aware of these policies. Journalists should hold officials accountable for preventable civilian deaths in wartime, as they should hold them accountable for decisions made during times of peace.

Some members of the media have acknowledged that the pressure to remain "patriotic" clouded their news judgment and that they were very aware of how their coverage of the war in Afghanistan would be received back home. Erik Sorenson, president of MSNBC, told the *Times:* "Any misstep and you can get into trouble with these guys and have the Patriotism Police hunt you down. These are hard jobs. Just getting the facts straight is monumentally difficult."[6]

As a result, when journalists were able to travel to places such as Kama Ado, the story they told often depended on whether they were filing for a U.S. or foreign media outlet.

British journalist Richard Lloyd Parry was one of the first to make the trip to the village after the bombing. He wrote:

> The village where nothing happened is reached by a steep climb at the end of a rattling three-hour drive along a stony road. Until nothing happened here, early on the morning of Saturday and again the following day, it was a large village with a small graveyard, but now that has been reversed. The cemetery on the hill contains 40 freshly dug graves, unmarked and identical. And the village of Kama Ado has ceased to exist.

Parry reported that 115 men, women, and children were killed.[7]

American journalists were more cautious in reporting the casualties, even after seeing the damage.

"Here We Come, Osama!—Battle at His Cave Fortress Has Begun," was the headline of a *New York Post* story that said: "Local officials took American journalists to the village of Kama Ado, which was flattened, apparently by errant U. S. bombs. Villagers said dozens of people were killed, and reporters saw nine craters and as many as 15 destroyed homes. Secretary of Defense Donald Rumsfeld said the United States cannot verify the claims of new civilian casualties."[8]

A day later, a CNN anchor began a news report by saying, "Three American soldiers and five allied soldiers killed when a B-52 bomber misses its target." Sandler stood in a decimated Afghan village in the Tora Bora region that was hit by

B-52 bombers that also missed their targets and reported: "If the assault achieves its objective, al-Qaeda might have nowhere to run. Confident-looking truck-loads of reinforcements are sent to join the fight. Drawn-out combat is likely on the way." He did not mention the devastation around him or the reports of civilian casualties. The program did, however, go on to show Marines in the des-ert discussing whether or not they had seen a puma; humanitarian efforts by the United States; and a segment that said, "some hope was returning for girls" who were able to attend school because of the U.S. presence.[9]

CNN missed an opportunity to explore how the U.S. military could deny civilian casualties despite its careful aim when it managed to accidentally drop bombs on its own men and women. With the barrage of bombs hitting the Tora Bora area, some were bound to miss their targets, and the consequence would be the death of innocent people.

Similarly, when 107 people were killed by bombs that hit the Afghan village of Qalaye Niazi, reportedly after a wedding celebration on December 29, 2001, the international media heavily reported the incident while the U.S. media played it down.

The British papers the *Guardian* and the *Independent* ran front-page stories the day after the bombing with the headlines, "U.S. Accused of Killing Over 100 Villagers in Airstrike" and "U.S. Accused of Killing 100 Civilians in Afghan Bombing Raid." The *New York Times* waited another day before writing a story that ran on page A1 with the headline: "Afghan Leader Warily Backs U.S. Bombing."

Journalists were told by a spokesman for U.S. Central Command, Commander Matthew Klee, that "follow-on reporting indicates that there was no collateral damage." The target was considered legitimate because the planes had hit a stockpile of weapons.

International journalists were incredulous and wrote scathing stories doubting the veracity of Klee's statement. Rory Carroll of the *Guardian* wrote,

> some of the things his reporters missed: bloodied children's shoes and skirts, bloodied schoolbooks, the scalp of a woman with braided grey hair. The charred meat sticking to rubble in black lumps could have been Osama bin Laden's henchmen, but survi-vors said it was the remains of farmers, their wives and children, and wedding guests.

Discussing the ammunition that was hit, "survivors say they stored the ammu-nition six weeks ago on the orders of retreating Taliban troops. When the regime fell, they notified authorities, but no one came to collect the ammunition. 'We left it. What else were we supposed to do with it?'"[10]

While it is difficult to know if the villagers were telling the truth about the ammunition, American journalists did not question the official assessment or wonder why civilians caught in a war zone are considered justifiable targets. The *New York Times* did mention Qalaye Niazi in a larger story that ran in Feb-ruary 2002 about civilian casualties and the difficulty of relying on potentially faulty intelligence. For the most part, however, these stories went unreported in the United States, far more so than in the international community. This is a problem for a variety of reasons, not the least of which is that it shields Americans from the consequences of war and makes it difficult to answer the question, "why do they hate us?"

Communication theorists have studied the dynamics of manipulation and the power of public opinion in politics for decades. Philosopher Jean-Jacques Rousseau believed that public opinion is "a compromise between social consensus and individual convictions."[11] Researcher Elisabeth Noelle-Neumann called the pressure people feel to suppress their views when they believe they are in the minority "the spiral of silence." She found that "individuals' opinions are more or less constant, but their willingness to express opinion changes depending on others' judgment."[12] The closer a person's opinion is to what he or she believes is the popular opinion, the more open that person is to discussing the viewpoint. The media obviously believed that popular opinion was opposed to discussing civilian casualties and avoided reports about it.

As journalists rode through Iraq with their embedded partners in the military, this belief grew. Very little attention was given to civilian casualties in Iraq—far less even than in Afghanistan.

This was very obvious in stories from Iraq. Consider media coverage of a roadside bomb that hit a U.S. military trailer as it traveled through Fallujah. Soldiers fled as a hostile Iraqi crowd set it ablaze and celebrated the successful hit against the United States. A *New York Times* reporter who was at the scene said in the second paragraph of a story: "It seemed a small miracle that no one was killed or even wounded here."[13]

Fifteen paragraphs later, the story said: "There were reports, unconfirmed, that at least one Iraqi had been killed in the exchange of fire that erupted after American soldiers returned several hours later." A British daily paper, the *Independent*, reported that at least one Iraqi did die and six were wounded at the scene, possibly from the spray of gunfire by troops as they fled the scene.[14]

The moral exclusion that Sternberg describes earlier seems to have taken hold: Only American deaths or injuries are considered relevant in the *Times* account; Iraqis were not counted among the humans on the scene that day. By beginning the article by hailing the "small miracle" that nobody was killed or injured, then casually mentioning late in the story that an Iraqi may have been killed, the paper effectively dehumanized the people who lived there.

"SHOCK-AND-AWE"

The conflict in Iraq began with the massive "shock-and-awe" campaign in which 3,000 "precision-guided bombs" were to fall on Baghdad in 48 hours. The international community reported that thousands of civilians would likely be killed in the attack.

Former British cabinet minister Robin Cook wrote in the *Guardian:* "None of us can predict the death toll of civilians in the forthcoming bombardment of Iraq. But the U.S. warning of a bombing campaign that will 'shock-and-awe' makes it likely that casualties will be numbered at the very least in the thousands."[15]

Rather than reflect as many international journalists did on the reality of what such brute force could mean to the general population of about 5.6 million people, American journalists seemed excited. U.S. journalists told Americans that few civilian casualties would result from the bombardment because military forces were being careful about their targets.

"Never have so many bombs been dropped so quickly with the aim of sparing so many lives," began a story by Gannett News Service on the day the campaign began. Rumsfeld said in the story's third paragraph: "What is taking place today is as precisely targeted as any campaign in history. Every single target has been analyzed and is being appropriately dealt with. It is an enormously impressive humane effort." Only at the end of the article did the writer mention that "even the world's best precision-guided bombs miss their targets 7 percent to 10 percent of the time." He did not explain how many deaths that might mean.[16]

The *Washington Times* wrote on page A1:

The United States and Britain unleashed a mighty bombardment yesterday on regime targets in Baghdad and other Iraqi cities as "the coalition of the willing" began the ballyhooed "shock-and-awe" phase of a war designed to bring down Saddam Hussein. By all accounts, it was both shocking and awesome. Torrents of satellite-guided bombs and Tomahawk missiles slammed into Saddam's main Baghdad palace and his security headquarters, setting them ablaze, as allied infantrymen formed the outline of a noose moving through the desert toward the city, the greatest prize of the war.[17]

At one point, American journalists became so cavalier about the bombings that Department of Defense spokeswoman Victoria Clarke asked for restraint.

At a press conference the day after "shock-and-awe" a journalist asked: "Are we likely to see another show like last evening?" Clarke interrupted, saying: "You know—let me stop you for a second. I know I am not always as careful with words as I should be. It's not a show; it's not a game. And I just think people should be really, really careful with the words."[18]

As some international journalists reported that there had been heavy civilian casualties in the first few days of bombing in Baghdad, the U.S. media reported that too many targets were being bypassed.

The *Washington Times* ran an A1 article that began, "the U.S.-led air war spared too many targets in Iraq in the war's first days, taking some of the shock out of a campaign billed as 'shock-and-awe,' say military officials and outside analysts."[19]

When a bomb missed its target and hit a crowded Baghdad market, killing at least 50 civilians, military commanders hinted that the destruction had been caused not by U.S. bombs but by Iraqi antiaircraft missiles. The idea played well in the U.S. media. The *New York Times* reported that "it was impossible to determine the cause" of the market bombing, adding that such "incidents threaten to become yet another major problem for the Bush administration."[20]

British journalist Robert Fisk did not agree that it was impossible to determine the cause. He ventured into the carnage and found a missile fragment with a visible identification number, which he reported in the *Independent*. A colleague later identified the missile as having been manufactured in Texas by Raytheon. "The identification of the missile as American is an embarrassing blow to Washington and London as they fight to match their promises of minimal civilian casualties with the reality of precision bombing," said the *Independent* article.

Media outlets in the United States had a different focus: how the military would have to spin the story to avoid the Arab world's anger.

Wolf Blitzer said:

> The pictures that are going to be seen on Al-Jazeera and Al Arabiya and all the Arab satellite channels are going to be further fodder for this anti-American attitude that is clearly escalating as this war continues....[The U.S. will] have an enormous amount of work to do to...point out that if, in fact, it was an errant U.S. bomb or missile, that it would be a mistake. It certainly wouldn't be deliberate.[21]

CBS Evening News anchor Dan Rather noted that "scenes of civilian carnage in Baghdad, however they happened and whoever caused them, today quickly became part of a propaganda war, the very thing U.S. military planners have tried to avoid."[22]

As the American media downplayed the incident, the Department of Defense acknowledged that the broadcast images of civilian deaths had affected its strategy in a humane way—it had become more conscious of how its actions may impact civilians and how this would be perceived by the outside world.

The *Washington Times* reported:

> Attacking U.S. and British troops have decided to bypass cities where there is likely to be heavy resistance rather than risk treating the war's critics to the televised sight of bloodied corpses or charred remains of civilian adults and children. The reason for the military's concern was apparent last night after a series of grisly pictures filled Arabic-language satellite television screens.[23]

The *Times* did not note that avoiding civilian casualties was what the U.S. military had claimed to be doing from the beginning.

In June 2003, the AP reported that it had documented 3,240 civilian deaths from March 20 to April 20 by surveying hospitals and added that the figure was certain to be lower than the reality. According to human rights organizations, including Amnesty International, Human Rights Watch, and the Red Crescent, as many as 10,000 civilians died during the initial U.S. military blitz through the country. It is a figure that would shock many Americans. By late 2004, some independent studies reported that 100,000 Iraqis had been killed in the conflict. The media's decision to ignore the carnage gave the military a lot of leverage with little accountability.[24]

THE HUMAN PRICE OF WAR

The human price of war is always great, but in recent conflicts, the United States has sought to minimize damage to its forces at the expense of those living in the country under attack. Often, that means teaming up with groups that are less than desirable or sacrificing the lives of innocent civilians. The conflict in Afghanistan is a good example of both. The United States sent a small number of ground troops—about 20,000 soldiers—and used massive firepower and new allies, the Northern Alliance, to do the bulk of the work.

Throughout the conflicts in Afghanistan and Iraq, Rumsfeld played down civilian deaths: "There probably has never in the history of the world been a conflict that has been done as carefully, and with such measure, and care, and with such minimal collateral damage to buildings and infrastructure, and with such small numbers of unintended civilian casualties."[25] His statements about the humanity of the U.S. decision to use massive firepower received attention by major networks and newspapers in the United States, with very few rebuttals by opponents of the plan to carpet bomb villages.

Pictures of Kabul were enough to dispel the notion that collateral damage was minimal, but journalists largely chose to ignore the obvious.

U.S. Army Major General Stanley McChrystal, vice director for operations for the Joint Chiefs of Staff, went even further when he told journalists that the United States has achieved "unprecedented precision" that enabled it "in most cases, to hit exactly what we are trying to hit, and scale the munitions appropriately to the task."[26]

Few journalists persistently questioned the validity of this or pointed out that in the first few weeks of the campaign, some U.S. and allied forces had been hit by so-called precision bombs that had missed their intended targets.

More than a year after the United States invaded Iraq, information was released that showed that precision bombs had hit civilian targets and missed the people they were supposed to kill. Marc Garlasco, a U.S. intelligence official during the war, who went to work for Human Rights Watch after he left the intelligence community, told the New York Times that the precision-bombing shock-and-awe campaign was an "abject failure." "We failed to kill the HVTs (high value targets) and instead killed civilians and engendered hatred and discontent in some of the population."[27]

At the time of the bombing campaigns in Afghanistan and Iraq, however, many American journalists agreed with the Pentagon's assessment that the war was going well and that civilian deaths were not newsworthy.

CNN correspondents were told to balance all civilian casualty stories with reminders about the 9/11 attacks. Rick Davis, CNN's head of standards and practices, provided examples for anchors to use in their stories, such as: "We must keep in mind, after seeing reports like this from Taliban-controlled areas, that these U.S. military actions are in response to a terrorist attack that killed close to 5,000 innocent people in the U.S." or "We must keep in mind, after seeing reports like this, that the Taliban regime in Afghanistan continues to harbor terrorists who have praised the September 11 attacks that killed close to 5,000 innocent people in the U.S." or "The Pentagon has repeatedly stressed that it is trying to minimize civilian casualties in Afghanistan, even as the Taliban regime continues to harbor terrorists who are connected to the September 11 attacks that claimed thousands of innocent lives in the U.S." Davis added: "Even though it may start sounding rote, it is important that we make this point each time."[28]

The *New York Times* noted the change in CNN's policy the day after it was revealed. The story began:

> CNN yesterday broadcast the latest images of bombing damage in Kandahar, panning across scenes of rubble and destruction on the streets of the Afghan city. The network then quickly switched to the rubble of the World Trade Center in New York City as the anchor, Bill Hemmer, reminded viewers of the deaths of as many as 5,000 people whose "biggest crime was going to work and getting there on time."[29]

The *Times* did not see a problem with CNN's decision to remind viewers about the 9/11 attacks in its broadcasts in the United States. According to the story, the problem was that the United States, despite its best efforts, including those of CNN, was losing the propaganda war.

The *Times* said:

> bombing victims are fleeting, cushioned between anchors or American officials explaining that such sights are only one side of the story. In the rest of the world, however, images of wounded Afghan children curled in hospital beds or women rocking in despair over a baby's corpse, beamed via satellite by the Qatar-based network, Al Jazeera, or CNN International, are more frequent and lingering.[30]

As civilian casualties in Afghanistan increased, reports began appearing more frequently in American publications, but they were usually minimized or accompanied by strong Pentagon denials or explanations.

After a series of mishaps caused a flutter of images of injured Afghanis in the media, Fox News' Hume asked: "Civilian casualties are historically, by definition, a part of war; really, should they be as big news as they've been?"[31] Air strikes and American soldiers' deaths are also, by definition, part of war. Should they be eliminated from coverage?

Time magazine reviewed an independent study that found that thousands of Afghani civilians had died in the first few weeks of conflict, only to dismiss it because it depended on "world press reports of questionable reliability." The magazine then discussed, as if it were fact, the Pentagon's claim that civilian casualties were the lowest in the history of war, without noting that these claims were unsubstantiated and therefore also had questionable reliability.[32]

Some journalists did attempt to file stories about the chaos in Afghanistan but were successfully restrained by the U.S. military. Once, journalists were held in a warehouse on a U.S. base to prevent them from photographing injured American soldiers and civilians who had been accidentally hit by a B-52 that missed its target. There were also reports of journalists traveling to sites within Afghanistan only to be turned back at gunpoint.

According to the Committee to Protect Journalists, *Washington Post* reporter Doug Struck was threatened by American soldiers and was not allowed near the site of a U.S. strike in Afghanistan that he suspected had killed civilians. U.S. soldiers held an M-16 rifle on him for about 15–20 minutes before refusing him access to a nearby village. "When Struck asked what would happen if he continued toward the village, according to the reporter, the soldier's commander said, 'You would be shot.' The commander refused to identify himself."[33]

There were some good examples of American journalists reporting military mistakes that led to civilian casualties. Shortly after U.S. troops arrived in Afghanistan, the *New York Times* reported, "American forces have mistakenly hit a residential area in Kabul." The paper also wrote that the Pentagon had admitted hitting a center for the elderly and another residential neighborhood northwest of Kabul. After U.N. officials told a reporter of more civilian deaths, the paper noted that it "was the latest of a growing number of accounts of American bombs going astray and causing civilian casualties."[34]

Still, most news organizations focused on ensuring that Americans did not forget why the United States was in Afghanistan. As they did, they missed a lot of important developments that could have helped forecast a growing animosity toward the military and the reasons why.

WE WILL TAKE NO PRISONERS

A few months after the U.S. campaign in Afghanistan began, Taliban leaders approached United Nations officials and, according to a *London Times* account, asked for them to arrange an unconditional surrender of as many as 30,000 Taliban troops, including 10,000 foreign fighters in Kunduz, a city with a general population of about 200,000. Kunduz was the last holdout of Taliban forces and signaled the end of the oppressive regime.

The paper wrote in a top-of-page A1 article: "The deal is being discussed to avoid massive bloodshed during any attempt to take the city by force.... [the commander of the Northern Alliance forces said]: 'If a country accepted them as refugees, we would have no problem; they can go free. We have been in contact with the U.N. over this.'"[35]

Rumsfeld was not pleased that potential al Qaeda members would be released, and told reporters: "The United States is not inclined to negotiate surrenders, nor are we in a position, with relatively small numbers of forces on the ground, to accept prisoners.... So my hope is that they will either be killed or taken prisoner [by the Northern Alliance]."[36]

The *Economist* said Rumsfeld "came horribly close to an invitation to kill even surrendering combatants, a practice long forbidden by the rules of war."[37]

In the United States, Rumsfeld's comment was barely reported or analyzed by members of the media. None of the major networks or newspapers appear to have mentioned it. The *Washington Times* was one of the few papers that noted Rumsfeld's policy announcement. On November 20, 2001, it ran a story on page A1 with the headline: "Rumsfeld Won't Deal on Taliban Surrender; Wants Terror Forces 'Killed or Taken Prisoner.'" Theodore Roosevelt once said, "no man is justified in doing evil on the grounds of expediency."

Had journalists paid closer attention, they could have anticipated potential catastrophic problems with the decision to allow Northern Alliance warlords to take prisoners. In late October, the *Chicago Sun-Times* ran a story on page 19 noting that the United States was befriending brutal murderers in Afghanistan. The article was headlined, "Uncle Sam's Shifty New Ally," and began:

> The United States has had to make some unsavory friends in its battle against Osama bin Laden's terrorist legions, but none more so than General Abdul Rashid Dostum, a cruel and cunning warlord who is fighting for control of the Afghanistan city of Mazar-e-Sharif. Even by the hardened standards of Afghanistan [he] stands out as by far the ablest practitioner of the double-cross.... Dostum reigned for years from Mazar, where he and his 50,000 ethnic Uzbek troops created a state within a state, surviving on smuggling, drug exports, and war before the Taliban ousted him. When [a] reporter...visited Dostum's medieval fortress...he found pools of blood and flesh in the dusty courtyard...the general had just finished punishing a soldier accused of theft. The man had been tied to a tank and crushed to a pulp under its steel treads. Another favorite punishment was ripping a victim in two by strapping him to tanks headed in opposite directions.[38]

The United Kingdom's *News Telegraph* said in a story about Dostum headlined "General's Name is Byword for Brutality": "His men, mainly Uzbeks from the area around Mazar, have a reputation for ferocity in battle and mercilessness if they carry the day."[39]

Sidney Jones, executive director of Human Rights Watch's Asia division, warned that Northern Alliance leaders were illegitimate warlords who could not be trusted and should not receive military assistance. She said: "The U.S. and its allies should not cooperate with commanders whose record of brutality raises questions about their legitimacy inside Afghanistan. Any country that gives assistance to the Afghan opposition must take responsibility for how this assistance is used." Jones noted that, "General Dostum has a particularly wretched record across the board."[40]

In 1997, when Dostum was driven out of Kabul by the Taliban, his troops are believed to have killed 50,000 people, raped any young female they found, and mutilated her breasts.[41]

After the U.N. declined to assist with the Taliban in Kunduz, Dostum, whose troops were part of the Northern Alliance forces surrounding the city, accepted the surrender of about 8,000 Taliban, including suspected members of al Qaeda, Chechens, Uzbeks, and Pakistanis. According to news reports, 400–500 suspected al Qaeda members were taken to Quila-e-Jhangi prison in Mazar-I-Sharif. Included in the group was American John Walker Lindh.

The remaining 7,500 were loaded into containers and transported by truck to the Qala-I-Zeini fortress almost halfway between Mazar-I-Sharif and Shebarghan prison. Human rights advocates say that as many as 5,000 of the original 8,000 taken by Dostum that day are missing.

Carlotta Gall of the *New York Times* did an excellent reporting job and was one of the few to hint at the brutal death of the Kunduz prisoners shortly after their surrender. In December 2001, she wrote:

> Dozens of Taliban prisoners died after surrendering to Northern Alliance forces, asphyxiated in the shipping containers used to transport them to prison, witnesses say. The deaths occurred as the prisoners, many of them foreign fighters for the Taliban, were brought from the town of Kunduz to the prison here, a journey that took two or three days for some.[42]

Dostum denied the charges. While the story was well done, discussed the brutal history of Afghanistan, and noted the fact that the atrocities were done by U. S. allies, it did not mention Dostum's record of abuse.

Physicians for Human Rights investigated the claims and concluded, "there is evidence of recent disposal of human remains at two mass grave sites near Mazar-I-Sharif.... This [is] of great concern as there still remains no reliable accounting for the numbers of prisoners who were captured in the fall of Kunduz and Mazar-I-Sharif in late 2001."[43]

The documentary "Afghan Massacre, Convoy of Death," by Irish filmmaker Jamie Doran, claims that U.S. troops were complicit in the mass murder of the prisoners. Afghanis appearing in the film made compelling statements about the death of the Taliban prisoners. One truck driver said he shot holes in a container that held 200–300 people. His shots killed some, and about half of his passengers died en route, he said. A truck driver said he drove into the desert with a container filled with about 300 men. He said those who had not suffocated during transport were shot as 30–40 U.S. soldiers watched. He saw 25 full containers in the desert. Other witnesses said that 150–200 American and British soldiers were at the Qala-I-Zeini prison when the containers arrived.

The film claims that U.S. forces were aware of the situation and participated in the torture and killing of prisoners. All of the witnesses said they would testify to an international court. Najibullah Quraishi, an Afghan journalist who worked with Doran, saw a video of American Special Forces troops beside the containers full of dead bodies being dumped into the desert graves. In the film he said he was copying the tape when he was brutally beaten and nearly killed.

In June 2002, Doran learned that the grave was being disturbed and evidence of the mass murder was being destroyed. He showed a 20-minute version of the film to the European Parliament and members of the media. The response was outrage and an immediate call for an investigation. The *Guardian*, *Le Monde*, *Suddeutsche Zeitung*, *Die Welt*, and other European publications all ran articles about the film. The *Scotsman* ran a story on June 14, 2002, with the headline: "U.S. Had Role in Taliban Prisoner Deaths."

No major U.S. paper or network mentioned the film or its allegations. In fact, an extensive Lexis/Nexus search found no mention of it anywhere in the U.S. media.

International outrage, combined with the stories in the foreign media claiming that U.S. troops may have engaged in torture, led to a Pentagon statement dismissing the allegations. "Our service members don't participate in torture of any type," Marine Lieutenant Colonel Dave Lapan told reporters.[44]

Two days after the film aired in Europe and media stories there focused on potential U.S. crimes in Afghanistan, the *New York Times* ran an article highlighting how military officials had coerced information from prisoners without resorting to torture.

> Military officials say torture is not an option. But, they said, under the Geneva Conventions, anything short of torture is permissible to get a hardened Qaeda operative to spill a few scraps of information that could prevent terrorist attacks. Interrogators acknowledge that they push psychological gamesmanship to the limits to prey on a prisoner's fears and desires, sexual stereotypes, and cultural sensitivities.[45]

The *Times* article did not mention the accusations made in "Afghan Massacre," nor did it note that according to Article 17 of the Geneva Conventions, the United States was engaging in unacceptable behavior. Article 17 states: "No physical or mental torture, nor any other form of coercion, may be inflicted on prisoners of war to secure from them information of any kind whatever. Prisoners of war who refuse to answer may not be threatened, insulted, or exposed to any unpleasant or disadvantageous treatment of any kind." The *Times* also neglected to note that the United States had admitted sending prisoners to Egypt

and Jordon where interrogation practices included torture and threats to prisoners' family members.[46]

The U.N. investigated the claims of Doran's film and released a report stating
that a forensic team had found a mass grave and that tests had revealed "the
cause of death was consistent with death due to suffocation."[47] A second grave
containing as many as 2,000 bodies was also found. Spent bullet shells littered
the site.

In August 2002, Newsweek reported that at least 1,000 bodies could be buried
in the Dasht-e Leili desert. The article said:

> The dead of Dasht-e Leili—and the horrific manner of their killing—are one of the
> dirty little secrets of the Afghan war.... The killings illustrate the problems America
> will face if it opts to fight wars by proxy, as the United States did in Afghanistan,
> using small numbers of U.S. Special Forces calling in air power to support local fight-
> ers on the ground. It also raises questions about the responsibility Americans have
> for the conduct of allies who may have no interest in applying protections of the
> Geneva Conventions. The benefit in fighting a proxy-style war in Afghanistan was
> victory on the cheap—cheap, at any rate, in American blood. The cost, Newsweek's
> investigation has established, is that American forces were working intimately with
> "allies" who committed what could well qualify as war crimes.

The Pentagon denied any knowledge of the atrocities, despite the presence of
U.S. forces in the area.[48]

State Department spokesman Philip Reeker skirted the issue when asked
about the mass graves: "I think it's very important that everyone within the
Afghan transitional administration remain united in their efforts to build a uni-
fied Afghanistan that rejoins the community of nations and can offer hope of
economic reconstruction and prosperity for all Afghans."[49] American journalists
did not press for an answer.

After Doran's film was broadcast on national television stations in Germany,
Great Britain, Italy, and Australia, the left-leaning radio program Democracy
Now! broadcast the audio portion of the film in the United States on May 26,
2003. No television station in the United States showed the film.

AMERICAN TALIBAN JOHN WALKER LINDH

The suspected al Qaeda members who were taken by Dostum from Kunduz to
Quila-e-Jhangi did not fare much better than those who died en route to Qala-
I-Zeini. As many as 450 were killed in a prison rebellion less than a week after
they arrived at Dostum's fortress. A CIA operative there to interrogate the prisoners was also killed. After a brief investigation of the incident, Mary Robinson,
then the U.N. high commissioner for human rights, called for a full inquiry. Her
spokesman explained: "There are a lot of unanswered questions," including

reports that some prisoners had their hands tied behind their backs when they were killed.

Afghan journalist Quraishi was in the prison when the riot erupted and got amazing footage, including American John Walker Lindh being questioned in the courtyard by CIA special agents. After the fighting had stopped, he filmed bodies littered throughout the compound, many face down with their hands securely tied behind their backs.

The British paper the *Independent* wrote that after the fighting was over, "General Dostum's political adviser, Ali Razim, said with simple satisfaction: 'The situation is completely under control. All of them have been killed.'"[50]

About 80 people survived the prison riot; among them was Lindh, the American who was later sentenced to 20 years in prison.

According to papers filed by his attorney, he had a bullet in his leg when he was taken into U.S. custody, but it went untreated for three weeks while he was in the care of U.S. Special Forces. His attorney described the conditions of his detention in U.S. custody:

> Completely naked, wearing nothing but his blindfold and shaking violently from the cold nighttime air, Mr. Lindh was then bound to the stretcher with heavy tape that was tightly wound around his chest, upper arms, shoulders, ankles and the stretcher itself...Next he was placed inside a rectangular, windowless metal shipping container...there was no light, heat source, or insulation inside the container...Mr. Lindh's hands and feet remained restrained such that his forearms were forced together and fully extended, pointing straight down toward his feet. Mr. Lindh remained fully exposed within the metal container until, after some time had passed, a single, thin blanket was placed over him and one beneath him.[51]

When interrogated by Special Forces, he was always blindfolded, sometimes hooded, and always restrained. "On December 7, 2001, heavily armed U.S. soldiers came into Mr. Lindh's room....The soldiers blindfolded Mr. Lindh and took several pictures of Mr. Lindh and themselves and Mr. Lindh. In one, soldiers scrawled 'shithead' across Mr. Lindh's blindfold and posed with him."[52]

The allegations of abuse were dismissed by the American media, which focused on the more exciting story of a citizen gone awry. The articles that did note his claims of abuse included vehement denials from Rumsfeld, who said they were "ridiculous."

Later it was revealed that Rumsfeld had told interrogators to "take the gloves off" when dealing with Lindh. Coffer Black, who was once the director of the CIA's counterterrorist unit, told Congress in early 2002 that the policy with regard to prisoners had changed in the aftermath of the 9/11 attacks. He would not go into specifics, saying only, "there was a before-9/11 and an after-9/11. After 9/11, the gloves came off." What he meant by "the gloves came off" was not explained and members of Congress did not ask. Lindh initially pleaded not guilty but later agreed to a plea bargain in which he dropped the torture claims.

A *Washington Post* article on December 26, 2002, provided clues as to what the new "gloves off" policy meant:

> Those who refuse to cooperate inside this secret CIA interrogation center, [at the Bagram air force base in Afghanistan] are sometimes kept standing or kneeling for hours, in black hoods or spray-painted goggles....At times, they are held in awkward, painful positions and deprived of sleep with a 24-hour bombardment of lights. ...The picture that emerges is of a brass-knuckled quest for information, often in concert with allies of dubious human rights reputation, in which the traditional lines between right and wrong, legal and inhumane, are evolving and blurred....While the U.S. government publicly denounces the use of torture, each of the current national security officials interviewed for this article defended the use of violence against captives as just and necessary...."If you don't violate someone's human rights some of the time, you probably aren't doing your job," said one official who has supervised the capture and transfer of accused terrorists.[53]

The military intelligence unit that oversaw interrogations at the Afghanistan base was later sent to Iraq where it controlled the Abu Ghraib prison. It was later discovered that prisoners were killed at three U.S. military bases in Afghanistan. Additionally, detainees at many of the Afghanistan camps complained about sexual abuse by U.S. forces.[54] At least 25 people reportedly died while in U.S. custody at prison camps in Iraq and Afghanistan.[55]

The *Washington Post* story about "stress and duress" at the detention camps was mentioned in the *Economist* and the *New Yorker* but was largely ignored by mainstream news organizations in the United States. The media trend to overlook key evidence of questionable practices by the U.S. military continued when the conflict spread to Iraq.

CONFUSION AND CHAOS

A year before pictures of torture and sexual abuse at Abu Ghraib prison were released, a Norwegian newspaper, *Dagbladet,* published an article that included pictures of Iraqis being marched, at gunpoint, naked through a public park outside Baghdad. Written in black marker across their chests were the Arabic words "ali-baba haram," roughly translated as *sinful thief.*

First Lieutenant Eric Canaday confirmed that his men had stripped the Iraqis. "We took their clothes and burned them, and then we pushed them out with thief written on them. It has actually been pretty successful. It's not as bad as it seems," a laughing Canaday was quoted as saying. "A little public shaming, no physical damage, and everything will be fine tomorrow. Hopefully, they will be embarrassed enough not to come back." He said he intended to continue the policy.[56]

One of the men, identified as 20-year-old Zian Djumma, said: "This was terrible. Now I only want to go home and find a hand grenade and throw it at the soldiers. Not only against those who did it to us but at everybody. I hate the Americans for this."[57]

Kate Allen, Amnesty International's director in London, said: "If these pictures are accurate, this is an appalling way to treat prisoners. Such degrading treatment is a clear violation of the responsibilities of the occupying powers. Whatever the reason, these men must at all times be treated humanely. The U.S. authorities must investigate this incident and publicly release their findings."[58]

A U.S. commander condemned the action and media attention quickly waned. There was little follow-up of the incident. The blatant decisions to ignore the Geneva Conventions' rules should have resulted in a barrage of stories in American publications and broadcasts.

The photos were not the first sign of trouble. Since labeling those picked up in Afghanistan as "enemy combatants" and "unlawful combatants," Rumsfeld had wavered about whether the United States had to abide by rules calling for the humane treatment of prisoners. "Unlawful combatants do not have any rights under the Geneva Convention," he told the *New York Times* in early 2002. He reassuringly added, "We have indicated that we do plan to, *for the most part*, treat them in a manner that is *reasonably consistent* with the Geneva Conventions to the *extent they are appropriate*"[59] (emphasis added). His quote was dutifully reported without many questions about what "reasonably consistent" or "to the extent they are appropriate" meant. Rumsfeld indicated that "stress and duress" techniques (deprivation of sleep or food, being stripped and paraded around naked, and being forced to sit for hours shackled and hooded in uncomfortable positions) were considered reasonable. All are against the Geneva Conventions' provisions.

As human rights organizations, including the International Red Cross (which stopped a tour of Abu Ghraib and demanded to know why so many prisoners were naked) and Amnesty International, grew increasingly alarmed at the treatment of prisoners in U.S. detention centers worldwide, the U.S. media did little investigation of the claims.

After the November 27, 2003, death in U.S. custody of Major General Abed Hamed Mowhoush, a senior official in Hussein's army, journalists wondered if his death was due to the "stress and duress" methods used by interrogators.

"Any suggestion that torture is used is false and offensive," Brigadier General Mark Kimmitt told reporters. Members of the military initially said Mowhoush had died of a heart attack while being interrogated. Later, his death was ruled a homicide by the Pentagon, which acknowledged that he died of "asphyxia due to smothering and chest compression."[60]

ABU GHRAIB

When Saddam Hussein ruled over Iraq, he ran a notorious prison where brutal torture and murder occurred daily. When Americans deposed him, they took over the prison, called Abu Ghraib. More than 7,000 Iraqis were placed in Abu Ghraib by American troops after being captured in sweeps throughout the country. After several complaints by human rights organizations, the military launched an investigation of possible abuses at the prison.

On January 16, 2004, the U.S. Command in Baghdad issued a one-paragraph press release: "An investigation has been initiated into reported incidents of detainee abuse at a Coalition Forces detention facility. The release of specific information concerning the incidents could hinder the investigation, which is in its early stages. The investigation will be conducted in a thorough and professional manner."[61]

The release was largely ignored by the media. According to the *American Journalism Review*,

> The *New York Times* published a 367-word report on page 7, noting that the inquiry was expected to "add fuel" to the burgeoning allegations of abuse. The *Philadelphia Inquirer* ran a 707-word story, also on page 7, and headlined, "U.S. Probes Report of Abuse of Iraqi Detainees." The *Washington Post* and *USA Today* did not run stories on the release, according to a Lexis/Nexus search. The *Boston Globe* had about 100 words on the investigation at the end of an 844-word Iraq story on page A4. The *Dallas Morning News* ran a 20-word brief on 26A. Television largely ignored the announcement: CNN and Fox News mentioned it briefly on January 16, NBC had a 41-word item the following morning. And that was about it.[62]

Later, *Washington Post* Executive Editor Leonard Downie Jr. said, "Have you ever read that paragraph? They made it as innocent-sounding as possible, and it just wasn't noticed the way it should have been."[63]

On April 4, 2004, U.S. Army Major General Antonio Taguba completed a 53-page "secret" report, which concluded that U.S. soldiers had committed "egregious acts and grave breaches of international law." The report said 60 percent of the prisoners at Abu Ghraib were "not a threat to society" and that innocent civilians were often detained indefinitely. Even worse, from October to December 2003, there were numerous instances of "sadistic, blatant, and wanton criminal abuses" of prisoners. Among other things, the report said, soldiers:

- Forced prisoners to strip and remain naked for days; videotaped and photographed the naked male and female detainees; and arranged detainees in sexually explicit positions and photographed them. Male detainees were forced to masturbate while being photographed and videotaped. Naked male detainees were forced to wear women's underwear. Naked male detainees were forced into a pile, and then soldiers jumped on them.
- A male MP guard raped a female detainee.
- A naked detainee was forced to stand on a box. A sandbag was placed on his head, and wires were attached to his fingers, toes, and penis. He was told that if he fell off the box, he would be electrocuted.

- A dog chain or strap was wrapped around a naked detainee's neck, and a female soldier posed for a picture dragging him across the floor.
- Dead Iraqi detainees were photographed with MPs posing with smiles and thumbs up signs.
- Chemical lights were broken and the phosphoric liquid poured on detainees. At least one detainee was sodomized with a chemical light and perhaps a broom stick.
- Unmuzzled dogs were used to frighten and intimidate detainees, and in one instance, a dog bit and severely injured a detainee.

After Taguba's report was completed, 17 soldiers and officers were reportedly removed from duty, and 6 were arrested and ordered to face courts marshal. In his report, Taguba said: "Specifically, I suspect that Colonel Thomas M. Pappas, Lieutenant Colonel Steve L. Jordan, Mr. Steven Stephanowicz, and Mr. John Israel were either directly or indirectly responsible for the abuses at Abu Ghraib and strongly recommend immediate disciplinary actions."

Reports show that Stephanowicz remained at Abu Ghraib at least until April 25, 2004, which suggests that little action was taken until it became clear that the media would run the story.[64]

Taguba's report was in startling contrast to what administration officials were publicly saying about the liberation of Iraq.

On September 2, 2003, Paul Bremer, administrator of the Coalition Provisional Authority, told journalists: "The Iraqi people are now free. And they do not have to worry about the secret police coming after them in the middle of the night, and they don't have to worry about their husbands and brothers being taken off and shot, or their wives being taken to rape rooms. Those days are over."[65]

President Bush repeatedly made similar statements the next month. "Iraq is free of a brutal dictator. Iraq is free of the man who caused there to be mass graves. Iraq is free of rape rooms and torture chambers. Iraq is free of a brutal thug. America did the right thing."[66]

Just one week before the announcement that allegations of abuse was being investigated in the prison, the president said: "One thing is for certain: There won't be any more mass graves and torture rooms and rape rooms."[67]

On April 28, 2004, 60 *Minutes II* ran a story about the abuse at Abu Ghraib. Anchor Rather admitted to viewers:

> Two weeks ago, we received an appeal from the Defense Department, and eventually from the chairman of the military Joint Chiefs of Staff, General Richard Myers, to delay this broadcast given the danger and tension on the ground in Iraq. We decided to honor that request while pressing for the Defense Department to add its perspective to the incidents at Abu Ghraib prison. This week, with the photos beginning to circulate elsewhere and with other journalists about to publish their versions of the story, the Defense Department agreed to cooperate in our report.

Rather admitted that CBS did not spend too much time worrying about the dehumanizing conditions in the prison or the innumerable Iraqis who were endangered during that two-week period. And rather than push for answers and uncover additional information—such as the existence of Taguba's report —CBS allowed Department of Defense officials to spin the story.

General Kimmitt told program viewers, "Frankly, I think all of us are disappointed at the actions of the few. You know, every day, we love our soldiers and—but frankly, some days we're not always proud of our soldiers."

He urged Iraqis to remember that the abuses were the work of a few and were not representative of all Americans. "So what would I tell the people of Iraq? This is wrong. This is reprehensible. But this is not representative of the 150,000 soldiers that are over here," Kimmitt added. "I'd say the same thing to the American people....Don't judge your army based on the actions of a few."

Most publications reported the abuses within a few days, but some major newspapers refused to print the horrendous pictures of naked prisoners piled high in a pyramid or the hooded man standing on a box, arms extended, wires attached to his body. The *Washington Post, Chicago Tribune,* and *Los Angeles Times* ran photographs of the abused Iraqis on page A1. The *New York Times, Pittsburgh Post-Gazette, Baltimore Sun, Miami Herald, Detroit News* and *Free Press, St. Paul Pioneer Press, Columbus Post-Dispatch,* and *Oakland Tribune* ran page-1 stories about the photos without publishing the pictures.[68]

The week the *New Yorker* published Seymour Hersh's investigation into the abuses at the prison, uncovering more brutality and providing excerpts from Taguba's report, the *New York Times* ran a story claiming the government was harsh in its interrogations but was careful not to torture even the most valuable prisoners.

"The Central Intelligence Agency has used coercive interrogation methods against a select group of high-level leaders and operatives of al-Qaeda that have produced growing concerns inside the agency about abuses," the story said. But the paper assured readers that, "defenders of the operation say the methods stopped short of torture, did not violate American anti-torture statutes, and were necessary to fight a war against a nebulous enemy whose strength and intentions could only be gleaned by extracting information from often uncooperative detainees." The "tactics *simulate torture,* but officials say they are supposed to stop short of serious injury." A former intelligence official said "there was a debate after 9/11 about how to make people disappear"[69] (emphasis added). The article did not quote humanitarian aid groups or an international legal expert who could clarify the definition of torture or the provisions of the Geneva Conventions.

With the Abu Ghraib prison pictures still fresh, the paper chose not to use the word torture in its headline, saying instead, "Harsh C.I.A. Methods Cited in Top Qaeda Interrogations." Had its reporters called even one human rights organization, they would have learned that the CIA was indeed violating international laws and was engaged in what has been defined as "torture."

Rumsfeld used the same strategy in defending the practices used on prisoners. "What has been charged so far is abuse, which I believe technically is different from torture. I'm not going to address the 'torture' word."[70]

The *Washington Post* was more accurate in a story it ran at about the same time:

> Many Muslims now see the American intervention as a devastating betrayal, starkly reflected by the Red Cross's recent conclusion that 70 to 90 percent of all Iraqis who were "deprived of their liberty"..."were arrested by mistake." Others in the region react with fury to the symbolism of a naked Arab male on a concrete floor tethered to a female American soldier looking down with disinterested arrogance on her prisoner at Abu Ghraib.[71]

It is difficult to know why journalists did not report the allegations of abuse and torture by the U.S. military sooner. It could be that they were afraid their reports about U.S. troops' bad behavior could spark outrage in the Arab world and cause additional violence against American soldiers. It could also be that journalists did not want to risk the harsh criticism from the administration that would follow the reports of torture and abuse, the anger of the American public, or a potential campaign against them that could lead to the loss of their jobs.

Social psychologist Albert Bandura has suggested that

> the moral disengagement that leads to inhumanity stems from a series of variables, including the cognitive restructuring of inhumane conduct into allegedly benign or worthy conduct by moral justification, sanitizing language, disavowal of a sense of personal agency by diffusion or displacement of responsibility, disregarding or minimizing the injurious effects of one's actions, and attribution of blame to, and dehumanization of, those who are victimized.[72]

All of these variables occurred during the wars in Afghanistan and Iraq. Journalists were not responsible for the torture or abuse and felt no responsibility toward civilians caught in the war. But they did feel a sense of responsibility toward American soldiers fighting abroad, and this perspective colored their coverage.

When the pictures taken in the prison were made public, it enraged Iraqis, who felt betrayed. Iraqi Hassan Saeed told *Newsday*: "That picture showed exactly the type of torture that Saddam's thugs used. The Americans promised us that things would be different from what they were under Saddam. They lied." Another said: "When I saw those pictures, I wanted to pick up a weapon, too."[73]

Most journalists shed their roles as pursuers of fact and became caretakers for American troops and the American perspective. Finding and reporting the news became secondary.

Peter Howe, author of *Shooting Under Fire: The World of the War Photographer*, said he was surprised at how sanitized the war in Iraq had become. "Unless we understand the full implication of our actions," he said, "as a democracy, we can't make a reasonable assessment of when it's the right time to go to war. If war is divorced from daily life, as a video game [is], we can't make judgments, and we find ourselves mired in something we did not expect."[74]

CHAPTER 7

A Propaganda Press

We must remember that in time of war, what is said on the enemy's side of the front is always propaganda, and what is said on our side of the front is truth and righteousness, the cause of humanity and a crusade for peace.
          —Walter Lippmann, journalist and former advisor to
                                President Woodrow Wilson

Government propaganda only has to work once to be successful.[1] Once an idea is sold to the public, it takes on a life of its own. Supporters lobby the cause and push for a budget. Hyperbole appears as headlines throughout the nation and is absorbed and accepted as truth.[2] Fox News, CNN, and others broadcast bold, unsubstantiated declarations that become "fact." Laws are enacted based on these "facts," and, much like what occurred with the war in Iraq, they move forward with little critical examination.

Once U.S. troops were in Iraq, there was no turning back—the mission to oust Saddam Hussein was accomplished and irreversible—no matter what independent investigations might uncover. In a sense, it did not matter how the United States had gotten there anymore; the issue became how to get out.

Throughout the years, for a variety of reasons, the once-sturdy line between publicity and news, advertising and editorial content, has eroded, making it difficult, if not impossible, for the public to distinguish between independent journalism and propaganda or spin.

This has been aided in large part by the growing pressure on journalists to comply with policies created by a corporate media concerned most about profit and stock prices. A May 2004 poll of journalists showed that the majority were concerned about the many factual errors in print and broadcast stories and felt that most news stories were superficial. They attributed many of the problems to bottom-line pressures.[3]

Pulitzer Prize-winning *Newsday* reporter Laurie Garrett expressed dismay about the profession in a resignation memo she sent to her colleagues:

> All across America, news organizations have been devoured by massive corporations, and allegiance to stockholders, the drive for higher share prices, and push for larger dividend returns trumps everything that the grunts in the newsrooms consider their missions....The sort of in-your-face challenge that the Fourth Estate once posed for politicians has been replaced by mud-slinging, lies, and, where it ought not be, timidity....And it's damned tough to find that truth every day with a mere skeleton crew of reporters and editors.[4]

According to the Project for Excellence in Journalism's State of the News Media Report 2004, most journalists said they

> think business pressures are making the news they produce thinner and shallower. And they report more cases of advertisers and owners breaching the independence of the newsroom. Most sectors of the media are cutting back in the newsroom, both in terms of staff and in the time they have to gather and report the news. While there are exceptions, in general, journalists face real pressures trying to maintain quality.

Sixty-six percent of journalists working on national news outlets said they believe "increased bottom line pressure is seriously hurting the quality of news coverage."

As corporations scaled back their news staffs, editors and producers were forced to look for other ways to fill news holes. The government was more than happy to help. In March 2005, the *New York Times* revealed that the Bush administration had spent $254 million on public relations contracts in its first term, nearly double the amount the Clinton administration spent.

Much of the money went toward producing prepackaged news segments in which public relations professionals pretended to be independent news reporters describing positive developments resulting from administration policy. The *Times* said,

> at least 20 federal agencies, including the Department of Defense and the Census Bureau have made and distributed hundreds of television news segments in the past four years....Some reports were produced to support the administration's most

cherished policy objectives, like regime change in Iraq or Medicare reform....The government's newsmaking apparatus has produced a quiet drumbeat of broadcasts describing a vigilant and compassionate administration.[5]

The segments were broadcast in some of the nation's largest television markets—including New York, Los Angeles, Chicago, Dallas, and Atlanta—without acknowledgement that the government had produced them. Some news organizations identified the government's reporter as their own, others had staff reporters do voice-overs in which they repeated the statements of the government "reporter," giving the appearance that the story was an independent piece.

The *Times* described

a world where government-produced reports disappear into a maze of satellite trans-missions, Web portals, syndicated news programs, and network feeds, only to emerge cleansed on the other side as "independent" news. It is also a world where all partic-ipants benefit. Local affiliates are spared the expense of digging up original material. Public relations firms secure government contracts worth millions of dollars. The major networks, which help distribute the releases, collect fees from the government agencies that produce segments and the affiliates that show them. The administration, meanwhile, gets out an unfiltered message, delivered in the guise of traditional reporting.[6]

Only the public and "grunts in newsrooms" who strive to bring truth to their audience lose in this world.

How does the maze work? Major networks have agreements with public rela-tions firms to send their pre-taped segments to affiliates worldwide. The *Times* explained that

Fox, for example, has an arrangement with Medialink Worldwide Inc. to distribute video news releases to 130 affiliates through its video feed service, Fox News Edge. CNN distributes releases to 750 stations in the United States and Canada through a similar feed service, CNN Newsource. Associated Press Television News does the same thing worldwide with its Global Video Wire.[7]

The affiliates, local stations often with small staffs and budgets, pick up the feeds, edit them, make them appear as though they were produced in-house, and broadcast them to an unwitting public.

After the segments were filtered through the process, even some journalists said they did not know the government had produced what they had aired. Mike Stutz, news director at KGTV, the ABC affiliate in San Diego, said he was against airing government-prepared videos and was surprised to learn that his station had done so. "It amounts to propaganda, doesn't it?" he said. "I thought we were pretty solid [in what we aired]." Stutz said the station would take more precautions against running government propaganda.[8]

It is admirable that the *Times* uncovered the story and prominently displayed it on page A1. However, it should have recognized that propaganda was being used to manipulate the media much earlier. Additionally, despite understanding (and acknowledging) how the flawed system allows such a pervasive manipulation of the media, journalists refused to take responsibility for their complicity in the distribution of propaganda. They largely placed blame on the public relations professionals the government hired to shoot the videos.

For example, Karen Ryan is a former ABC and PBS journalist who changed careers and opened a PR firm. She was hired by the government to "report" in dozens of prepackaged news items, many of which made it onto news broadcasts around the country. Her segments typically ended: "In Washington, I'm Karen Ryan reporting" in a tone and cadence used by television reporters. The signoff got her into trouble when it was discovered she was not a journalist but a flack peddling a product. Journalists ridiculed her and labeled her a propagandist. The criticism may be well deserved, but so is self-reflection by members of the media and acknowledgement of their errors. If they had done their jobs properly, Ryan's reports would not have made it into mainstream news broadcasts.

The GAO denounced the segments, calling them "covert propaganda" and telling government agencies they may not produce reports "that conceal or do not clearly identify for the television viewing audience that the agency was the source of those materials."[9]

President Bush defended the packages: "There is a Justice Department opinion that says these pieces are within the law so long as they're based upon facts, not advocacy."[10]

David Walker, who heads the GAO, said he was dismayed by the president's reaction. "This is not just a legal issue; it's also an ethical matter. The taxpayers have a right to know when the government is trying to influence them with their own money."[11]

Journalists have since allowed the issue to die; it is unclear whether government officials have continued the practice.

PROPAGANDA, SPIN, AND WAR

Journalists were aware that governments use propaganda and spin in a buildup to war. The *Christian Science Monitor* ran a piece about the need to question government information in September 2002, the same month the Bush administration's public relations campaign for war with Iraq began, and six months before the war started. The story recalled that during the 1991 Persian Gulf war, the government claimed the invasion was necessary not because Hussein was in Kuwait but because United States ally Saudi Arabia was next on his list. The Pentagon cited top-secret satellite images that it said showed as many as 250,000 troops and 1,500 tanks at the border of Saudi Arabia, ready to advance.[12]

The *Christian Science Monitor* explained, however, that, "when the *St. Peters-burg Times* in Florida acquired two commercial Soviet satellite images of the same area, taken at the same time, no Iraqi troops were visible near the Saudi border—just empty desert." The justification for the war, the reporter who stud-ied the satellite images concluded, "was a pretty serious fib....That [Iraqi buildup] was the whole justification for Bush sending troops in there, and it just didn't exist." The reporter who broke the story said she had tried to contact the Office of the Secretary of Defense but was told: "Trust us." Dick Cheney was secretary of defense at the time.[13]

The administration's justification for the current war in Iraq, WMD, also did not exist (as many in the administration now admit).

Bush advisor Karl Rove once told writer Ken Auletta that members of the press "don't represent the public any more than other people do. I don't believe you have a check-and-balance function." Auletta concluded that the Bush administration considered the press corps just another special-interest lobbying group.

In fact, some members were. Armstrong Williams, a conservative columnist, promoted the administration's No Child Left Behind Act in his columns without disclosing that the Department of Education paid him $240,000 to do so. His columns ran in several large newspapers. James D. Guckert—who used the pseudonym Jeff Gannon—wrote for Talon News, a conservative online publica-tion owned by Bobby Eberle, a prominent Texas-based Republican. Gannon was paid to ask President Bush and White House officials preordained questions (some would say "softball" questions) at press conferences. He was the author of such Talon News exclusives as "Kerry Could Become First Gay President."[14] After he was discredited as a fraud, journalists debated how he had been able to receive a White House press pass when many legitimate journalists had been denied one.

The American press corps reacts with indignation when compared with public relations professionals, but the reality is that they are becoming more and more like flacks and less and less like reporters. Journalism schools have picked up on this trend and include marketing classes in their curricula. Most graduate jour-nalism students have no intention of becoming reporters.

Newsday's Garrett, who has worked as a visiting professor at several univer-sities, said: "The lines are getting very, very blurred, even at the level of basic training in journalism school....When you ask the students why public relations as opposed to journalism, often they would say to me, 'well, there really isn't that much of a distinction, but you can make more money on the PR side.'..."[15]

In the past decade, the balance of power between the government and the press has been quietly tilted toward government. The traditional media, long dis-dainful of staged photo ops, and propaganda rallies, slowly came to accept them as newsworthy. They are no longer relegated to back pages but have become front-page news, printed and aired without critical examination.

This has occurred for a variety of reasons, including the fear of losing further access and the gaining of financial benefits from such "political image-making" events.[16] As the media's influence diminished, the influence of public relations professionals thrived. The marketing of a product, the president, became as important as his message.

As the prepackaged news segments illustrate, members of the Bush administration were masters of spin. Many of the same officials who successfully sold the first Persian Gulf war (Dick Cheney, Donald Rumsfeld, Paul Wolfowitz, Colin Powell) were back for the second turn in Iraq. What should be noted is that so were many of the same journalists.

The administration was not secretive about its belief that spin was an important part of its operations. Top-level public relations professionals were hired to fill key administration posts, and officials announced at several turns that they were launching PR campaigns.

Before becoming the top Pentagon spokeswoman, Victoria Clarke ran the Washington office of one of the world's largest PR firms, Hill & Knowlton. Hill & Knowlton created the successful multimillion-dollar "Free Kuwait" ad campaign in the buildup to the Persian Gulf war. As part of that campaign, the company coached a young woman who testified to a congressional committee that she saw Iraqi soldiers remove babies from hospital incubators and leave them "on the cold floor to die." After the war, reporters learned that she was the daughter of Kuwait's ambassador to the United States and had never actually seen the incident she described taking place.[17]

As a member of the Pentagon's team for the Iraq war, Clarke is widely credited with the idea of embedding reporters with soldiers in Iraq.

John Rendon, CEO of the public relations firm the Rendon Group, was hired shortly after the 9/11 attacks as a consultant for the Pentagon and the CIA. He also helped promote the first Gulf war. He told cadets at the U.S. Air Force Academy in 1996: "I am not a national security strategist or a military tactician. I am a politician, and a person who uses communication to meet public policy or corporate policy objectives. In fact, I am an information warrior and a perception manager."

He reminded cadets that the troops who rolled into Kuwait City at the end of the first Gulf War were greeted by Kuwaitis waving small American flags. "Did you ever stop to wonder," Rendon asked, "how the people of Kuwait City, after being held hostage for seven long and painful months, were able to get hand-held American, and for that matter, the flags of other coalition countries? Well, you now know the answer. That was one of my jobs then."[18]

Administration officials told the media, very specifically, that they were launching a publicity campaign to garner support for their policies. In a discussion with the *New York Times* in September 2002, Bush's chief of staff, Andrew Card, described a $200 million campaign that the paper called a "meticulously planned strategy to persuade the public, the Congress, and the allies of the need to confront the threat from Saddam Hussein."[19] The administration decided that the president's speech on the anniversary of the terrorist attacks (with the Statue of Liberty glowing from behind as he spoke) would be an appropriate time to introduce the campaign to the American public. Members of Congress were lobbied when they returned from a Labor Day break. The administration did not begin the push earlier, Card said, because "from a marketing point of view, you don't introduce new products in August."[20]

The *Times* of London reported that a newly created department was planning a "multimillion-dollar PR blitz against Saddam Hussein, using advertising techniques to persuade crucial target groups that the Iraqi leader must be ousted." The blitz would be directed "at American and foreign audiences, particularly in Arab nations skeptical of U.S. policy in the region."[21]

Card essentially told the world that the administration was going to peddle the war like a consumer product and that he expected a media frenzy to soon follow.

And sure enough, Iraqi dissidents soon began dominating news stories with tales of Hussein's brutality and his weapons programs. NPR's *On the Media* reported in August 2002 that the State Department had provided media training to help the dissidents "effectively spread their message against Saddam Hussein" and push for war in Iraq. As part of the training, 17 Iraqis learned how to write effective op-ed articles and speeches, and how to stay "on message" during interviews so they could more effectively convince the American public of the need to topple Hussein.[22]

Undersecretary of State Douglas Feith discussed the reasons the Iraqis were being trained on a U.S.-funded Arab language radio station. "Ratcheting up the rhetoric is the kind of thing we can do now," he said. "We can stir the pot and see what happens."[23]

The INC, headed by Ahmad Chalabi, supplied many of these Iraqis, then called "defectors" by journalists. Chalabi received $340,000 a month from the U.S. government before and during the Iraq war. It is now believed that the INC may have spent some of the $18 million it received from the U.S. Congress to plant false news stories supporting its position to oust Hussein and lobbying for the war. The group claims to have placed 108 stories in newspapers and magazines in 2002. Most of the stories have been proven false with time. The GAO is investigating the claims since it is illegal to use government funds to spread false stories. The investigation marks the second time the United States has looked into how Chalabi and the INC spent money provided by the American government. It is a story that was not well reported in the United States.

Instead of exhibiting skepticism as the propaganda was distributed, reporters largely printed official statements without challenge and became participants in the publicity campaign.

For example, during a joint press conference with British ally Tony Blair on September 7, 2002, Bush said an IAEA report had claimed that Hussein could produce nuclear weapons within six months. Bush said: "I would remind you that when the inspectors first went into Iraq and were denied—finally denied access, a report came out of the Atomic—the IAEA that they were six months away from developing a weapon. I don't know what more evidence we need."[24]

It was startling news that was widely reported as fact in the United States. Journalists did not hunt down the report or call the IAEA for confirmation that such a report existed. If they had, they would have learned that there was no such report and the agency had never said Hussein was six months away from developing a nuclear weapon. The British paper the *Independent* did call the agency the day Bush made his statement. An agency spokesman told a reporter: "We don't know where he got that figure from."

Ideally, papers and broadcast news outlets would have presented this information in their original stories, as did the *Independent*. This type of proactive reporting could have slowed the resulting repetition of misinformation in editorials and on radio talk shows. False information and misstatements by Bush and his staff were repeatedly drilled into the collective consciousness of the American public by the media, usually without further reflection.

In the case of Bush's IAEA statement, a few U.S. papers did revisit the subject and reveal the errors.

Ten days after its original story about Bush's reference to the IAEA report, the *Washington Times* wrote that the report did not exist. "There's never been a report like that issued from this agency," Mark Gwozdecky, the IAEA's chief spokesman, told the paper "We've never put a time frame on how long it might take Iraq to construct a nuclear weapon in 1998."[25]

The newspaper wrote:

> The White House says Mr. Bush was referring to an earlier IAEA report. "He's referring to 1991 there," said Deputy Press Secretary Scott McClellan. "In '91, there was a report saying that after the war, they found out they were about six months away." Mr. Gwozdecky said no such report was issued by the IAEA in 1991....To clear up the confusion, Mr. McClellan cited two news articles from 1991....But neither article cites an IAEA report on Iraq's nuclear-weapons program or states that Saddam was only six months away from "developing a weapon"—as claimed by Mr. Bush.[26]

On October 22, 2002, the *Washington Post* wrote an article titled, "For Bush, Facts Are Malleable." The story, written by Dana Milbank, said: "As Bush leads the nation toward a confrontation with Iraq and his party into battle in midterm elections, his rhetoric has taken some flights of fancy in recent weeks." The president's assertions, including mention of the nonexistent IAEA report, were "powerful arguments for the actions Bush sought" but were "dubious, if not wrong....The White House, while acknowledging that on one occasion, the president was 'imprecise,' said it stands by his words."[27] To the *Post*'s credit, the story ran on page A1.

The two articles show how a free media should work to expose falsehoods and set the record straight. Unfortunately, as time progressed and the war in Iraq became viewed as inevitable, there were progressively fewer of such examples.

This occurred for a variety of reasons, including the fact that the administration was very adept at staying on-message. Journalists had to search hard for an official who would give an answer that had not been written by the White House communications team. Compounding the problem, some government employees risk jail for talking to reporters. The Department of Homeland Security implemented a policy requiring employees to sign a nondisclosure agreement that threatens them with "administrative, disciplinary, civil, or criminal action" for revealing "sensitive but unclassified" information including anything that could "adversely affect the national interest or the conduct of federal programs" if disclosed. One government worker was sentenced to a year in prison for giving a British reporter "sensitive but unclassified information."[28]

A GLOBAL EFFORT

The creation of the OGC (Office of Global Communications) provided another clue that spin was a large part of administration policy. In July 2002, the *Washington Post* reported on page A1: "The office, due to be up and running by fall, will allow the White House to exert more control over what has become one of the hottest areas of government and private-sector initiatives since September 11. Known as 'public diplomacy,' it attempts to address the question President Bush posed in his speech to Congress the week after the terrorist attacks: 'Why do they hate us?'"[29]

OGC produces the Global Messenger, a one-page e-mail of talking points sent daily to administration officials, embassies, members of Congress, and other interested parties. The office "helps develop and coordinate mid-range themes and events to support presidential initiatives, such as his drive for congressional and U.N. support for disarming Saddam Hussein." It also coordinates communication about U.S. humanitarian and pro-democracy efforts by working with the international media and producing U.S.-supported broadcasts in Muslim regions.

The campaign to convince Americans of the need for war succeeded in large part because of the uniformity of the message.

In November 2002, when polls suggested the American public was concerned about going to war with Iraq without international support (27 percent favored using force if the United States were acting alone, down from 33 percent a few weeks earlier), independent groups, supported by the administration, were formed to sway opinion toward the view that a war was necessary. Buried on page A15, the *Washington Post* said in November 2002:

> With the administration's blessing, a new group is forming to press the case in the United States and Europe for ejecting Hussein from power. Called the Committee for the Liberation of Iraq, the organization is modeled on a successful lobbying campaign to expand the NATO alliance. Members include former Secretary of State George P. Shultz, Senator John McCain (R-Ariz.), and former Senator Bob Kerrey

(D-Neb.).... While the Iraq committee is an independent entity, committee officers said they expect to work closely with the administration.[30]

Members were urged to write opinion pieces and columns, give lectures and presentations, and meet with reporters and editors to make the case for war. It was during this time that much of the information became skewed. A great deal of what was said in the buildup to war was true, such as Hussein's brutality. What was omitted was an accurate timeline of the incidents that supporters of the war used to make their case. Hussein did use chemical weapons against his own people and Iraq's neighbors and did kill thousands of innocent civilians. But these things occurred 20 years earlier, during a time when the United States was supporting the dictator. Members of the media rarely pointed this out when reporting the administration's statements, and the public was given the impression that mass murder was occurring on a daily basis.

There is no way members of the media could have known definitively that there were no links between Hussein and al Qaeda or that Hussein did not have WMD. But what they should have known was that public relations professionals were distributing the information supporting the administration's view and that it needed to be balanced with alternative perspectives. Whether journalists believed Hussein had WMD or not, they should have promoted open discussion of the issues.

In fact, the opposite occurred. Rather than seek opposing viewpoints, the media favored sources that supported administration claims. In the two-week period before Powell's U.N. speech presenting the U.S. evidence for the need to go to war with Iraq, ABC, CBS, NBC, and the PBS *NewsHour with Jim Lehrer* conducted 393 interviews about the proposed war. Three were with people holding antiwar views. The public was being primed for the speech. Polls at the time showed that about two-thirds of the population was opposed to the invasion and wanted more inspections and diplomacy.[31]

Noam Chomsky once said:

> The smart way to keep people passive and obedient is to strictly limit the spectrum of acceptable opinion but allow very lively debate within that spectrum—even encourage the more critical and dissident views. That gives people the sense that there's free thinking going on, while all the time the presuppositions of the system are being reinforced by the limits put on the range of the debate.

This occurred in the aftermath of the 9/11 attacks and was most obvious in the buildup to the war in Iraq. Very little discussion focused on whether the United States should attack Iraq. The debate centered on whether the United States should wait for an international consensus to go to war or launch a pre-emptive attack and go to war with its few allies. The international conversation was broader and centered on whether Hussein's threat justified the consequences of going to war.

GOOD VERSUS EVIL

Before a war can begin, the public in the nation waging the war needs to be anesthetized to its horrific reality. The enemy cannot be perceived as being human, or the inevitable deaths of innocent people are difficult to sell. Propaganda creates a public irrationality that makes war seem rational.[32]

After 9/11, bin Laden, Hussein, and al Qaeda were portrayed as devils, out to destroy the good in this world. The United States was described as God's country, the land of freedom and opportunity, fighting to liberate Iraqis from an evil dictator.

The president used biblical terminology to make his case for war, something that resonated with the largely Christian country. He also assured Americans that God was on their side in this fight.

"We will rid the world of evil-doers," he said on September 17, 2001. "This crusade, this war on terrorism, is going to take a while. And the American people must be patient."[33]

During a press conference with the prime minister of Japan, Bush said: "Make no mistake about it: This is good vs. evil. These are evildoers. They have no justification for their actions. There's no religious justification; there's no political justification. The only motivation is evil."[34] "God is not neutral in this war," Bush said on November 16, 2001.[35] No reporter questioned these statements or noted that some political motivations had been mentioned by bin Laden and his followers.

Lieutenant General William "Jerry" Boykin, the deputy undersecretary of defense for intelligence, publicly took it further, proposing that Bush had been anointed by God: "Why is this man in the White House? The majority of Americans did not vote for him. He's in the White House because God put him there for a time such as this."[36]

Eventually, the rhetoric became so outlandish that Pope John Paul II felt compelled to speak out and urged leaders to strive for peace. He told Bush, "God is a neutral observer in the affairs of man. Man cannot march into war and assume God will be at his side."[37]

Joseph Goebbels, Hitler's propagandist, once said: "If you tell a lie big enough and keep repeating it, people will eventually come to believe it. The lie can be maintained only for such time as the state can shield the people from the political, economic, and/or military consequences of the lie."

In making the case for war in Iraq, Bush and administration officials asserted that Hussein had a decade-long relationship with al Qaeda operatives and that he had been plotting against the United States for years. During the buildup to war, these alarmist statements by officials ran as headlines in major publications, giving them credibility without accountability.

Nancy Snow, a propaganda expert who worked for the U.S. Information Agency during the Clinton administration, explained it this way:

[The] American people were repeatedly told by the president and his inner circle that Saddam's evil alone was enough to be linked to 9/11 and that given time, he would have used his weapons against us. With propaganda, you don't need facts per se, just the best facts put forward. If these facts make sense to people, then they don't need proof like one might need in a courtroom.[38]

In September 2002, Bush said: "You can't distinguish between al Qaeda and Saddam when you talk about the war on terror."[39]

A month later, Bush acknowledged that he had no hard proof to back his claims but said ignoring Hussein would be akin to inviting a nuclear attack.

We have seen that those who hate America are willing to crash airplanes into buildings full of innocent people. Our enemies would be no less willing—in fact, they would be eager—to use biological or chemical, or a nuclear weapon. Knowing these realities, America must not ignore the threat gathering against us. Facing clear evidence of peril, we cannot wait for the final proof—the smoking gun—that could come in the form of a mushroom cloud.[40]

The *New York Times* reported on page A1: "President Bush declared tonight that Saddam Hussein could attack the United States or its allies 'on any given day' with chemical or biological weapons. In a forceful argument for disarming Iraq or going to war with that country, he argued that 'we have an urgent duty to prevent the worst from occurring.'"[41]

The repetitive coupling of Hussein, bin Laden, al Qaeda, and the September 11 attacks worked—the American public thought of them as an indistinguishable evil lump. An opinion survey by the Pew Research Center for the People and the Press found that in February 2003, the month before Bush began his attack on Iraq, 63 percent of those interviewed said they believed the war in Iraq would help the war on terrorism.

The fresh memories of 9/11 were amplified by the grim terrorist-filled future portrayed by the administration.

Condoleezza Rice made headlines worldwide when she said: "We don't want the smoking gun to be a mushroom cloud."[42]

Members of Congress voted to go to war in Iraq based on these fearful images.

"I refuse to sit back and wait for another September 11 to occur," said Republican Congressman Mark Foley. "We know who the enemy is. We know what he does, and we know what we must do."

The lack of questions from journalists and politicians enabled the administration to frame and reframe the debate at will. Iraq had nothing to do with 9/11, but repeated coupling of Hussein, bin Laden, and the 9/11 attacks made the connections seem rational. Members of the administration, when pressed for proof, simply repeated the coupling, which was then repeated in journalists' stories.

Similarly, when the original premise for war, Iraq's alleged possession of WMD, became problematic, the Bush administration subtly changed the context of the debate. Bush went from saying that Hussein "possessed weapons of mass destruction" to saying he had the "capability" to build the weapons.[43]

"Even though we did not find the stockpiles that we thought we would find, we did the right thing. He had the capability, and he could have passed that capability on to our enemies," Bush said in August 2004.[44]

It is a subtle difference that few noticed, but the media took the bait and began changing the angle of its stories. Troops may not have found the weapons, but Hussein *could* have acquired them and given them to enemies of the United States. That is a far cry from a mushroom cloud.

PROPAGANDA AND MEDIA COMPLIANCE

One of the most visually momentous images during the war in Iraq was the toppling of the statue of Hussein in central Baghdad's Freedom Square on April 9, 2003. It is also one of the most obvious signs that the media lost touch with its primary responsibility, which is to present an accurate accounting of an event. The statue was located in front of the hotel where most foreign journalists stayed during the conflict.

To the world watching the images on the television screen, jubilant Iraqi civilians spontaneously placed a rope around the enormous statue, tore it down with assistance from U.S. troops, and began beating it with hammers. They seemed to be ecstatic, and images of Iraqi men kissing American soldiers appeared in newspapers the following day. Broadcast journalists fostered the belief that it was an "historic moment" that defined the fall of Hussein's regime and the liberation of the Iraqi people.

The *Washington Post's* Ceci Connelly told Fox News: "It was reminiscent, I think, of the fall of the Berlin Wall. And just sort of that pure emotional expression, not choreographed, not stage-managed, the way so many things these days seem to be. Really breathtaking."[45]

The *San Francisco Chronicle* wrote:

Several hundred Iraqis poured into the square. "Saddam no, Bush yes," a gleeful boy shouted. Then some in the crowd attacked a giant statue of Hussein that dominated the square. First, a couple of sturdy young men climbed the 25-foot pedestal and tied a rope about the statue. Then, they moved to the base and used sledgehammers, breaking chunks out of it.[46]

In reality, a few dozen Iraqis and a few dozen U.S. Marines were in the square, which was surrounded by American tanks. And the idea of toppling the statue was not a spontaneous show by jubilant Iraqis but a planned event by a media savvy marine colonel.

Journalists who were at the event knew there were not hundreds but dozens of people in the square that day. A long shot by a Reuters' photographer clearly showed a nearly empty square. How, then, could the international viewing community be led to believe that "hundreds" of Iraqis had taken fate into their hands that day? The media complicity in the propaganda event is startling.

There were a few attempts by reporters at the scene to set the record straight.

The *Boston Globe* noted that, "whenever the cameras pulled back, they revealed a relatively small crowd at the statue." The headline of the story was prescient: "Snap Judgments; Did Iconic Images From Baghdad Reveal More About the Media Than Iraq?"[47]

In July 2004, the *Los Angeles Times* revealed that the Army had released a report acknowledging that it had staged the event.

> It was a marine colonel—not joyous Iraqi civilians, as was widely assumed from the TV images—who decided to topple the statue, the army report said. And it was a quick-thinking Army psychological operations team that made it appear to be a spontaneous Iraqi undertaking. The colonel—who was not named in the report—selected the statue as a "target of opportunity," the psychological team used loud-speakers to encourage Iraqi civilians to assist....Ultimately, a marine recovery vehicle toppled the statue with a chain, but the effort appeared to be Iraqi-inspired because the psychological team had managed to pack the vehicle with cheering Iraqi children.[48]

The quick-thinking psychological operations team had even found a spin for what it considered the only misstep in the successful propaganda event, the placement of an American flag on the statue. BBC reported the day the statue tumbled: "We've just learned from the U.S. Marines that the U.S. flag that was put on the face of Saddam yesterday—it was replaced by an Iraqi flag when the people shouted for that—was the flag that was flying over the Pentagon on September 11."[49] It was not, of course, but journalists did take the time to consider how unlikely it was that a flag that flew over the Pentagon on 9/11 ended up on a statue of Hussein that was "spontaneously" toppled by "jubilant Iraqis."

The "rescue" of Private (Pfc.) Jessica Lynch is another example of journalists' deciding not to let facts get in the way of a good story.

The *Cleveland Plain Dealer* began a story about Lynch by saying, "For many Americans...the face of Gulf War II will forever be the smiling young woman under the camo-colored Army cap against the background of an American flag."[50] The propaganda machine had placed yet another indelible image in the memory of the unwitting American public, again with assistance from the media.

As *Washington Post* ombudsman Michael Getler said in criticizing his paper's coverage of the event, "this was the single most memorable story of the war, and it had huge propaganda value. It was false, but it didn't get knocked down until it didn't matter quite so much."[51]

The "rescue" contained so many elements of a propaganda plan that it was hard to miss: The Iraqis were portrayed as sadistic killers who ambushed heroic

Americans who were returning to base. As bullets felled her colleagues, the brave, young American fought until her ammunition ran out. Information from the Pentagon said she was then shot and stabbed. In an Iraqi hospital, officials said, she was interrogated and slapped.

Lynch later said her gun had jammed and she never fired a shot. Instead, she dropped to her knees and prayed as her unit came under attack. She was not shot or stabbed, and she said those in the hospital had treated her very well.

Even the Pentagon's presentation to journalists was dramatic: "In the early hours of April 2," the *Guardian* reported, "correspondents in Doha were summoned from their beds to Centcom, the military and media nerve centre for the war.... The journalists rushed in, thinking Saddam had been captured."[52] What they got was the dramatic story of the rescue. The next day, the media were flooded with stories of the heroism involved in storming into enemy territory and bringing out an injured soldier.

Oddly enough, the rescue was filmed. When five minutes of edited footage was released, General Vincent Brooks said: "Some brave souls put their lives on the line to make this happen, loyal to a creed that they know that they'll never leave a fallen comrade."

Time magazine said the story was better than a Hollywood movie.

The *Washington Post* ran an "exclusive" story about the capture and "rescue" effort:

> Pfc. Jessica Lynch, rescued Tuesday from an Iraqi hospital, fought fiercely and shot several enemy soldiers after Iraqi forces ambushed the Army's 507th Ordnance Maintenance Company, firing her weapon until she ran out of ammunition, U.S. officials said yesterday. Lynch, a 19-year-old supply clerk, continued firing at the Iraqis even after she sustained multiple gunshot wounds and watched several other soldiers in her unit die around her.... "She was fighting to the death," the official said. "She did not want to be taken alive." Lynch was also stabbed when Iraqi forces closed in on her position, the official said, noting that initial intelligence reports indicated that she had been stabbed to death.[53]

Since the *Post* had the exclusive story, its version of events was picked up by papers around the country. Unfortunately, it was almost all wrong.

The day after the *Post* story ran, the *Toronto Star* reported that Lynch was rescued from a hospital that had tried to return her to U.S. forces. The doctor who tended to Lynch said,

> the most important thing to know is that the Iraqi soldiers and commanders had left the hospital almost two days earlier. The night they left, a few of the senior medical staff tried to give Jessica back. We carefully moved her out of intensive care and into an ambulance and began to drive to the Americans, who were just one kilometer away. But when the ambulance got within 300 meters, they began to shoot. There wasn't even a chance to tell them "We have Jessica. Take her."[54]

Lynch's father also began to question the official reports, telling reporters she had broken bones but no bullet or stab wounds.

The *Guardian* went to the hospital in Iraq where the doctor who had treated Lynch said: "We were surprised. Why do this? There was no military; there were no soldiers in the hospital. It was like a Hollywood film. They cried, 'Go, go, go,' with guns and blanks and the sound of explosions. They made a show—an action movie like Sylvester Stallone or Jackie Chan, with jumping and shouting, break-ing down doors."[55]

The *Washington Post* attempted to correct the record in a 5,000-word story more than two months after its original article. The story began on page A1 and filled nearly two and a half inside pages. In the article, the *Post* retracted much of its original story, but most of the new facts were buried on the inside pages.

In his critique of the paper's coverage, *Post* ombudsman Getler said that in its original story, the paper wrote on page A1 that Lynch had fought bravely and was shot and stabbed before being overtaken by Iraqis. "None of that actually happened, according to unnamed military officials cited in the June 17 *Post* account. But readers didn't find this out on the front-page portion of that story; it was in the continuation on page A-16."[56]

He noted:

> Colonel David Rubenstein, commander of the Army hospital at Landstuhl, Ger-many, where Lynch had been taken, was widely quoted as saying that medical evi-dence did "not suggest that any of her wounds were caused by either gunshots or stabbing."...We now know that Rubenstein spoke the truth, but he has disappeared from print. He was the only one to speak on the record for months, but there is no indication that the *Post* ever went back to ask him what happened after he made those remarks and whether he was told not to say any more.[57]

Once Lynch was able to speak for herself, the story fell apart completely. She accused the Pentagon of using her for propaganda purposes.

> It hurt in a way that people would make up stories that they had no truth about. Only I would have been able to know that, because the other four people on my vehicle aren't here to tell the story. So I would have been the only one able to say, yeah, I went down shooting. But I didn't. I did not shoot, not a round, nothing. I went down praying to my knees....From the time I woke up in that hospital, no one beat me, no one slapped me, no one, nothing. I'm so thankful for those people, because that's why I'm alive today.[58]

Lynch said one Iraqi in the hospital sang to comfort her when she was dis-tressed and helped her sleep despite the pain from her injuries.

Most Americans continue to believe that Lynch was gloriously rescued by brave members of the U.S. military who refused to leave one of their own behind. It was something they had been conditioned to believe from movies like *Black Hawk Down*.

The media's unexamined repetition of government information certainly helped foster such conditioning.

CHAPTER 8

Hurricane Katrina and Its Effect on News Reporting

I would say the best moment of all was when I caught a 7.5 pound perch in my lake.

—George W. Bush, on his best moment in office[1]

On August 29, 2005, one of the largest hurricanes ever to hit the United States barreled through the Gulf Coast. While the damage from Katrina was extensive throughout the region, the devastation was at its worst in New Orleans, where the storm destroyed the levies protecting the city and caused torrents of water to flood the streets and homes.

More than 1,600 people died and 700 more were listed as missing in March 2006, making it one of the worst natural disasters in the country's history. The storm caused more than $75 billion in damages.

It was the first major crisis handled by the Department of Homeland Security, which had taken control of the FEMA (Federal Emergency Management Agency) in 2004. For days, people were stranded within the city limits, unable to find food, potable water, or shelter, and the government's slow response angered journalists and the public.

What made Katrina such a disaster was the way the government handled it. Even though Katrina moved slowly toward New Orleans and there were plenty of warnings about its force, local, state, and federal officials failed to evacuate thousands of people in its path.

This lack of action opened a host of questions about the new Department of Homeland Security, which was formed after 9/11 to protect the country. If the department could not take the necessary steps to protect citizens from a storm that had been predicted, could it protect against a terrorist plot? The fear that followed 9/11 turned to anger as journalists wondered about the competence of the administration and the safety of the nation.

The hurricane galvanized the press and the president faced the first serious criticism of his leadership since before the 9/11 attacks. Images of Bush on vacation playing guitar with a country singer shortly after the levies broke and pictures of Condoleezza Rice shopping at an expensive Manhattan boutique infuriated journalists who wrote stories about the administration's lack of compassion.

Reporters became extremely emotional covering the victims of the flood; several cried on camera. CNN's Andersen Cooper was among the first to express his frustration about the relief effort while on air:

> Shocking images from New Orleans. What is happening there is an outrage...And what you are about to see in this next hour is going to shock you, that this is taking place in the United States of America in this day and age. Why is it happening, and what can be done to stop it.

Throughout the report he asked relevant questions:

> What is the federal government doing? Should more have been done early? I mean we knew this storm was coming. If we knew an attack on the south of the United States was coming, you would think some military forces, National Guard forces would be mobilized in a high degree. Was that done?... Does the federal government bear responsibility for what is happening now?[2]

The report, with all its questions, is dramatically different from those that followed the 9/11 attacks.

Similarly, during an interview that day with Homeland Security chief Michael Chertoff, NPR's Robert Siegel repeatedly asked why no food and water was being delivered to the hurricane victims and insisted that Chertoff provide a date when help would arrive.[3] Siegel also told Chertoff that 2,000 people were living at the convention center, something Chertoff said he did not know.

This led Ted Koppel to complain to FEMA director Michael Brown: "You just found out about [the people at the convention center] today? Don't you guys watch television? Don't you guys listen to the radio? Our reporters have been reporting about it for more than just today?"

He aggressively questioned Brown:

Mr. Brown, some of these people are dead. They're beyond your help. Some of these people have died because they needed insulin and they couldn't get it. Some of the people died because they were in hospitals and they couldn't get the assistance that they needed. You say you were surprised by the fact that so many people didn't make it out. It's no surprise to anyone that you had at least 100,000 people in the city of New Orleans who are dirt poor; who don't have cars, who don't have access to public transportation, who don't have any way of getting out of the city simply because somebody says, "You know, there's a force five storm coming, you ought to get out." If you didn't have buses there to get them out, why should it be a surprise to you that they stayed?[4]

The anger about the government's inaction was palpable. Ben Morris, the mayor of Slidell, Louisiana, complained seven days after Katrina:

We are still hampered by some of the most stupid, idiotic regulations by FEMA. They have turned away generators, we've heard that they've gone around seizing equipment from our contractors. If they do so, they'd better be armed because I'll be damned if I'm going to let them deprive our citizens. I'm pissed off, and tired of this horseshit.[5]

Firefighters told reporters they were being forced to take classes on sexual harassment before being allowed to rescue victims. Historically, the National Guard rushes to scenes like this to help with rescue efforts. They were slow to arrive in New Orleans and people began to wonder aloud whether the wars in Iraq and Afghanistan had left the country vulnerable rather than protected.

In the weeks that followed the storm, journalists began to take a critical look at Bush's leadership from the day of 9/11 through the botched hurricane relief effort. They also began to question the honesty of the administration.

Koppel said: "To hear federal and local officials describing what is happening on the ground in New Orleans is to know that one group or the other is seriously out of touch or incapable of confronting the truth."[6]

New York Times columnist Frank Rich wrote: "The administration and its apologists erect every possible barrier to keep us from learning the truth."[7]

MSNBC's Joe Scarborough said on November 30, 2005: "These storms raised serious questions about our government's ability to protect its citizens and left Americans with many questions about the problems that were exposed."

Bush was described by *USA Today* as "detached and unaware of the message conveyed by his words and conduct....He didn't cancel his vacation until two days after Katrina struck and didn't visit the region until four days after the storm....Bush's critics say his response to the hurricane proves that he's not a leader."

Shortly after the hurricane more than 42 percent polled said Bush has done a "bad or terrible job responding to the hurricane."[8] Later 67 percent said they felt the federal government had been unprepared and 75 percent said the state/ local government was unprepared. It was the first of many downward slides in the polls for the president; by May 2006 his approval rating was down to 30 percent.

Even administration-friendly Fox News criticized the administration, saying conditions in New Orleans were "not acceptable."

While the aggressive questioning was positive, as time progressed many of the shortcomings journalists had exhibited during and after 9/11 surfaced again. Instead of carefully examining and verifying information they received, reporters stenographically recorded what they were told and they got many of the facts wrong.

Reports about the slow emergency response were accurate, but other allegations were not. Stories about dead bodies stacked in the Superdome and convention center were false, as were the reports of a large number of rapes and murders there. Looting was not as extensive as reported; studies later found that most of the belongings taken were not televisions and electronic equipment, but food, water, and toiletries necessary for survival.

This type of error-ridden reporting led conservative radio talk show host Hugh Hewitt to complain that the

> American media threw everything they had at this story, all the bureaus, all the networks, all the newspapers, everything went to New Orleans, and yet they could not get inside the convention center, they could not get inside the Superdome to dispel the lurid, the hysterical, the salaciousness of the reporting...the media's coverage of New Orleans was one of the worst weeks of reporting in the history of the American media and it raises this question: If all of that amount of resources was given over to this story and they got it all wrong, how can we trust American media in a place far away like Iraq where they don't speak the language, where there is an insurgency, and I think the question comes back we really can't.[9]

He makes a good point. Years ago, journalists would not have mentioned the rapes and murders until verifying that the information was true. If they did mention it before confirmation was received, they would have noted that there were "rumors" of "alleged" crimes in the facilities. The unsubstantiated allegations about rapes and murders in New Orleans were reported as fact.

AP wrote:

> Katrina's winds have left behind an information vacuum. And that vacuum has been filled by rumor. There is nothing to correct wild reports that armed gangs have taken over the convention center. That two babies had their throats slit in the night. That a 7-year-old girl was raped and killed at the Superdome.

Another journalist complained, "you can report them but you at least have to say they are unsubstantiated and not pass them off as fact....But nobody is doing that."[10]

Within days of the hurricane grim, rumor-based stories began to dominate news coverage. Lootings became the headline news.

The administration reacted by sending in the military. The governor of Louisiana said, "these troops are battle-tested. They have M-16s and are locked and loaded. These troops know how to shoot and kill, and I expect they will."[11]

As time progressed, the manner in which the victims were portrayed revealed a fundamental problem with the Fourth Estate—many reporters for the large networks and newspapers tend to present news in terms of race and class, albeit unconsciously.

The media was accused of racism in its coverage of the victims. An AP picture caption of a black man wading in the flooded city was compared to an AFP caption of a white couple wading through the same waters. AP's caption: "A young man wades in chest deep flood water after looting a grocery store in New Orleans." AFP's: "Two residents wade through chest deep water after finding bread and water from a local grocery store after Hurricane Katrina."

CNN's Wolf Blitzer said on September 1: "You simply get chills every time you see these poor individuals...many of these people, almost all of them that we see are so poor and they are so black, and this is going to raise lots of questions for people who are watching this story unfold."[12]

In his groundbreaking book *Breaking the News*, James Fallows described how the journalism profession changed as television became popular and those entering the profession moved from the working class to the college educated. In the 1960s and 1970s many reporters lived in the same neighborhoods as the people they covered and had a good grasp of the issues that affected their audience. However, as reporters' salaries increased, their perspectives changed and they lost touch with the issues that affect average Americans.[13] Today top journalists are among the highest paid people in the country. Blitzer, for example, earns millions each year as anchor at CNN and lives in one of the wealthiest suburbs of Washington, D.C.

Had correspondents exhibited less bias and paid closer attention, they would have realized that the crime they were focusing on was not a major issue. There was looting, as often occurs after a catastrophe. But the crimes were not as prevalent as news stories indicated. This was something Blitzer and his colleagues did not seem to be able to comprehend.

Here is a conversation Blitzer had on September 5, 2005, with Nic Robertson who was reporting from Canal Street in New Orleans.

Blitzer:
What about all those shops, those stores, the restaurant behind you, along those streets? Are most of them—have most of them been looted?

Robertson:
They haven't, that's the very surprising thing.[14]

In October, the *Washington Post* reported that

claims of widespread looting, gunfire directed at helicopters and rescuers, homicides, and rapes...frequently turned out to be overblown, if not completely untrue.... The sensational accounts delayed rescue and evacuation efforts already hampered by poor planning and a lack of coordination among local, state and federal agencies. People rushing to the Gulf Coast to fly rescue helicopters or to distribute food, water and other aid steeled themselves for battle. In communities near and far, the seeds were planted that the victims of Katrina should be kept away, or at least handled with extreme caution.[15]

The *New York Times* later wrote that a Wal-Mart, three auto parts shops, a pawn shop, and some pharmacies were looted but that most of the stores in the historic district, including jewelry stores, remained untouched. The paper said "faced with reports that 400 to 500 armed looters were advancing on the town of Westwego, two police officers quit on the spot. The looters never appeared."[16]

However, the abundance of reports about bad behavior demonized the victims and made relocation even more difficult. When residents were bussed out of the flooded city, local TV and radio stations spread rumors about car-jackings and riots at Baton Rouge shelters.

The *Chicago Tribune*'s Howard Witt wrote:

By Thursday, local TV and radio stations in Baton Rouge—the only ones in the metro area still able to broadcast—were breezily passing along reports of cars being hijacked at gunpoint by New Orleans refugees, riots breaking out in the shelters set up in Baton Rouge to house the displaced, and guns and knives being seized. Scarcely any of it was true.... There were no riots in Baton Rouge. There were no armed hordes.... But the damage had been done.[17]

After a while, stories about Katrina faded away. Victims were shipped to cities across the country, and the issue was largely forgotten. Author and historian Arthur M. Schlesinger Jr. once said "issues that once galvanized the electorate fade into irrelevance." This is often aided by the lack of attention by the press. By the end of October, stories about the Katrina refugees disappeared from news reports and public anger dissolved.

"THE FAKE NEWS"

In the years that followed the 9/11 attacks, Americans grew tired of the lack of questions being asked by reporters and sought alternative sources of information. One of the most startling places that they turned for news was late-night television comedians. Comedy Central's *The Daily Show with Jon Stewart* became a primary place where people got their news—despite the fact that he calls his program "the fake news."

In an interview in 2003, Bill Moyers introduced Stewart by saying when future historians come to write the political story of our times, they will first have to review hundreds of hours of a cable television program called the Daily Show. You simply can't understand American politics in the new millennium without the Daily Show...[He is] a man many consider to be the preeminent political analyst of our time, the distinguished commentator and anchorman, Jon Stewart.

Moyers then made this confession: "I do not know whether you are practicing a old form of parody and satire. Or a new form of journalism."[18]

Oddly enough, many journalists seemed to agree. While Stewart is not a journalist and often reminds his audience that he is a comedian, his success can be attributed to the fact that he asks questions that journalists avoid and he repeats the question until he receives an answer.

Here is an exchange with Blitzer after a Senate Intelligence Committee report acknowledged that the purported reasons for the Iraq war were false.

Stewart:
Taking the country to war based on information that was totally wrong because it was told to you by a guy called Curveball—shouldn't that be the biggest scandal we ever had in the country?

Blitzer:
You never made a mistake in your life? The CIA is not perfect, sometimes they get it wrong. They got it wrong.

Stewart:
But in that situation, shouldn't someone get fired?

Blitzer:
Well, [CIA director] George Tenet did leave this weekend.

Stewart:
After being told he was doing a superb job.

Blitzer:
In defense of George Tenet, we never know the successes because they're kept secret. The failures we all know.

During this exchange, the gap between the comedian and journalist is alarming. Stewart is angry and wants answers; Blitzer is passive and provides excuses for the administration.

Stewart seems baffled and turns his attention to the media.

Stewart:
...At CNN do they have meetings where they say we should have asked that?

Blitzer:
We do that. We have meetings. We have conference calls, too.

Stewart:
What does the media do differently?

Blitzer:
We learn from our mistakes and try to do it better next time.

Stewart:
Specifically (emphasis added).

Blitzer:
We learn from our mistakes and try to do it better the next time...

Stewart:
Is the media suffering from groupthink or retardation?

Here Stewart did something that few journalists have dared to do—he pressed for specifics.

Many established journalists are offended by Stewart's popularity because they believe he has the freedom to express himself more honestly than they do; he is not constrained by journalistic rules. Stewart often tries to convince them that they can be more effective than comedians by asking straightforward questions and persistently pursuing facts.

During a brief encounter on the floor of the 2004 Democratic National Convention, Koppel said: "A lot of television viewers, more, quite frankly, than I'm comfortable with, get their news from the comedy channel on a program called 'The Daily Show.' Its host is Jon Stewart."

Koppel complained to Stewart:
Those who watch say, at least when I'm watching Jon, he can use humor to say BS, that's a crock...I can't [use satire to] do that.

Stewart:
You can say, "That's B.S." You don't need humor, because you have what I wish I had, which is credibility and gravitas. And it's all part of the discussion, and I think it's a good discussion to have, but I also think that it's important to take a more critical look, you know? Don't you think?

Koppel:
No[19]

Stewart also appeared on CNN's Crossfire to beg its hosts to "stop hurting America...and come work for us because we as the people...we need your help. Right now you're helping the politicians and the corporations...you're part of their strategies. You're partisan...hacks....When you talk about holding politicians' feet to fire I think that's disingenuous."[20]

It is this type of honest, passionate discourse that has brought Stewart viewers. In time people who were given access to officials started asking the questions the press had long ignored.

There are several examples of this. On April 7, 2006, a man named Harry Taylor stood up at a Charlotte, South Carolina, town hall meeting and scolded the president.

> You never stop talking about freedom, and I appreciate that. But while I listen to you talk about freedom, I see you assert your right to tap my telephone, to arrest me and hold me without charges, to try to preclude me from breathing clean air and drinking clean water and eating safe food.... What I want to say to you is that I, in my lifetime, I have never felt more ashamed of, nor more frightened by, my leadership in Washington. I would hope, from time to time, that you have the humility and the grace to be ashamed of yourself.

The media coverage that followed Taylor's monologue largely centered on how Bush had received some criticism but had handled it well. The *Washington Post* wrote in its news story, "...until Taylor came along, no one had really gotten in Bush's face. No one had really confronted him so directly on the issues of war and liberty that are at the heart of both his presidency and his political troubles. And no one had given him the opportunity to look unbothered by dissent."[21]

The question that immediately comes to mind is, why not? Reporters had written critically about the war in Iraq, but none had taken the hard questions directly to the nation's leaders.

Editor & Publisher's Greg Mitchell put it this way:

> While reporters and commentators continue to tiptoe around the question of whether Bush administration officials, right up to the president, deliberately misled the nation into the war, average and not-so-average citizens have raised the charge of "lies" and caused a stir usually reserved for reporters.[22]

An explanation about the media's passivity was provided by MSNBC's Chris Matthews. Matthews belittled comedian Stephen Colbert, who poked fun at Bush at the 2006 White House Correspondents' dinner. According to Matthews, Colbert's sharp criticism of Bush was bad because "the president is our head of state, not just a politician."[23]

The reactions of Matthews and Blitzer to criticisms of the Bush administration show that the media has not returned to its adversarial role. Instead, some journalists seem to believe that their responsibility is to protect government officials.

Colbert, who on his Comedy Central program portrays a conservative talk show host, was extremely critical of both Bush (who was on the podium) and the media during the correspondents' dinner. He told Bush to ignore his low poll ratings because they were based on reality, "and reality has a well known liberal bias." He said about the war in Iraq: "I believe that the government that governs best is a government that governs least, and by these standards we have set up a fabulous government in Iraq." He noted that Bush was a man of principles and decision: "When the president decides something on Monday, he still believes it on Wednesday—no matter what happened Tuesday."[24]

After Colbert was through roasting the president, he turned on the media.

> Over the last five years, you people were so good over tax cuts, WMD intelligence, the effect of global warming. We Americans didn't want to know, and you had the courtesy not to try to find out. Those were good times, as far as we knew. But, listen, let's review the rules. Here's how it works. The president makes decisions, he's the decider. The press secretary announces those decisions, and you people of the press type those decisions down. Make, announce, type. Put them through a spell check and go home. Get to know your family again. Make love to your wife. Write that novel you got kicking around in your head. You know, the one about the intrepid Washington reporter with the courage to stand up to the administration. You know, fiction.[25]

Shortly after Colbert's performance, former CIA analyst Ray McGovern made headlines when he persistently questioned Rumsfeld at an open forum in Atlanta. The exchange was broadcast live on CNN and became widely available online. For the first time Rumsfeld was asked to defend his own public statements. McGovern asked a question and was told by Rumsfeld that his question was inaccurate. In response, McGovern quoted Rumsfeld's own words back to him and repeated his question.

The manner in which this short discussion was reported is a clear example of how the mainstream media has softened the news. The web site "Media Matters For America" did an extensive analysis of how the exchange was covered by several major newspapers, and ABC, NBC, and Fox News. None of the major networks broadcast the part of the exchange in which McGovern challenges Rumsfeld with his own quote. Most major newspapers also ignored the challenge (the *Los Angeles Times* was an exception).[26]

In defense of the print media, most major newspapers picked up the AP story, which omitted the quote. Here is how the AP covered the exchange:

"Ray McGovern, a former CIA analyst and noted critic of the war in Iraq, waited patiently in line to question Rumsfeld, *then let loose* (emphasis added).

'Why did you lie to get us into a war that caused these kind of casualties and was not necessary?' McGovern said.

'I did not lie,' shot back a feisty Rumsfeld, who waved off security guards ready to remove McGovern from the hall at the Southern Center for International Studies."[27]

News broadcasts also ended the exchange there.

In April 2006, investigative journalist John Pilger wrote a column recounting a lesson he had learned from Czech dissident writer Zdenek Urbánek, who said, "in one respect, we are more fortunate than you in the west. We believe nothing of what we read in the newspapers and watch on television, nothing of the official truth. Unlike you, we have learned to read between the lines, because real truth is always subversive."

Pilger notes

> this acute skepticism, this skill of reading between the lines, is urgently needed in supposedly free societies today.... The oldest cliche is that truth is the first casualty of war. I disagree. Journalism is the first casualty. Not only that: it has become a weapon of war, a virulent censorship that goes unrecognized in the United States, Britain, and other democracies; censorship by omission, whose power is such that, in war, it can mean the difference between life and death for people in faraway countries, such as Iraq.[28]

American journalists have shown at times that they are up to the challenge of asking the tough questions and digging as far down as they need to go to find the facts. Unfortunately, all too often, they are content to lob soft balls or simply regurgitate what they are handed by government officials.

It is not good enough, as both 9/11 and Katrina showed, for the media to perform its job half-heartedly. There is just too much at stake.

CHAPTER 9

Lessons Learned

I ask you in this room tonight whether you know what it must be like to spend all your working life scared. Scared of being shot, of being kidnapped, of being raped by some lunatic who may not want your story or who blames you for bringing NATO bombs down around them.

—Christiane Amanpour, CNN correspondent[1]

As Christiane Amanpour's quote makes clear, journalism is not an easy profession. It is dangerous, often frustrating; the hours are terrible, and for the vast majority, it does not pay well. I have a deep respect for the journalists who risk their lives to gather the news in areas where simply asking the wrong question can get them killed.

But it is also an incredibly important profession, and it warrants careful scrutiny. When the media fails the public, the results can be disastrous.

Amanpour said those words in a speech at the Radio-Television News Association's Murrow Awards Ceremony in 2000. It was an emotionally honest speech during which she acknowledged wondering whether it was worth risking her life in war zones when networks had become more interested in discussing diet fads than genocide.

"Think how much more of a contribution we could make to this great society if we weren't so dependent on what I call those hocus-focus-pocus awful groups who tell us what people are not interested in," she said.

> They tell us that Americans don't care about serious news; Americans don't care about this presidential election; Americans don't care about foreign news; Americans don't care about anything except contemplating their own navels. That's what they tell us.... The way the mass media treats the democratic process and the truly poisonous relationship between government and the press right now must have something to do with why Americans are so alienated from it.[2]

Something has gone terribly wrong with the American media. Thirty years ago, *Washington Post* reporters Bob Woodward and Carl Bernstein pursued every lead, scrutinized every possible scenario, and uncovered Watergate, one of the greatest scandals in American history. The press realized back then that it had the power to undermine leadership and the responsibility to pursue the facts.

Today, there is little evidence of that passion and determination. Woodward acknowledged that he had information that would have cast doubt on President Bush's argument for the need for war in Iraq but did not write stories about it. He blames "groupthink" for his decisions. Reporters on the *Post* who did not succumb to groupthink saw their stories buried on back pages. The *Post* executive editor, Leonard Downie Jr., said he does not believe his paper could have prevented the president from building his case for war and for the events that followed: "People who were opposed to the war from the beginning and have been critical of the media's coverage in the period before the war have this belief that somehow the media should have crusaded against the war. They have the mistaken impression that somehow if the media's coverage had been different, there wouldn't have been a war."[3]

If the American press is to flourish, some basic changes need to be made, including the belief that objectivity means passive acceptance of information. It may sound simplistic, but just because an official says something is true does not make it so. Journalists need to forcefully and persistently search for information that either supports what the official says or disproves it. Sometimes, verifying a claim seems next to impossible. But a diligent search will turn up something—a document with a clue or a person willing to talk.

Additionally, a simple he said/she said presentation of politicians' interpretations of the facts is no longer an option in an era when government spin has become an art. If journalists feel uncomfortable saying outright that an official's statement is a lie, then they should approach the official with the information that indicates it is and ask for an explanation.

In the buildup to the war in Iraq, the media accepted official explanations without pushing for proof or attempting to discredit the claims. When Colin Powell preceded his U.N. report on Iraq's weapons capabilities by saying, "What we are giving you are facts and conclusions based on solid intelligence," members of the American media agreed and allowed him to largely dictate their stories. Few journalists outside the United States were as passive as those in this country. As uncomfortable as it may be, journalists have a responsibility to ask the questions that come to mind. Debate does not endanger a country; passive acceptance of ideas does.

When the president or a member of Congress says the United States must go to war to fight a "rogue nation" or terrorists, reporters should wonder what the repercussions will be. How will the government measure success against terrorism? How will the United States extricate itself from a war on terror? What will the government do to leave a country or a region it invaded more stable than it found it? How much will the war cost in terms of both dollars and lost lives? Asking such questions is not exhibiting bias; it is an attempt to honestly examine the issues and allows the potential ramifications of decisions to be exposed and understood by leaders and the public.

It was not until right before the war began, when the president proclaimed that Iraq would become a model of democracy for the entire Middle East, that American journalists began to address what that meant and how it might be accomplished. The press corps acted as if the issue became a story only after officials discussed it. It was as if the administration had now given them permission to explore the subject without feeling they had stepped over the line from objectivity to bias.[4]

The media did the same thing in the 2004 presidential election campaign. Journalists rarely told the public whether candidates were manipulating the facts or lying outright until, during televised debates, the candidates accused each other and partisan groups of "misleading" the public. After distortions were made an issue by officials, journalists—in particular, print journalists—did a fantastic job of clearly laying out each candidate's record and discussing whether their statements matched their actions. The examination was damning for both candidates—both stretched the truth during the debates, and both suffered the consequences of seeing their lies exposed in print.

Yet even this coverage became mired in debate among journalists who wondered whether they should pointedly tell the public that one candidate was lying more egregiously than the other.

For years, the media refrained from saying that false statements by Bush and members of his administration were false, and from setting the record straight. The idea that journalists are simply "the mouthpiece for whatever administration is in power," as the *Washington Post*'s Karen DeYoung put it, needs to be abandoned. Journalists should be aggressive in the pursuit of information, unafraid to analyze what the information means, and willing to explore the ramifications. Facts do not taint a process or favor one candidate over another; fuzzy details, rumors, and unsubstantiated accusations do.

Additionally, most journalists have stopped reading reports and documents and rely instead on executive summaries and official explanations. Journalists need to return to the basics and read the documents that are available.

They should go through planning board minutes, congressional hearing records, Defense Department reports, the *Federal Register*, and whatever else falls under their beat. There is a treasure trove of stories that go undetected by journalists.

I say this knowing that it grows more difficult by the day to keep up with the pace required to do a good job. Newsroom staffs are smaller and the workload bigger. One solution would be to bypass some of the rumor and celebrity stories that "sell" in favor of a few investigative pieces that explore issues in depth.

If staffs are smaller, they must be used better. Reporters in war zones should be teamed with others on the home front who can fact-check the information that is being distributed. Those at home should work their sources in Congress and the Pentagon to provide a broader understanding of the war. Many stories uncovered during past wars (including the My Lai massacre) were found by persistent Washington reporters. If journalists are embedded with troops, then independent correspondents from the same media organizations should work with them to verify that what military officials are saying is, in fact, true.

During presidential campaigns, reporters (or even interns) should collaborate with the journalists following the candidates. Statements should be checked and clarified, records dug up, and distortions revealed. If a conflict is found, the reporter with the candidate can ask for clarification.

The goal should be to provide accurate information to the public so it can form opinions based on facts, not rumor and innuendo.

THE GROWING MEDIA MONOPOLY

An issue this book has not addressed is media ownership and the growing monopoly power of a few over the print, radio, and television media. The fact is that these "money handlers," as Amanpour called them, do manipulate what correspondents focus on. Consumers should know who owns their favorite news station or newspaper and the particular slant its reporters take. Fox News obviously leans right. Others, such as CNN, are not as obvious. But all media outlets have an agenda and a target audience. Many of them view the news through a lens that softens the information to suit the perspective of their audience and to minimize the negative impact for their owners.

The Pew Research Center for the People and the Press found in a survey of journalists in 2000 that a third of local reporters admitted softening a news story in the interests of their media organizations. Twenty-five percent said editors had told them to drop a story because it was dull but that they suspected the real reason was that the story could harm the company's financial interests.

The Center for Public Integrity has an excellent web site that tracks media ownership. Its home page is http://www.publicintegrity.com. You can access the ownership section by typing in http://www.publicintegrity.org/telecom/report.aspx?aid=146.

Similarly, Free Press is a nonprofit group that focuses on the media. Its web site, http://www.freepress.net/, provides information about media ownership and helps consumers understand why the media is an important tool for democracy. MediaChannel.org, at http://www.mediachannel.org/, provides media criticism and some information on stories missed by the mainstream media. The Reporters Committee for Freedom of the Press publishes a roundup of news about homeland security and public information at http://www.rcfp.org/behindthehomefront/.

In addition to reading American news sources, consider adding an international publication to your Internet bookmarks. The U.K.'s *Guardian* and *Independent* are two sources whose information can add perspective to the U.S. news media's reports. If these sites do not appeal to you, search for one that does and visit it occasionally for an international perspective on events.

A WORD TO JOURNALISM STUDENTS—AND TO JOURNALISTS

Journalism is an extremely complex job in which ethical dilemmas come up daily. It is easy to become entangled in a web of information or to trust a source who ultimately uses you for his or her own agenda. The best journalists in the world have been duped by a source; it is part of the learning process. But there are things you can do to minimize your vulnerability to such manipulation. Before sitting down to write or broadcast a report, ask yourself:[5]

- Did you ask all the questions that needed to be asked, or did you simply accept what public officials said? Have you asked for clarification of definitions or terms that may have multiple meanings?

- Are there any documents that can confirm or refute what officials said? Have you aggressively attempted to obtain these documents? If officials refused to hand them over, should you include this information in your story and pursue them further?

- Did you talk to people who have a different position than the public officials? How will you prominently display their opinions in your report?

- If the subject is complex, do you have a clear understanding of the issues? If not, who can you call to clarify a few points? Are there experts who can provide a balanced explanation for readers?

- If you were tipped off by a source, what is the source's motive? Did you attempt to get all your sources on the record?

- If you could not corroborate officials' claims, will you do a follow-up the next day, and who will you call?

These seem like basic questions, but if you ask and answer them consistently, your stories will be better balanced and your audience better informed.

Notes

PREFACE

1. The PIPA/Knowledge Networks Poll, "Misperceptions, the Media and the War in Iraq," 3.
2. Peter Johnson, "Media Mix: Amanpour: CNN Practiced Self-Censorship," *USA Today*, September 15, 2003.
3. Ibid.
4. *Late Night with David Letterman* transcript, September 17, 2001.

INTRODUCTION

1. The Pew Research Center for the People and the Press, "Global Opinion: The Spread of Anti-Americanism," January 24, 2005.
2. The Pew Research Center for the People and the Press, "Bottom-Line Pressures Now Hurting Coverage, Say Journalists: Press Going too Easy on Bush," May 23, 2004. Susan D. Moeller, "Media Coverage of Weapons of Mass Destruction," Center for International and Security Studies, University of Maryland, March 9, 2004.
3. David E. Sanger and Don Van Natta Jr., "In Four Days, a National Crisis Changes Bush's Presidency," *New York Times*, September 16, 2001. Allan Wood and Paul Thompson: Center for Cooperative Research, "An Interesting Day: President Bush's Movements and Actions on 9/11," May 9, 2003, http://www.cooperativeresearch.net/timeline/main/essayaninterestingday.html.
4. *The News with Brian Williams*, NBC News transcript, September 9, 2002.
5. Andrew Card, "9.11 Voices/What If You Had To Tell The President?" *San Francisco Chronicle*, September 11, 2002.
6. Amy Patterson-Neubert, "Study: Columbine News Coverage Misled Nation Down Fearful Road," *Purdue News*, April 9, 2003.
7. Ibid.
8. Nicholas Confessore, "Beat the Press: Does the White House Have a Blacklist?" *American Prospect*, March 11, 2002.
9. *Nightline with Ted Koppel*, ABC News transcript, April 30, 2004.
10. Elizabeth Birge and June Nicholson, "Terrorists Increased Attacks Difficulty In Keeping Personal Biases In Check," *Quill*, August 2004.

11. Ibid.

12. Joe Strupp, "Editors Grapple With How to Cover Swift Boat Controversy," *Editor & Publisher*, August 24, 2004.

13. UPI Hears, "Insider Notes From United Press International for March 6, 2002."

14. Justin Pope, "Officials Investigate How Security at Boston's Logan Airport was Breached on Two Flights," Associated Press story as appeared in the *Courier Journal*, September 12, 2001.

15. Blake Morrison, "Agent Blew Whistle 'for American People'," *USA Today*, February 25, 2002.

16. Statement of Bogdan John Dzakovic, "The Paul Revere Forum: National Security Whistleblowers Speak," February 27, 2002. Canon House Office Building, Room 402.

17. David Stout, "Nine Hijackers Drew Scrutiny on September 11, Officials Say," *New York Times*, March 2, 2002.

18. Trudy Lieberman, "State of the Beat: Imagining Evil; What We Don't Know Can Hurt Us," *Columbia Journalism Review*, September 2004.

19. John R. MacArthur, *Second Front: Censorship and Propaganda in the Gulf War* (New York: Hill and Wang, 1992), 213.

20. Ibid., 216.

21. Lisa F. Abdolian and Harold Takooshian, "The USA PATRIOT Act: Civil Liberties, The Media and Public Opinion," *Fordham Urban Law Journal*, 30 (May 2003): 1436.

22. Lynda Hurst, "From Tiger to Pussycat: America's Press Defanged," *Toronto Star*, September 8, 2002.

23. Abdolian and Takooshian, "USA PATRIOT Act."

24. Johnson, "Media Mix: Amanpour."

25. Now with Bill Moyers, "Secret Government: History of the Freedom of Information Act," April 5, 2002.

26. Human Rights First, "A Year of Loss: Reexamining Civil Liberties Since September 11," September 2002, 15.

27. Adam Clymer, "Government Openness at Issue as Bush Holds onto Records," *New York Times*, January 3, 2003.

28. Ruth Rosen, "The Day Ashcroft Foiled FOIA," *San Francisco Chronicle*, January 7, 2002.

29. Joe Strupp, "Media Vows to Pry Open Closed Doors in Washington," *Editor & Publisher*, June 3, 2004.

30. Ibid.

31. Ibid.

32. White House transcript, "Remarks by the President in Photo Opportunity with National Security Team," September 12, 2001.

33. Robert M. Entman, "Cascading Activation: Contesting the White House's Frame After 9/11," *Political Communication*, October–December 2003, 417.

34. William Grieder, "Under the Banner of the War on Terror," *Nation*, June 21, 2004.

35. "A Call To Arms; President Bush Prepares The Nation For A Long Struggle Against Terrorism," *Times Union*, September 21, 2001.

36. Jacob Levenson, "The War on What, Exactly? Why The Press Must Be Precise," *Columbia Journalism Review*, November/December 2004.

37. Meet the Press, NBC News transcript.

38. Elisabeth Bumiller, "Bush Vowes to Aide Other Countries in War on Terror," *New York Times,* March 11, 2002.

39. Ibid.

40. Mike Allen and Karen Deyoung, "'This nation will act'; President outlines new first-strike policy during speech at West Point," *Washington Post,* June 2, 2002.

41. Geov Parrish, "Helen Thomas' Legacy for Truth," http://www.workingforchange.com/article.cfm?ItemID=16639

42. Parrish, "Helen Thomas."

43. "What they said," *Baltimore Sun,* March 22, 2004.

44. George H.W. Bush quoted in "A World Transformed" (1998) George H.W. Bush and Brent Scowcroft.

CHAPTER 1

1. Bob Woodward, *Bush at War* (New York: Simon and Shuster, 2002), 145.

2. Stacey Frank Kanihan and Kendra L. Gale, "Within Three Hours 97 Percent Learn About the Terrorist Attacks," Media Studies of September 11, *Newspaper Research Journal,* 24 (Winter 2003): 78.

3. Jaeho Cho, Michael P. Boyle, Heejo Keum, Mark D. Shevy, "Media, Terrorism and Emotionality: Emotional Differences in Media Content and Public Reactions to the Sept. 11 Terrorist Attacks," *Journal of Broadcasting and Electronic Media,* 47, no. 3 (September 2003): 309.

4. Glenn Guzzo, "Thinking Big: Covering Major International Stories Can Pay Significant Dividends For Regional Newspapers," *American Journalism Review,* June/July 2004.

5. Sasha Abramsky, "Journalists Who Survived Ground Zero," *Editor & Publisher,* September 5, 2002.

6. Ibid.

7. Ibid.

8. George Gerbner, "Reclaiming our Own Cultural Mythology; Television's Global Marketing Strategy Creates a Damaging and Alienated Window on the World," *In Context, A Quarterly of Humane Sustainable Culture, Ecology of Justice,* no. 38 (Spring 1994): 40.

9. John E. Newhagen, "TV News Images That Induce Anger, Fear, and Disgust: Effects on Approach-Avoidance and Memory," *Journal of Broadcasting and Electronic Media,* (Spring 1998): 265.

10. Kanihan and Gale, "Within Three Hours."

11. Ibid.

12. Marc Siegel, "How Terror Fears Can You Sick," *USA Today,* November 14, 2004.

13. Christopher Hanson, "We're All War Correspondents Now," *Columbia Journalism Review,* November/December 2001

14. Ronald Brownstein, "The Government Once Scorned Becomes Savior," *Los Angeles Times,* September 19, 2001.

15. Albert Hunt, "Government to the Rescue," *Wall Street Journal,* September 27, 2001.

16. Jim Hoagland, "Putting Doubts to Rest," *Washington Post,* September 23, 2001.

17. "Mr. Bush's New Gravitas," *New York Times* editorial, October 12, 2001.

18. Jeffrey H. Birnbaum, "The Making of the President 2001," *Fortune Magazine,* November 2001.

19. James Bovard, "Government Trust Grows Despite Its Inability to Protect," *Investor's Business Daily,* October 2, 2001.

20. "How the Public Assesses the News Coverage Since September 11th," The Pew Research Center for the People and the Press, November 2001.

21. Alexander Stille, "Suddenly, Americans Trust Uncle Sam," *New York Times,* November 3, 2001; Gary Langer, "Trust in Government to Do What?" *Public Perspective,* July/August 2002.

22. Ron Suskind, "Without a Doubt," *New York Times Magazine,* October 17, 2004.

23. Elliot Aronson, *The Social Animal* (New York: Worth Publishers, 1999). *In Playboy,* January 1975, 78.

24. White House transcript, "Address to a Joint Session of Congress and the American People," September 20, 2001.

25. Rivera Live, CNBC News transcript, "Osama Bin Laden's Role in the World Trade Center and Pentagon Bombings and How the US Should Deal With Terrorists," September 13, 2001.

26. Sam Keen, *Faces of the Enemy: Reflections of the Hostile Imagination: The Psychology of Enmity* (San Francisco: Harper & Row, 1986).

27. The Point With Greta Van Susteren, CNN transcript, "Tracking the Terrorists," September 17, 2001.

28. Jim Lobe, "Post-9/11 Immigrant Roundup Backfired – Report," http://www.commondreams.org/headlines03/0627-03.htm, June 27, 2003.

29. CBS Evening News with Connie Chung, CBS News transcript, "Investigators Look For Link Between Middle East Terrorists and Bombing in Oklahoma City," April 19, 1995.

30. Jeff Cohen, "Rule of Law Vs. Rule of War: Are Media Missing the Lesson of Oklahoma City?" FAIR, September 19, 2001.

31. Deborah Potter, CNN Reliable Source, April 25, 1995.

32. ABC News transcript, "Special Report: America Under Attack," 11 a.m. September 11, 2001.

33. Osama bin Laden, "Letter to the American People," November 24, 2002. Translated version from *The Wednesday Report, Canada's Aerospace and Defence Weekly.*

34. Special Report with Brit Hume, Fox News transcript, September 12, 2001.

35. White House transcript, "Address to a Joint Session."

36. David Shaw, "News Shrinks in Era of Globalization," *Los Angeles Times,* September 27, 2001.

37. Ibid.

38. Hurst, "America's Press Defanged."

CHAPTER 2

1. Stanley Milgram, "The Perils of Obedience" as it appeared in *Harper's Magazine.* Abridged and adapted from *Obedience to Authority* by Stanley Milgram, 1974.

2. Ibid.

3. Ibid.

4. Ibid.

5. Ibid.

6. Daniel Lewis, "Tad Salc, Times Correspondent Who Uncovered Bay of Pigs Imbroglio, Dies at 74," *New York Times*, May 22, 2001; Carl Jensen, *20 Years of Censored News* (New York: Seven Stories Press, 1997).

7. FAIR, "Networks Accept Government Guidance," October 11, 2001.

8. Peter Hart and Seth Ackerman, "Patriotism & Censorship. Some Journalists are Silenced, While Others Seem Happy to Silence Themselves," *Extra!* November/December 2001.

9. Ken Fireman, "U.S. Asks of Newspapers: No Unedited bin Laden Comments," *Newsday*, October 12, 2001.

10. Hart and Ackerman, "Patriotism & Censorship."

11. Hanson, "We're All War Correspondents Now."

12. Alessandra Stanley, "A Nation Challenged: The Media; Opponents of the War are Scarce on Television," *New York Times*, November 9, 2001.

13. Irving L. Janis, "Groupthink," *Psychology Today*, November 1971.

14. Amy Goodman, "Koppel Defends Iraq Coverage," Democracy Now!, July 29, 2004.

15. *The Daily Show with Jon Stewart*, transcript, July 13, 2004.

16. Aronson, *The Social Animal*.

17. Philip Zimbardo, Stanford Prison Experiment slide show, http://www.prisonexp.org/

18. Howard Kurtz, "CNN Chief Orders CNN 'Balance' in War News; Reporters Are Told To Remind Viewers Why U.S. Is Bombing," *Washington Post*, October 31, 2001.

19. "War Declared on Resistance," Reuters, November 7, 2003, in *Sydney Morning Herald*.

20. Brian Lambert, "Media: Koppel Says War Coverage Will Change," *Pioneer Press*, September 21, 2002.

21. Dennis Pluchinsky, "They Heard it All Here and That's the Trouble," *Washington Post*, June 16, 2002.

22. Steve Ritea, "Going it Alone," *American Journalism Review*, August/September 2004.

23. Nicholas Professore, "Beat the Press: Does the White House Have a Blacklist?" *American Prospect*, March 11, 2002.

24. Howard Kurtz, "The Post on WMDs: An Inside Story; Prewar Articles Questioning Threat Often Didn't Make Front Page," *Washington Post*, August 12, 2004.

25. Hart and Ackerman, "Patriotism & Censorship."

26. *Politically Incorrect*, transcript, September 17, 2001.

27. Hanson, "We're All War Correspondents Now."

28. Jamie Dettmer, "Media MIA in Fight For Civil Liberties," *Insight on the News*, a *Washington Times* publication, December 17, 2001.

29. Rick Ellis, "The Surrender of MSNBC," All Your TV, February 25, 2003.

30. The Pew Research Center for the People and the Press, "How the Public Assesses the News Coverage Since September 11th," November 2001.

31. Caryn James, "A Nation Challenged: News Coverage—Critic's Notebook; British Take Blunter Approach to War Reporting," *New York Times*, November 9, 2001.

32. "Ashcroft: Critics of New Terror Measures Undermine Effort," CNN.com, December 7, 2001.

33. White House press briefing transcript, Ari Fleischer, May 7, 2003.

34. "Powell Criticizes Kennedy for Iraq Remarks," Associated Press in *Modesto Bee*, April 7, 2004.

35. Steven R. Weisman, "White House Says Iraq Sovereignty Could be Limited," *New York Times*, April 23, 2004.

36. Paul Farhi, "The Soothing Sound of Fighting Words," *Washington Post*, March 26, 2003.

37. Cynthia Cotts, "Moral Clarity: An Unauthorized Glossary of War," *Village Voice*, April 2–8, 2003.

CHAPTER 3

1. Gustav Gilbert, *Nuremberg Diary* (New York: Da Capo Press edition, 1995), 279.

2. Senate Judiciary Committee transcript, testimony of John Ashcroft, December 6, 2001.

3. James X. Dempsey and David Cole, *Terrorism and the Constitution: Sacrificing Civil Liberties in the Name of National Security* (Washington D.C.: First Amendment Foundation, 2002) 2.

4. Attorney General John Ashcroft Testimony Before the House Judiciary Committee, September 24, 2001.

5. Sam Stanton and Emily Bazar, "Security Collides with Civil Liberties; Debate Intensifies Over War on Terrorism," *Sacramento Bee*, September 21, 2003.

6. Jonathan Krim and Robert O'Harrow Jr., "Bush Signs into Law New Enforcement Era: U.S. Gets Broad Electronic Powers," *Washington Post*, October 27, 2001.

7. John F. Harris, "Behind the Show of Bipartisanship: Muted Dissent," *Washington Post*, September 17, 2001.

8. Ibid.

9. John Lancaster, "Anti-Terrorism Bill Hits Snag on the Hill; Dispute Between Democrats, White House Threatens Committee Approval," *Washington Post*, October 3, 2001.

10. Ibid.

11. Ibid.

12. Joint Inquiry into Intelligence Community Activities Before and After the Terrorist Attacks of September 11, 2001, available on the Memory Hole: http://thememoryhole.org/911/phoenix-memo/01.htm.

13. Sibel Edmonds, "An Open Letter to 9/11 Chairman Thomas Kean," August 4, 2004.

14. *60 Minutes*, CBS News transcript, "Lost in Translation," August 8, 2004.

15. US Department of Justice, "A Review of the FBI's Handing of Intelligence Information Related to the 9/11 Attacks," Finished November 2004, released to the public June 2005.

16. Eric Lichtblau, "Report Details F.B.I.'s Failure on 2 Hijackers," *New York Times*, June 10, 2005.

17. Elisabeth Bumiller, "New Slogan in Washington: Watch What You Say," *New York Times*, October 7, 2001.

18. Tony Blankley, "Trade Civil Liberties for Security," *Washington Times*, September 26, 2001.

19. Dettmer, "Media MIA in fight."

20. Karen Masterson, "Ashcroft is Ready to Unleash Agents Power," *Houston Chronicle*, October 26, 2001.

21. Abdolian and Takooshian, "USA PATRIOT Act."

22. Stanton and Bazar, "Security Collides with Civil Liberties."

23. Hannity & Colmes, Fox News Transcript, December 2, 2002.

24. "Patriot Act II," *New York Times* editorial, September 22, 2003.

25. Audrey Hudson, "Bill Seen as Threat to Civil Liberties; Intelligence Provision Broadens Powers to Probe Financial Records," *Washington Times*, December 5, 2003.

26. Eric Lichtblau and James Risen, "Broad Domestic Role Asked for the CIA and Pentagon," *New York Times*, May 2, 2003.

27. Eric Boehlert, "Too Hot to Handle," Salon.com, August 26, 2002.

28. Steve Friess, "Patriot Act Gets Mixed Review in Vegas Its Use in Investigation of Strip Clubs Questioned," *Boston Globe*, November 8, 2003.

29. Clymer, "Government Openness at Issue."

30. Eric Lichtblau, "F.B.I. Scrutinizes Antiwar Rallies," *New York Times*, November 23, 2003.

31. Clay Reddick, "Undercover Officers at Anti-war Meetings," *Daily Texan*, February 21, 2004.

32. KCCI.com, "Feds Drop All Subpoenas Against Peace Protestors," February 9, 2004.

33. Will Potter, "L.A. Activists Tailed, Arrested On Way to Liberation Weekend Conference," *In These Times*, June 12, 2004.

34. "FBI Keeps Eye on Antiwar Protesters," CNN.com, November 24, 2003.

35. Chris Brauchli, "So This is 'Success' in War on Terror," http://www.common-dreams.org/views04/0927-09.htm, September 27, 2004.

36. Dan Eggen, "Report Scolds Terrorism Prosecutors; U.S. to Drop Convictions Against Trio in Detroit," *Washington Post*, September 2, 2004.

37. "Dangerous Errors," *Washington Post* editorial, September 6, 2004.

38. Phil Hirschkorn, "US Blunder May Save Moussaoui," CNN.com, March 13, 2006.

39. Matthew Barakat, "Death Penalty Back On Table," Associated Press in *Portsmouth Herald*, March 15, 2006.

40. "House Renews Patriot Act Renewal; Approval Sends Measure to Bush's Desk Before Expiration," CNN.com, March 7, 2006.

41. TRAC Report, "Investigators Seek Prosecution of More Than 6,400 But Only Five Get Twenty Years or More in Prison Median or Typical Sentence for Those Classified as International Terrorists is 14 days," December 8, 2003.

42. Matthew Purdy and Lowell Bergman, "Unclear Danger: Inside the Lackawanna Terror Case," *New York Times*, October 12, 2003.

43. Remarks by Al Gore, "Freedom and Security," New York University, November 9, 2003.

CHAPTER 4

1. "Wolfowitz Comments Revive Doubts over Iraq's WMD," AP story in *USA Today*, May 30, 2003.

2. Dick Gordon, The Connection, "The War's Discontents," WBUR Boston, February 3, 2004.

3. Kurtz, "Post on WMDs."

4. Judith Miller, "Illicit Arms Kept Till Eve of War, An Iraqi Scientist is Said to Assert," *New York Times*, April 21, 2003.

5. *The NewsHour with Jim Lehrer*, PBS transcript, "Search for Evidence," April 22, 2003.

6. From the Editors, "The Times and Iraq," *New York Times*, May 26, 2004.

7. Ibid.

8. Michael Massing, "Now They Tell Us," *New York Review of Books*, February 26, 2004.

9. Dale T. Miller, "The Norm of Self-Interest," *American Psychologist*, 54, no. 12 (December 1999): 1053–60

10. Mary McGrory, "Beyond Recognition," *Washington Post*, September 16, 2001.

11. Kurtz, "Post on WMDs."

12. Miller, "The Norm of Self-Interest."

13. Miller, "The Norm of Self-Interest."

14. Russ Baker, "Scoops and the Truth at the Times," *Nation*, June 23, 2003.

15. Daniel Okrent, "The Times and Judith Miller's WMD Coverage," *New York Times*, March 25, 2004.

16. Kurtz, "Post on WMDs."

17. Allen J. Hart, "Naturally Occurring Expectation Effects," *Journal of Personality and Social Psychology*, 68, no. 1 (January 1995): 109–15.

18. Moeller, "Media Coverage of Weapons."

19. Ibid.

20. Mike Allen, "Bush: 'We Found' Banned Weapons; President Cites Trailers in Iraq as Proof," *Washington Post*, May 31, 2003.

21. Moeller, "Media Coverage of Weapons," 47; also Allen, "'We Found' Banned Weapons."

22. "U.S. Confident Saddam Had Mobile WMD Lab," Associated Press, on Foxnews.com, May 28, 2003.

23. Ibid.

24. Steven Kull, Clay Ramsay, Stefan Subias, Evan Lewis, Phillip Warf, "Misperceptions, the Media and the War In Iraq," pg. 2, Program on International Policy Studies, Knowledge Networks, October 3, 2003.

25. Richard Sale, "Sources Say Intercepts Prove Iraq has WMDs," UPI, December 18, 2002.

26. Patrick Tyler, "Intelligence Break Led U.S. to Tie Envoy Killing to Iraqi Qaeda Cell," *New York Times*, February 6, 2003.

27. David Martin, "US: Iraq Set to Use Chemical Weapons," CBS News, March 25, 2003.

28. "Coalition Discovers Suspicious Site Near Baghdad," Fox News, April 4, 2003.

29. "Powell Concedes UN Speech Probably Wrong; WMD Evidence 'appears not to be the case that it was that solid,' he says," Associated Press in *Toronto Star*, April 3, 2004.

30. Chris Mooney, "The Editorial Pages and the Case for War: Did Our Leading Newspapers Set Too Low a Bar for a Preemptive Attack?" *Columbia Journalism Review*, March/April 2004.

31. Russell Mokhiber and Robert Weissman, "The Unbalanced Hawks at the Washington Post," *Jackson Progressive*, March 6, 2003.

32. "'Drumbeat' on Iraq? A Response to Readers," *Washington Post*, February 27, 2003.

33. Sam Gardiner, "The Truth from These Podia," independent study, October 8, 2003, on George Washington University website, http://www.gwu.edu/~nsarchiv/NSAEBB/NSAEBB177/Info%20Operations%20Roadmap%20Truth%20from%20These%20Podia.pdf.

34. Warren P. Strobel and Jonathan S. Landay, "Pentagon Hires Image Firm to Explain Airstrikes to World; U.S. Trying to Reverse Rise in Muslims' Outrage," *San Jose Mercury News*, October 19, 2001.

35. James Dao and Eric Schmitt, "Pentagon Readies Efforts to Sway Opinion Abroad," *New York Times*, February 19, 2002.

36. Strobel and Landay, "Pentagon Hires Image Firm."

37. Ibid.

38. Warren P. Strobel and Jonathan S. Landay, "Pentagon Hires Image Firm to Explain Air Strikes to the World; U.S. Trying to Reverse Rise in Muslim's Rage," *San Jose Mercury News*, October 19, 2001.

39. Dao and Schmitt, "Pentagon Readies Efforts."

40. Tom Carver, "Pentagon Plans Propaganda War," BBC.com, February 20, 2002.

41. Defense Department News Briefing Secretary of Defense Donald H. Rumsfeld, official transcript, February 26, 2002.

42. Seymour M. Hersch, "The Debate Within; The Objective is Clear-Topple Saddam. But How?" *New Yorker*, March 11, 2002.

43. James Dao, "Rumsfeld Says Pentagon Plan Won't Include Lies," *New York Times*, February 20, 2002.

44. Ibid.

45. Donald Rumsfeld, Department of Defense transcript, November 18, 2002; Steven Aftergood, SECRECY NEWS, from the FAS Project on Government Secrecy, November 27, 2002.

46. Gardiner, "Truth From These Podia."

47. Ibid., 7.

48. Jonathan S. Landay and Tish Wells, "Iraqi Exile Group Fed False Claims to Media," Knight Ridder Washington Bureau, March 16, 2004.

49. Ibid.

50. From the Editors, "The Times and Iraq."

51. Richard Goldstein, "Fessing Up How Guilty is the Times?" *Village Voice*, June 1, 2004.

52. Joe Strupp, "'N.Y. Times' Correction Causes Other Papers that Ran Stories to Scramble for Explanation," *Editor & Publisher*, May 26, 2004.

53. Ibid.

54. Richard W. Stevenson and Eric Lichtblau, "As Ashcroft Warns of Attack, Some Question Threat and Its Timing," *New York Times*, May 27, 2004.

55. Kurtz, "Post on WMDs."

56. Amy Goodman, "Koppel Defends Iraq Coverage," Democracy Now transcript, July 31, 2004.

57. Michael Massing, "Now They Tell Us."

58. Powell Testimony Before the United Nations, February 5, 2003.

59. "Leaked Report Rejects Iraqi al-Qaeda Link; Bin Laden 'Does Not Agree With Saddam's Regime'," BBC, February 5, 2003.

60. White House transcript, "U.S. Secretary of State Colin Powell Addresses U.N. Security Council," February 5, 2003.

61. Mooney, "Editorial Pages and Case for War."

62. Michael R. Gordon, "Powell's Trademark: Overwhelm Them," *New York Times*, February 6, 2003.

63. "The Case Against Iraq," *New York Times*, February 6, 2003.

64. "Irrefutable," *Washington Post* editorial, February 6, 2003.

65. "Powell's Smoking Gun; His Presentation Persuades All But Saddam's Diehard Backers," *Wall Street Journal*, February 6, 2003.

66. Audrey Gillan, "US Recycles Human Test Claims; Iraq Accused of Using Prisoners as Guinea Pigs," *Guardian*, February 6, 2003.

67. Jeevan Vasagar, "All Too Human Failings of 'Human Intelligence'; Information From Defectors, Spies and Prisoners May be Unreliable, Say Experts," *Guardian*, February 6, 2003.

68. Richard Wallace, "Powell's Lack of Proof Exposes War of Flaws; Dodgy Tapes, Grainy Videos, Great Rhetoric, But Where's the PROOF Colin?" *Daily Mirror*, February 6, 2003.

69. Today Show, NBC News transcript, February 6, 2003.

70. John Pilger, Documentary Film: "Breaking the Silence," Russ Kick, "The Memory Hole," http://www.thememoryhole.org/war/powell-no-wmd.htm; Press Remarks with Foreign Minister of Egypt Amre Moussa Secretary Colin L. Powell Cairo, Egypt (Ittihadiya Palace), February 24, 2001.

71. Kick, "The Memory Hole."

72. Pilger, "Breaking the Silence," Kick, "The Memory Hole," CNN Late Edition with Wolf Blitzer, "Rice Discusses Role of U.S. Military Overseas," transcript, July 29, 2001.

73. Laura Kurtzman, "Arabs Will Blame U.S. 'Forever' If Iraq Falls Apart, Critic Says," *San Jose Mercury News*, March 18, 2004.

74. Greg Mitchell, "Will Press Roll Over Again on New WMD Report?" *Editor & Publisher*, September 9, 2003.

75. Charles J. Hanley, "Powell's Battle Cry Fails Test of Time; Six Months After His Case Swung Opinion Toward Attacking Iraq, His Intelligence File Looks Thin," , August 10, 2003.

76. Walter Pincus, "Experts Say U.S. Never Spoke to Source of Tip On Bioweapons; Information From Iraqi Relayed By Foreign Agency, CIA Notes," *Washington Post*, March 5, 2004.

77. Bob Drogin and Greg Miller "Iraqi Defector's Tales Bolstered U.S. Case for War; Colin Powell Presented the U.N. With Details on Mobile Germ Factories, Which Came from a Now-Discredited Source Known As 'Curveball'." *Los Angeles Times*, March 28, 2004.

78. Jack Fairweather in Baghdad and Anton La Guardia, "Chalabi Stands by Faulty Intelligence That Toppled Saddam's Regime," *Daily Telegraph* (London), February 19, 2004.

79. "Bush Still Confident in U.S. Spies," CBS News, January 28, 2004.

80. White House transcript, "President Bush Discusses Top Priorities for the U.S.," Press Conference of the President, July 30, 2003.

CHAPTER 5

1 Statement by Lieutenant Colonel Rick Long made during a panel discussion with journalists at the University of California at Berkeley, March 18, 2004.

2. "Pubic Affairs Guidelines on Embedding Media," http://www.defenselink.mil/news/Feb2003/d20030228pag.pdf.

3. Mark Mazzetti, "Dispatches from Media Boot Camp," *Slate*, November 22, 2002.

4. David Shaw, "Boot Camps Give Hope the Media will be on the Front Lines," *Los Angeles Times*, December 1, 2002.

5. Peter Johnson, "Media Mix: Boot Camp Prepares Journalists for Iraq," *USA Today*, December 11, 2002.

6. Ibid.

7. Mazzetti, "Dispatches from Boot Camp."

8. Ibid.

9. Shaw, "Boot Camps Give Hope."

10. Christian Lowe, "The Pentagon and the Press: In an Effort to Counter Saddam Hussein's Propaganda, the Pentagon is Embedding Reporters in Military Units for the Iraq Campaign," *Daily Standard*, February 20, 2003.

11. Ibid.

12. Dan Wilcox, "Propaganda or News? Embedded Journalists Say They Provided Both," Investigative Reporters and Editors Annual Conference, June 7, 2003, http://www.ire.umd.edu/

13. Christian Lowe, "All Embeds are Not Created Equal; Embedded Journalists are Paying Big Dividends for the Pentagon So Far. Except that Some Commanders Refuse to Take Advantage of Them," *Daily Standard*, March 21, 2003.

14. Verne Gay, "Back From the Front; A Year Later, TV's Embedded Reporters Ponder the Merits of How They Covered the 'Drive-By War'," *Newsday*, March 18, 2004.

15. Chip Reid, "Recalling Life as an Embedded Reporter; Digging Ditches to Sleep In, Dodging Gunfire—A Long Way From D.C.," NBC News, March 15, 2004.

16. Ibid.

17. Howard Kurtz, "For Media After Iraq, A Case of Shell Shock; Battle Assessment Begins for Saturation Reporting," *Washington Post*, April 28, 2003.

18. Ibid.

19. "Marines in Fallujah Appear 'Geared Up'," CNN.com, April 27, 2004.

20. *The Early Show*, CBS News transcript, "Correspondents Share War Stories," April 15, 2003.

21. CBS Evening News, transcript, "CBS News Embeds' War Journals," March 13, 2004.

22. John Burnett, "War Stories," *Texas Observer*, June 6, 2003.

23. Wilcox, "Propaganda or News?"

24. Kurtz, "For Media After Iraq."

25. "Embedded Journalist Program in Iraq Seen as Success," *Japan Today*, April 20, 2003.

26. CBS Evening News, "CBS News Embeds' War Journals."

27. Burnett, "War Stories."

28. John Simpson, BBC News transcript, "This is Just a Scene from Hell," April 10, 2003.

29. Vinay Menon, "CNN Won't Let the Facts in Iraq Get in the Way," *Toronto Star*, April 7, 2003.

30. Robert Jensen, "The Military's Media," *Progressive*, May 2003.

31. Maj. Mike Donnelly, MSgt. Mitch Gettle, 1st Lt. Greg Scott, and Petty Officer 2nd Class Dana War, "Embedded Journalism: How the War is Viewed Differently from the Front Lines than the Sidelines," http://www.ou.edu/deptcomm/dodjcc/groups/03D1/INDEX.htm.

32. "Mixed Verdict on Iraq 'Embedded' Reporters," News Wales, July 11, 2003, http://www.newswales.co.uk/?section=Media&F=1&id=6569.

33. Japantoday.

34. Greg Mitchell, "15 Stories They've Already Bungled," *Editor & Publisher*, March 27, 2003.

35. Jensen, "The Military's Media."

36. Ibid.

37. Kurtz, "For Media After Iraq."

38. Associated Press, "TV Doctor Drafted to do Brain Surgery; CNN Correspondent Fails to Save Iraqi Boy, Defends Involvement," March 4, 2003.

39. Jim Naureckas, "Official Story vs. Eyewitness Account; Some Outlets Preferred Sanitized Version of Checkpoint Killings," FAIR, May/June 2003.

40. Ibid.; William Branigin, "A Gruesome Scene on Highway 9; 10 Dead After Vehicle Shelled at Checkpoint," *Washington Post*, March 31, 2003.

41. Naureckas, "Official Story."

42. Burnett, "War Stories."

43. Rachel Coen and Peter Hart, "Brushing Aside the Pentagon's 'Accidents'; U.S. Media Minimized, Sanitized Iraq War's Civilian Toll," FAIR, May/June 2003; NBC Nightly News Special Edition transcript, "US Pounds Baghdad with Missiles as Saddam's Palaces Destroyed," March 21, 2003.

44. Project for Excellence in Journalism Study, "Embedded Reporters: What Are Americans Getting?" April 3, 2003.

45. Eric Boehlert, "Reality Check; The Media are Finally Showing the War in Its Full Horror. What Took Them So Long?" Salon.com, May 6, 2004.

46. *The Early Show*, CBS News transcript, "Correspondents Share War Stories."

47. Jason Vest, "On-the-Ground Reality TV," *Boston Phoenix*, May 27, 2004.

48. Ibid.

49. Ibid.

50. Jessica Pitts, "Explaining the News, Banfield Delivers 129th Landon Lecture," *Kansas State Collegian*, April 25, 2003.

51. Hal Bernton, "The Somber Task of Honoring the Fallen," *Seattle Times*, April 18, 2004.

52. Deborah Norville, "Worth a Thousand Words, Three Sets of Photographs have Defined This War So Far," MSNBC, May 13, 2004.

53. Ray Rivera, "Images of the Dead a Sensitive Subject," *Seattle Times*, April 22, 2004.

54. Seth Porges, "Newspapers Change Reporting on Iraqi Deaths," *Editor & Publisher*, November 4, 2003.

55. Harley Sorensen, "The Wounded Who Never Die," *San Francisco Chronicle*, November 3, 2003.

56. Tom McGurk, Transcript RTE1 Radio Sunday Show, Irish Public Radio, March 9, 2003.

57. Rory McCarthy, Jonathan Steele, and Brian Whitaker, "Three Die in Attacks on Media Bases: Journalists 'Target' as Hotel and Al-Jazeera Bombed," *Guardian*, April 9, 2003.

58. Ibid.

59. Emma Daly with Jim Rutenberg, "Powell Defends Shelling Journalists' Hotel in Letter," *New York Times News Service*, April 25, 2003.

60. FAIR Media Advisory: "Is Killing Part of Pentagon Press Policy?" April 10, 2003.

61. Ibid.

62. Ibid.

63. Alastair Macdonald, "Inquiry Demanded into Death of Cameraman: U.S. Soldier Mistook TV Equipment for Rocket Launcher," *National Post* (Canada), August 19, 2003.

64. Barry Moody, "Reuters Death 'Due' to U.S. Military Flaws," Reuters, May 20, 2004.

65. Paul Workman, "Embedded Journalists Versus 'Unilateral' Reporters," CBC News Online, April 7, 2003.

66. Ibid.

67. Vest, "On-the-Ground."

68. Barbara Bedway, "MacArthur Warns Press About Pentagon Control," *Editor & Publisher*, March 18, 2003.

69. Burnett, "War Stories."

CHAPTER 6

1. Good Morning America with Diane Sawyer, ABC News transcript, March 18, 2003.

2. Martin Savidge, Brent Sandler, Jonathan Aiken, and Don Shepperd, "Massive Civilian Casualties Reported Near Tora Bora," CNN transcript, December 1, 2001.

3. Jim Rutenberg and Bill Carter, "Network Coverage a Target of Fire from Conservatives," *New York Times*, November 7, 2001.

4. Robert J. Sternberg, "A Duplex Theory of Hate: Development and Application to Terrorism, Massacres, and Genocide," *Review of General Psychology*, (September 2003) 299–328.

5. Ibid.

6. Rutenberg and Carter, "Network Coverage."

7. Richard Lloyd Parry, "A Village is Destroyed. And America Says Nothing Happened," *Independent*, December 4, 2001.

8. Niles Lathem, "Here We Come, Osama!—Battle at His Cave Fortress Has Begun," *New York Post*, December 5, 2001.

9. CNN Transcript, "Live From Afghanistan with Nic Robertson," December 5, 2001.

10. Rory Carroll, "Bloody Evidence of U.S. Blunder," *Guardian*, January 7, 2001.

11. Adam Rogers, "Selling a War Through the Mass Media: Cunning Communications or Brilliant Brainwashing?" http://www.whywehatebush.com/news/04_04_brainwashing.html.

12. Ibid.; Elisabeth Noelle-Neumann, *The Spiral of Silence: Public Opinion—Our Social Skin* (Chicago: University of Chicago, 1984).

13. Ian Fisher, "G.I.'s Escape Roadside Bombing, But 2 are Killed in Northern Iraq," *New York Times*, October 20, 2003.

14. Dave Lindorff, "God's on Our Side," Counterpunch.com, October 21, 2003.

15. Robin Cook, "Why I Had to Leave the Cabinet; This Will be a War Without Support at Home or Agreement Abroad," *Guardian*, March 8, 2003; Jefferson Morle, "As U. S. Attacks Begin, World Recoils from 'Shock-and-Awe'," Washingtonpost.com, March 20, 2003.

16. John Yaukey, "'Shock-and-Awe' Combines Destruction, Protection," Gannett News Service, March 21, 2003.

17. Rowan Scarborough and Bill Gertz, "Coalition Lets Loose 'Shock-and-Awe,' Starts to Draw Noose Around Capital," *Washington Times*, March 22, 2003.

18. DoD News Briefing—ASD PA Clarke and Maj. Gen. McChrystal; transcript from the United States Department of Defense, March 23, 2003.

19. Rowan Scarborough, "Sparing Targets Softens Effect of 'Shock-and-Awe'," *Washington Times*, March 31, 2003.

20. FAIR: Action Alert, "Media Should Follow Up on Civilian Deaths: Journalist's Evidence that U.S. Bombed Market Ignored by U.S. Press," April 4, 2003.

21. Jensen, "The Military's Media."

22. FAIR, "Media Should Follow Up."

23. Paul Martin, "Allied Troops Skirt Cities to Limit Civilian Casualties; The Military Outlines Policy as Arabic, British Television Highlight Injured Women and Children," *Washington Times*, May 23, 2003.

24. Peter Ford, "Surveys Pointing to High Civilian Death Toll in Iraq," *Christian Science Monitor*, May 22, 2003.

25. C-Span transcript, "War on Terrorism Unfinished," January 8, 2002.

26. David Anthony Denny, "General Describes U.S. Efforts to Minimize Civilian Casualties," *Washington File*, U.S. Department of State, April 3, 2003.

27. Douglas Jehl and Eric Schmitt, "The Struggle for Iraq: Intelligence; Errors are Seen in Early Attacks on Iraqi Leaders," *New York Times*, June 13, 2004.

28. Kurtz, "CNN 'Balance' in War News;" FAIR, "CNN Says Focus on Civilian Casualties Would Be 'Perverse'," November 1, 2001.

29. Alessandra Stanley, "A Nation Challenged: The Images; Battling the Skepticism of a Global TV Audience," *New York Times*, November 1, 2001.

30. Ibid.

31. Special Report with Brit Hume, Fox News transcript, November 5, 2001.

32. Peter Phillips, "Media Dropped Ball After Sept. 11," *Evening Sun*, June 11, 2002.

33. Committee to Protect Journalists, "Attacks on the Press 2002: Afghanistan," http://www.CPJ.org/attacks02/asia02/afghan.html.

34. Howard Zinn, "Just Cause, Not a Just War," *Progressive*, December 2001.

35. Ian Cobain and Damian Whitworth, "America Will Take No Prisoners," *London Times*, November 21, 2002.

36. CNN transcript, "Secretary of Defense, Donald Rumsfeld Holds a Press Conference," November 19, 2001.

37. "On the Ground," *Economist*, November 29, 2001.

38. Jan Cienski, "Uncle Sam's Shifty New Ally," *Chicago Sun-Times*, October 21, 2001.

39. Julius Strauss, "General's Name is Byword for Brutality," *Independent*, October 24, 2001.

40. BBC, "Afghan Opposition's 'Record of Brutality'," October 19, 2001; Ross Benson, "The Chilling Truth About the Butchers Who Routed the Taliban," *Daily Mail*, November 14, 2001.

41. Benson, "Chilling Truth."

42. Carlotta Gall, "Witnesses Say Many Taliban Died in Custody," *New York Times*, December 11, 2001.

43. Physicians for Human Rights Press Release, "PHR Calls upon Interim Administration of Afghanistan, International Community to Protect Alleged Mass Gravesites in Afghanistan," May 2, 2002.

44. Gareth Harding and Elizabeth Manning, "Pentagon Denies Afghan Torture Claim," UPI, June 13, 2002.

45. Eric Schmitt, "There are Ways to Make Them Talk," *New York Times*, June 16, 2002.

46. Rajiv Chandrasekaran and Peter Finn, "US Behind Secret Transfer of Terror Suspects," *Washington Post*, March 10, 2002.

47. CNN transcript, "U.N.: Massacre Probe Up To Afghans," August 21, 2002.

48. Babak Dehghanpisheh, John Barry and Roy Gutman, "The Death Convoy of Afghanistan," *Newsweek*, August 26, 2002.

49. U.S. Embassy release, "State's Reeker Urges Afghan Authorities to Investigate Reports," August 20, 2002.

50. Kim Sengupta, "Three-Day Fight for Fortress leaves Hundreds Dead," *Independent*, November 28, 2001.

51. Ibid.

52. United States of America v. John Philip Walker Lindh, "Memorandum of Points and Authorities in Support of Release Pending Trial," The United States District Court for the Eastern District of Virginia.

53. Dana Priest and Barton Gellman, "U.S. Decries Abuse But Defends Interrogations 'Stress and Duress' Tactics Used on Terrorism Suspects Held in Secret Overseas Facilities," *Washington Post*, December 26, 2002.

54. "Report Completed on U.S. Prisons in Afghanistan," Associated Press in *Globe and Mail*, July 7, 2004.

55. "25 Died While Held by U.S. Forces," Agence France-Presse, May 5, 2004.

56. Line Fransson, "Vi tok klærne og brente dem før vi dyttet dem ut med 'tjuv' skrevet på brystet," *Dagblat*, April 25, 2003; Chris Hughes, "Suspects Stripped and Paraded at Gunpoint," *Daily Mirror*, April 28, 2003.

57. Ibid.

58. Hughes, "Suspects Stripped and Paraded."

59. Katharine Q. Seelye, "First 'Unlawful Combatants' Seized in Afghanistan Arrive at U.S. Base in Cuba," *New York Times*, January 11, 2002.

60. Robert Weller, "Soldier Investigated in Iraqi General's Death: Officer at Fort Carson Says There Is an 'Agenda'," Associated Press, May 29, 2004; also, Arthur Kane and Miles Moffeit, "Carson GI Eyed in Jail Death," *Denver Post*, May 28, 2004.

61. Sherry Ricchiardi, "Why Did It Take So Long for the News Media to Break the Story of Prisoner Abuse at Abu Ghraib?" *American Journalism Review*, August/September 2004.

62. Ibid.

63. Ibid.

64. Ellen McCarthy, "Media's Most Wanted Today is Blogger from Iraqi Prison," *Washington Post*, May 5, 2004.

65. Transcript, Department of Defense Press Briefing, "Coalition Provisional Authority Update Briefing from Baghdad, Iraq," Paul Bremer, September 2, 2003.

66. Remarks by the President at the 2003 Republican National Committee Presidential Gala, Washington Hilton, October 8, 2003.

67. White House transcript, "President Bush, President Fox Meet with Reporters in Mexico; Remarks by President Bush and President Fox of Mexico in Press Availability," Quinta Real Hotel, Monterrey, Mexico, January 12, 2004.

68. Boehlert, "Reality Check."

69. James Risen, David Johnston, and Neil A. Lewis, "Harsh C.I.A. Methods Cited in Top Qaeda Interrogations," *New York Times*, May 13, 2004.

70. David Folkenflik, "Dodging Using Words Like 'Torture'," *Baltimore Sun*, May 26, 2004.

71. Robin Wright, "Iraq Occupation Has Affirmed the Islamic World's Worst Fear," *Washington Post*, May 22, 2004.

72. Sternberg, "Duplex Theory of Hate."

73. Mohamad Bazzi, "Photos of U.S. Abuse of Prisoners Enrage Iraqis," *Newsday*, August 23, 2004.

74. Boehlert, "Reality Check."

CHAPTER 7

1. James T. Bennett and Thomas J. DiLorenzo, *Official Lies, How Washington Misleads Us* (Alexandria, VA: Groom Books, 1992).

2. Ibid.

3. The Pew Research Center, "Bottom-Line Pressures Hurting Coverage."

4. "Garrett Quits Newsday, Bemoans State of News Business," *Romenesco News*, Poynter Online, February 28, 2005.

5. David Barstow and Robin Stein, "Under Bush, A New Age of Prepackaged TV News," *New York Times*, March 15, 2005.

6. Ibid.

7. Ibid.

8. Ibid.

9. Ibid.

10. Ibid.

11. Ibid.

12. Caren Bohen, "Bush Defends Packaged News Stories from Government," Reuters, March 16, 2005.

13. Scott Peterson, "In War, Some Facts Less Factual; Some US Assertions from the Last War on Iraq Still Appear Dubious," *Christian Science Monitor*, September 6, 2002.

14. Ibid.

15. Frank Rich, "The White House Stages Its 'Daily Show'," *New York Times*, February 20, 2005.

16. Amy Goodman, "Koppel Defends Iraq Coverage," Democracy Now transcript, July 29, 2004.

17. Orville Schell, "Why the Media Failed US in Iraq," book preface, in *Now They Tell Us (Michael Massing)* (New York: The New York Review of Books, 2004).

18. Peter Wirth, "Selling a War," http://www.commondreams.org/views03/0213-04.htm, February 13, 2003.

19. Sheldon Rampton and John Stauber, "How to Sell a War," *In these Times*, August 4, 2003.

20. Elisabeth Bumiller, "Traces of Terror: The Strategy; Bush Aides Set Strategy to Sell Policy on Iraq," *New York Times*, September 6, 2002.

21. Ibid.

22. Tim Reid, "America Plans PR Blitz on Saddam," *London Times*, September 17, 2002.

23. Bob Garfield and Brooke Gladstone, "On the Media," National Public Radio on WNYC, August 30, 2002; Laura Miller, "War is Sell," Center for Media and Democracy PR Watch, 2002.

24. Garfield and Gladstone, "On the Media."

25. White House transcript, "President Bush, Prime Minister Blair Discuss Keeping the Peace, Remarks by the President and Prime Minister Tony Blair in Photo Opportunity," Camp David, Maryland, September 7, 2002.

26. Joseph Curl, "Agency Disavows Report on Iraq Arms," *Washington Times*, September 27, 2002.

27. Dana Milbank, "For Bush, Facts Are Malleable; Presidential Tradition of Embroidering Key Assertions Continues," *Washington Post*, October 22, 2002.

28. Lori Robertson, "In Control," *American Journalism Review*, February/March 2005.

29. Karen DeYoung, "Bush to Create Formal Office to Shape U.S. Image Abroad," *Washington Post*, July 30, 2002.

30. Peter Slevin, "New Group Aims to Drum Up Backing for Ousting Hussein; Effort Seeks to Reverse Decline in Support for Attacking Iraq," *Washington Post*, November 4, 2002; also Miller, "War is Sell."

31. FAIR Action Alert, "Iraq Crisis, Networks are Megaphones for Official Views," March 18, 2003.

32. Keen, *Faces of the Enemy*.

33. "Bush Pledges Crusade Against 'Evil-Doers'," the Associated Press, September 17, 2001.

34. White House transcripts, "International Campaign Against Terror Grows; Remarks by President Bush and Prime Minister Koizumi of Japan in Photo Opportunity," The Colonnade, September 25, 2001.

35. "Bush a Fight Vs. Evil, Bush and Cabinet Tell U.S.," *Daily News*, November 17, 2001.

36. David Rennie, "God Put Bush In Charge, Says the General Hunting Bin Laden," *Daily Telegraph*, October 17, 2003.

37. "Pope to Bush: Go into Iraq and You Go Without God," *Capitol Hill Blue*, March 5, 2003.

38. Miren Gutierrez, "The 'prop-agenda' war," Inter Press Service in *Asia Times*, July 2, 2004.

39. White House transcript, "President Bush and Columbian President Uribe Discuss Terrorism," September 26, 2002.

40. Transcript, "President Bush Outlines Iraqi Threat Remarks by the President on Iraq," Cincinnati Museum Center—Cincinnati Union Terminal, Cincinnati, Ohio, October 7, 2002.

41. David E. Sanger, "Bush Sees 'Urgent Duty' to Pre-empt Attack by Iraq," *New York Times*, October 7, 2002.

42. *Late Edition with Wolf Blitzer*, CNN transcript, "Top Bush Officials Push Case Against Saddam," September 8, 2002.

43. "Poll: Many Americans Still Believe Iraq Had WMDs," The Associated Press, August 20, 2004.

44. "President's Remarks at Stratham, New Hampshire, Picnic," Bittersweet Farm, Stratham, New Hampshire, August 6, 2004.

45. Fox News Special with Brit Hume, transcript, "All-Star Panel Discusses Liberation of Baghdad, Arab World Opinion," April 9, 2003.

46. John Koopman, "Marines Stumble upon a Moment Frozen in History," *San Francisco Chronicle*, April 10, 2003.

47. Matthew Gilbert and Suzanne C. Ryan, "Snap Judgments; Did Iconic Images From Baghdad Reveal More About the Media Than Iraq," *Boston Globe*, April 10, 2003.

48. David Zucchino, "Army Stage-Managed Fall of Hussein Statue," *Los Angeles Times*, July 3, 2004.

49. Paul Wood, "9/11 Pentagon Flag Used to Cover Saddam's Face in Baghdad," BBC, April 10, 2003.

50. Bill Lubinger, "And In W.Va., A Time of Joy; Jessica Lynch's Hometown Praises Local Hero," *Cleveland Plain Dealer*, April 13, 2003.

51. Michael Getler, "A Long, and Incomplete, Correction," *Washington Post*, June 29, 2003.

52. John Kampfner, "The Truth About Jessica," *Guardian*, May 15, 2003.

53. Susan Schmidt and Vernon Loeb, "'She was Fighting to the Death'; Details Emerging of W. Va. Soldier's Capture and Rescue," *Washington Post*, April 3, 2003.

54. Mitch Potter, "The Real 'Saving of Private Lynch' Iraqi Medical Staff Tell a Different Story Than US Military 'We All Became Friends With Her, We Liked Her So Much'," *Toronto Star*, May 4, 2003.

55. Kampfner, "Truth About Jessica."

56. Getler, "Long Correction."

57. Ibid.

58. David D. Kirkpatrick, "Jessica Lynch Criticizes U.S. Accounts of Her Ordeal," *New York Times*, November 7, 2003.

CHAPTER 8

1. George W. Bush Comment during interview with German Newspaper *Bildam Sonntag*, May 7, 2006.

2. Anderson Cooper 360°, News transcript, Special Edition: Hurricane Katrina, September 1, 2005.

3. NPR All Things Considered, "U.S. Aid Effort Criticized in New Orleans," Robert Seigel, September 1, 2005.

4. *Nightline with Ted Koppel,* transcript, September 1, 2005.

5. WWLTV.com Louisiana's News Leader, "Updates as They Come in on Katrina," September 6, 2005.

6. Chuck Taylor, "Bush Blows Katrina," *Seattle Weekly,* September 7, 2005.

7. Ibid.

8. Judy Keen and Richard Benendetto, "A Compassionate Bush was Absent Right After Katrina," *USA Today,* September 8, 2005.

9. NewsHour with Jim Leher, PBS transcript, Katrina Media Coverage, September 29, 2005.

10. Gary Younge, "Murder and Rape—Fact or Fiction?" *Guardian,* September 6, 2005.

11. ABC News Online, "In Quotes: Chaos in New Orleans," September 2, 2005.

12. The Situation Room, CNN transcript, September 1, 2005.

13. James Fallows, *Breaking the News: How the Media Are Undermining Democracy* (New York: Pantheon, 1996).

14. The Situation Room, CNN transcript, September 2, 2005; also see, "Demonizing the Victims of Hurricane Katrina," *FAIR Extra!,* November/December 2005.

15. Robert E. Pierre and Ann Gerhart, "News of Pandemonium May Have Slowed Aid," *Washington Post,* October 5, 2005.

16. Jim Dwyer and Christopher Drew, "Fear Exceeds Crime's Reality in New Orleans," *New York Times,* September 29, 2005.

17. Howard Witt, "Spreading Bigotry," *Chicago Tribune,* September 4, 2005.

18. NOW, Transcript of Bill Moyers interviews Jon Stewart, July 11, 2003.

19. *Nightline with Ted Koppel,* Transcript, Democratic National Convention, July 28, 2004.

20. Crossfire, CNN transcript, October 15, 2004.

21. Pete Baker, "Bush Faces Rare Audience Challenge in NC; President Defends Warrantless Spying Program After Criticism at Open Forum Event," *Washington Post,* April 7, 2006.

22. Greg Mitchell, Pressing Issues, "Neil Young and the Restless," *Editor & Publisher,* May 5, 2006.

23. *Hardball with Chris Matthews,* CNN transcript, May 1, 2006.

24. The White House Correspondents' Dinner 2006, April 29, 2006.

25. Ibid.

26. Media Matters For America, "NBC, CBS, Fox cropped Rumsfeld questioner's challenges, Rumsfeld's "stammer[ing]" replies," May 5, 2006.

27. Media Matters for America, "NBC, CBS, Fox Cropped Rumsfeld's 'Stammering' Replies," May 5, 2006.

28. "Reporting War and Empire," by John Pilger at Columbia University, New York, in company with Seymour Hersh, Robert Fisk, and Charles Glass.

CHAPTER 9

1. Christiane Amanpour, "Why We're in the Fight of Our Lives," Radio-Television News Directors Association Convention 2000.

2. Ibid.

3. Kurtz, "Post on WMDs."

4. Brent Cunningham, "Re-Thinking Objectivity," *Columbia Journalism Review*, July/August 2003.

5. John Hanrahan, "Missing Before the War: Journalism 101 Questions," Neiman Watchdog, Neiman Foundation for Journalism, Harvard University, May 7, 2004.

Bibliography

BOOKS

Bennett, James T., and Thomas J. DiLorenzo. *Official Lies: How Washington Misleads Us.* Alexandria, VA: Groom Books, 1992.

Fallows, James. *Breaking the News: How the Media Undermine American Democracy.* New York: Pantheon, 1996.

Fisk, Robert. *The Great War for Civilisation: The Conquest of the Middle East.* New York: Alfred A. Knopf, 2005.

Keen, Sam. *Faces of the Enemy: Reflections of the Hostile Imagination: The Psychology of Enmity.* New Hampshire: Olympic Marketing Corp., 1986.

Massing, Michael. *Now They Tell Us: The American Press and Iraq.* New York: New York Review of Books, 2004.

Palast, Greg. *The Best Democracy Money Can Buy.* New York: Penguin Books, 2003.

Rashid, Ahmed. *Taliban: Militant Islam, Oil and Fundamentalism in Central Asia.* New Haven: Yale University Press, 2001.

Solomon, Norman. *War Made Easy: How Presidents and Pundits Keep Spinning Us to Death.* Hobokon, NJ: John Wiley & Sons, 2005.

MEDIA WEB SITES

The Center for Public Integrity, http://www.publicintegrity.com/default.aspx.

Common Dreams News Center, http://www.commondreams.org/

Democracy Now Radio Program, http://democracynow.org/

Fairness and Accuracy in Reporting (FAIR), http://www.fair.org/index.php.

Free Press, http://www.freepress.net/

John Pilger's Web site, http://www.johnpilger.com/page.asp?partID=6.

Media Matters For America, http://mediamatters.org/

Noam Chomsky's Web site, http://www.chomsky.info/

Norman Solomon's Web site, http://www.normansolomon.com/

The Pew Research Center for the People and the Press, http://people-press.org/

The Reporters Committee for Freedom of the Press, http://www.rcfp.org/behindthehome-front/

TomDispatch.com, http://www.tomdispatch.com/

PERIODICALS

ASAP, Analyses of Social Issues and Public Policy (The Society for the Psychological
    Study of Social Issues), http://www.spssi.org/
The Guardian Magazine, http://www.guardian.co.uk/
Harper's Magazine, http://www.harpers.org/
The Nation, http://www.thenation.com/
The New York Review of Books, http://www.nybooks.com/
The New Yorker, http://www.newyorker.com/

Index

ABOUT THE AUTHOR

LISA FINNEGAN is an independent award-winning journalist who has spent nearly two decades reporting for newspapers and magazines in the United States and abroad. After the 9/11 attacks she began to focus on the psychology of terrorism and its impact on the media. She has published articles on the subject in professional journals and has spoken at conferences around the United States.